W9-DCX-973

BY THE EDITORS OF CONSUMER GUIDE®

ANNUALS

Contributing Authors:
Carol Landa Christensen
Ted Marston

Consultant:
Judy Glattstein

Illustrator:
Mike Muir

PUBLICATIONS INTERNATIONAL, LTD.

Photo credits:

Front cover photo: Derek Fell

Greg Crisci: Photo/Nats: p. 119
Derek Fell: pp. 6, 8, 13, 15, 20, 21, 22, 24, 34, 42, 43, 52, 54, 56, 60, 64, 68, 69, 70, 76, 80, 86, 88, 89, 91, 92, 97, 98, 100, 102, 103, 104, 107, 109, 111, 112, 114, 115, 117, 119, 122, 123, 124, 125, 127, 131, 133, 134, 135, 138, 139, 140
Don Johnston: Photo/Nats: p. 44
Robert E. Lyons: Photo/Nats: p. 106
Ivan Massar: Photo/Nats: p. 82
Elvin McDonald: pp. 91, 93, 111, 118, 120
Julie O'Neil: Photo/Nats: p. 115
Ann Reilly: pp. 4, 5, 10, 26, 32, 36, 39, 47, 50, 73, 92, 101, 107, 112, 114, 118, 121, 137, 139, 141
Ann Reilly: Photo/Nats: pp. 104, 106, 113, 126, 128, 130, 131, 135, 136
Steven M. Still: pp. 90, 91, 93, 94, 95, 96, 97, 98, 99, 100, 101, 102, 103, 105, 106, 108, 109, 110, 113, 114, 115, 116, 117, 118, 119, 120, 121, 122, 123, 124, 125, 126, 127, 128, 129, 130, 131, 132, 133, 135, 136, 137, 138, 139, 140, 141
David M. Stone: Photo/Nats: pp. 110, 116, 117, 141

Contributors:

Ted Marston (encyclopedia) of Kirkland, Washington, has been writing about gardens and gardening for over 20 years. During that time, he has written for national publications such as *The New York Times, Family Circle,* and *Flower & Garden,* and has edited several gardening periodicals and books, including *Plants Alive.* His spare time is spent gardening.

Carol Landa Christensen (chapters 1-4) graduated *cum laude* from the Pennsylvania School of Horticulture for Women, and went on to work at Longwood Gardens as a Horticulture Information Specialist and as a floral decorator. For the past seven years, she has been a feature writer for the Springfield (Massachusetts) newspapers, and was a frequent contributor to *Gurney's Gardening News* until it ceased publication.

Judy Glattstein (consultant) of Wilton, Connecticut, has been a landscape consultant since 1976. She is a frequent contributor to national horticultural publications such as *Horticulture, Garden Design, Flower and Garden,* and the Brooklyn Botanic Garden Handbook, *Plants for Problem Places.* Ms. Glattstein is also a workshop instructor and lecturer to garden clubs and nature centers.

Copyright © 1989 Publications International, Ltd. All rights reserved. This publication may not be reproduced or quoted in whole or in part by mimeograph or any other printed or electronic means, or for presentation on radio, television, videotape, or film without written permission from:

Louis Weber, C.E.O.
Publications International, Ltd.
7373 North Cicero Avenue
Lincolnwood, Illinois 60646

Permission is never granted for commercial purposes.

Manufactured in Yugoslavia

h g f e d c b a

ISBN 0-88176-619-4

CONTENTS

This lovely annuals garden is awash with the many colors of lobelias, verbenas, zinnias, petunias, and plumed cockscomb. Note the various shades—whites, pinks, lavenders, purples, and reds—that blend so harmoniously to create this garden.

PLANNING A SEASONAL KALEIDOSCOPE OF COLOR

Annuals are those plants that go through an entire life cycle—germinate, grow, flower, produce seed, and die—all in a single growing season. Generally, they reach the point of flower production within six to eight weeks after sprouting and continue in abundant bloom until they're killed by frost. In some parts of the United States, perennials that would not survive a severe winter are used as annuals for seasonal color as well.

No wonder, then, that annuals are such a boon to gardeners! Most grow quickly and easily, provide a long season of color, and require minimal special care at very low cost. They also offer a wondrous variety of sizes, flower forms, and leaf types from which to choose. A gardener's problem is not whether to grow annuals—it's how to narrow the choice to those few that space allows.

In this first chapter, we'll discuss some of the important factors to be considered when planning the planting of annuals. Subjects such as soil and light conditions and how they affect plant choices; the palette of colors, forms, and textures available from different annuals; and the attractive ways in which various plantings of annuals can beautify your yard will all be dealt with. These basics will get you started properly toward successful use of annuals in your garden.

Soil & Light

Soil and light are especially important factors to consider when planning the use of annuals. Let's talk about soil first.

Soil types vary from the extremes of constantly dry, nutrient-poor sand to 90 percent rocks held together with 10 percent soil to rich, heavy clay (which forms a slick, sticky, shoe-grabbing mass when wet, then dries to brick hardness). Fortunately, most soil conditions fall somewhere between these extremes. Still, very few homeowners find they have that ideal "rich garden loam" to work with!

Therefore, the first order of business is to learn just what kind of soil you *do* have. The way to do this is to have your soil tested. In some states, the county Cooperative Extension office will do soil tests; in others, it's necessary to use the services of a private testing lab.

To obtain a representative sample of the soil in your flower bed, take a tablespoonful from each end of the bed and another from somewhere in the middle. Dig 4 to 6 inches down before taking each sample. Mix all of the samples together thoroughly in a single container. Then hand carry or mail the mixture to those doing the testing.

You'll want a complete soil test. One part will be a pH test that reads for acidity or alkalinity. A pH test result between 6.0 and 7.0 is ideal and requires no adjustment. A result below 6.0 indicates the soil is too acid. Ground limestone should be added to correct this problem. If the reading is over 7.2, the soil is too alkaline. To solve this problem, add powdered sulfur or, for quicker results, iron sulfate.

In addition to pH, you'll receive information about the nutrients in your soil. If there is a deficiency in any of these, you'll need to add the missing elements as recommended in the report. A third result will tell you the percentage of organic materials contained in your soil; this information will help you decide whether or not you need to supplement your soil with additional organic matter. (Further details on fertilizing and improving garden soil can be found in Chapter 2 in the section "Preparing the Soil," page 24.)

Some homesites have so little soil or the soil is so poor that it cannot—or should not—be used at all. One solution in these situations is to build raised beds and fill them with high-quality soil brought in from elsewhere. Such beds should be at least 6 inches deep to allow good root penetration. This may seem a costly solution in the short-term, but the beds will last for years and prove themselves well worth your initial investment.

Crested cockscomb, sweet alyssum, and dusty miller combine beautifully in a well-designed garden.

Another solution, especially in a small area, is to garden entirely in containers. An imaginative approach, such as installing a deck or patio over the useless ground and then decorating it with container-grown plants, can transform a sad eyesore into an oasis. (You'll find more details on container gardening in Chapter 4, page 76.)

Light is another important factor in gardening. How much is there and for how many hours each day? In other words, does the area where you want to grow your flowers have full sun, partial shade, or full shade?

At least to some extent, the amount of light the flower bed receives will dictate the plant species you'll be able to grow. Those plants that love full sun may become leggy and produce very few flowers if they're planted in a shady spot. By the same token, some plants are sensitive to too much light and will burn when placed in bright sunlight. Fortunately, there are annuals for all lighting conditions. Therefore, except for those places of deepest shade, there are many different annuals from which to choose.

Obtaining a Soil Sample

To obtain a good representative sample of garden soil for testing, dig down 4 to 6 inches below the surface in several different locations in the planting bed. Take a tablespoonful from each hole. Mix all of the samples together thoroughly to make one single large sample. Then hand carry or mail this single sample to the testing lab for analysis.

Soil samples can be taken in the fall if you want to add slow-acting pH adjusters during the fall or winter months.

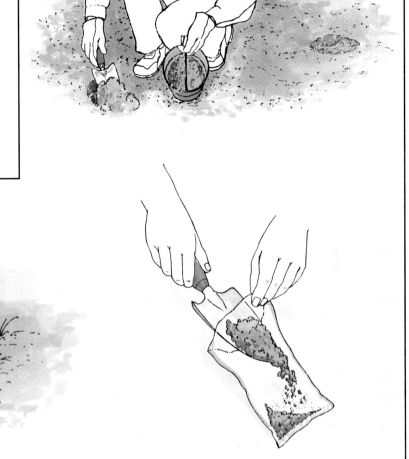

Gardening with Raised Beds

Raised beds are a good choice where soil is either of particularly poor quality or nonexistent. Constructed of pressure-treated wood, reinforced concrete, or mortared brick, stone, or blocks, these beds can be of any length, but should have a soil depth of at least 6 inches. For easy maintenance, beds should be no wider than 4 feet. By filling some beds with a rich loam mixture and others with a more sandy, well-drained mix, it's possible to provide the ideal soil requirements for a wide range of plants.

Color/Form/ Texture/Scale

A very dramatic effect can be created by combining different-colored flowers in various forms with foliage of varied texture.

Annual plantings will have more impact if, as part of the planning process, you consider *all* that each variety has to offer. Frequently, we only think about the color of the flowers annuals produce: Will a pale pink petunia look best beside blue ageratum, or would a bright pink be better?

Color *is* an important factor, but many plants have even more to offer. They may have both colorful blooms *and* foliage of an unusual texture or color: bold-leaved geraniums and nasturtiums; heart-shaped morning glory and moon vine foliage; purple-red cockscomb leaves; feathery cosmos and baby's breath.

Or they may be grown primarily, or even exclusively, for their foliage. Outstanding examples are silvery gray dusty miller, rich purple basil and perilla, and the myriad colors of coleus. Finally, there are those annuals primarily treasured for their seedpods. This group includes decorative peppers, ornamental eggplants, and purple-beaned dolichos.

We see, then, that color comes not only from bloom. It can come from foliage and seedpods as well. The same is true of texture, or surface. Most often we think of foliage as the sole textural source, when in fact texture can be added equally often by flowers themselves.

Besides color and texture, form of both flowers and of the overall growth habit of the plant needs to be considered. Flower forms include tall spikes, round globes, sprays, and clusters. Plant forms range from tall and skinny to low and spreading.

In addition, scale (the size of the plant) also must be kept in mind. Miniature plants are great to use in small spaces and where people are close enough to see them, but in a large area, they can become completely lost. On the other hand, large growing plants such as cleomes, cosmos, and nasturtiums may dominate and even smother out smaller neighbors when space is limited.

When selecting plants to be combined in a garden, all of these factors should be taken into consideration at the time of planning. The design will be more effective if a pleasing mixture of contrasting textures, colors, and plant and flower forms is used.

Learn to look for the bonus a plant may offer. Try to discover the best plant for a given location, rather than settling for one that happens to be readily available. Above all, don't worry about making a bad choice. The beauty of annuals is that you get another chance every growing season!

8

The Varied Characteristics of Annuals

Flowers are not the sole source of color in annual gardens. Many plants such as this dramatic purple perilla and more muted silver-gray dusty miller are treasured for their foliage alone. Others such as cockscombs have both colorful foliage *and* flowers. Still others—ornamental peppers, corn, and castor beans, for instance—provide garden color with their attractive fruits.

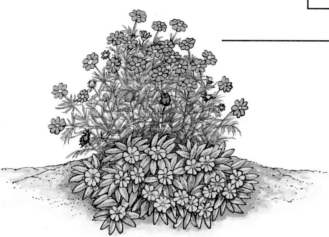

Variety of scale can be provided by both flowers and plants. Here, a large, wide-spreading cosmos and compact calliopsis provide similar flowers on very different-sized plants. Other species, zinnias, for example, offer a wide range of flower sizes and forms on plants that are all very much alike in form and size. Make use of this full range of flower and plant size to provide interest in your garden.

The broad, velvety leaves of this nicotiana, as well as its tall spikes of trumpet-shaped flowers, are a complete contrast in form to the low-spreading impatiens. A garden is more visually stimulating when a variety of forms are used.

This cloud of baby's breath illustrates the role that texture can play in a garden. A flower bed planted exclusively with such open, airy plants would appear to be a floating mist. By contrast, a bed planted entirely with bold, massive plants such as these marigolds would be heavy and solid-looking. Mixing plants of differing textures provides a pleasant variety and balance.

Massing Colors

Plumed cockscomb in bold colors of red and yellow give this massed garden a dramatic tone.

The easiest, most straightforward way to use annuals is to select one favorite and flood the entire planting area with it. This approach eliminates deciding where to plant a particular variety, selecting colors and textures that blend together effectively, or learning the cultural requirements for more than one kind of plant. It can be a money-saving solution as well: You only need to purchase one or two packets of seed to obtain enough plants to fill an entire planting area.

Certainly, the impact of all one kind and color of bloom can be very dramatic. Imagine an entire garden awash with fiery red geraniums or bold, yellow marigolds; fluorescent-pink fibrous begonias, or cooling white petunias!

Variations of this approach are also possible. For those who prefer variety of color, but all the same kind of plant, a checkerboard design would allow the use of large clumps of several different colors in a single species. The lipstick shades of impatiens work well in this kind of massing. Geraniums would, too.

Alternatively, some species come in an abundant variety of flower and plant sizes. A bed filled with zinnias, for example, could include everything from dwarf 10- to 12-inch mounds in front to giant 3- to 4-foot tall background clumps, with a wide range of flower colors and sizes in double, single, and spider forms. Marigolds are another species that grow in great variety, all of which are extremely vigorous and foolproof.

Another way to mass annuals is to keep to a single color but use several different plant varieties. The resulting garden would contain plants of different forms and heights with a variety of different flower shapes, all in varying shades of one color. A unique option for this style of massing would be a silver-gray garden!

Whichever design option is selected, massed plantings are generally rather formal looking—bold and dramatic rather than homey or quaint. They're the perfect complement to a large or formal house. Massing can also provide a clean, uncluttered look where garden space is severely limited.

For something simple, something easy, something different, consider the massed approach. Using annuals for this purpose allows the added option of changing the entire look of your yard every growing season simply by selecting a different plant or color. However, if that's too much bother, you can always repeat the same theme year after year.

GOOD CHOICES FOR MASSED PLANTINGS

Globe Amaranth	Marigold
Fibrous Begonia	Ornamental Kale
Canna	Ornamental Pepper
Chrysanthemum	Petunia
Cleome	Pocketbook Plant
Cockscomb	Red Salvia
Coleus	Snapdragon
Dusty Miller	Zinnia
Geranium	

Simple Massed Layout

This simple massed garden layout uses bedding geraniums in several varieties. All of the bed sections are the same size. Note that white varieties have been used as buffers between flower shades that might possibly clash. This garden is full of color all at one height.

15'						
Orbit Apple Blossom	Orbit Violet	Sprinter White	Orbit Cherry	Hollywood Star	Orbit White	Elite Salmon

3'

Elaborate Massed Layout

Here is a more elaborate massed layout for the same garden bed, using the same geranium varieties. Two standard or tree geraniums have been added as focal points that will stand above the rest of the flowers in the bed. Potted plants on pedestals could be substituted for the tree geraniums. Other possible substitutes include a pair of dwarf columnar evergreens, small boxwood bushes, or clumps of tall, decorative grasses.

Tree Geranium   15'   Tree Geranium

Sprinter White	Elite Salmon	Orbit Cherry	Elite Salmon	Sprinter White
Orbit Violet	Orbit Apple Blossom	Orbit White	Orbit Apple Blossom	Orbit Violet

3'

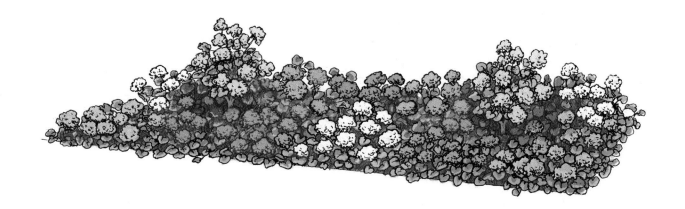

11

Gardening in a Single Color

This all-yellow garden plan utilizes many different annuals. A variety of plant and flower forms, as well as different plant heights, add interest to this planting. As the color-coding shows, the tallest varieties are located in the center back of the bed and the low-growing varieties at the front, with intermediate heights filling in between. As a result, none of the plants will be hidden from view.

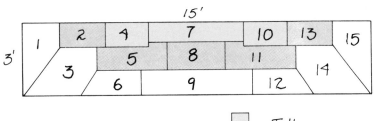

☐ = Tall

☐ = Intermediate

☐ = Low

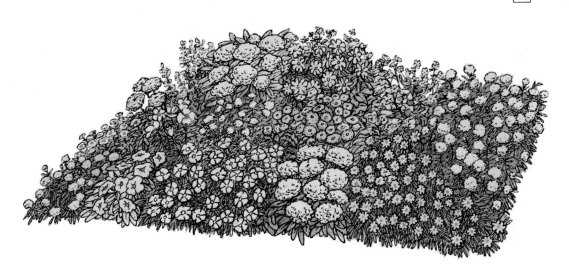

ALL YELLOW GARDEN:

1. Pot Marigold - Yellow
2. Zinnia - Yellow Zenith
3. Marigold - Gold Lady
4. Snapdragon - Golden Rocket
5. California Poppy - Sunlite
6. Petunia - California Girl
7. Crested Cockscomb - Yellow
8. Marigold - Yellow Fireworks

9. Marigold - Signet Lemon Gem
10. Dahlia - Sunny Yellow
11. Feverfew - Gold Ball
12. Crested Cockscomb - Yellow
13. Nasturtium - Golden
14. Cosmos - Sunny Yellow
15. Marigold - Yellow Nugget

Mingling Annuals with Other Plantings

Just take a look at this glorious garden of candytuft, cosmos, China pinks, and perennials.

Although annuals make a splendid display on their own, they also combine effectively with other plants. Any dull spot can be brightened almost immediately with the addition of a few colorful annuals.

If, as you look at your garden, you feel something is lacking, see if you can identify one or more areas where accents of color would improve it. For example, although shrub borders are flower-filled in spring and early summer, they often provide only a few blooms the rest of the season. In many gardens, shrub plantings provide no summer color at all. It's amazing how much more attractive such an area becomes when just a few groupings of annuals are inserted. It's not necessary to plant a large bed in front of the entire length of the shrub border. Several strategically located accent clumps are usually all that is needed.

Annuals can also provide the perfect midsummer boost a perennial border may need. Plant them in the spaces where spring bulbs and some perennials are dying back, or where early flowering biennials such as foxgloves and English daisies have been removed—anyplace an empty spot occurs.

If a perennial bed is so packed that there is no free space in which to plant annuals, consider another approach: Place pots or boxes of annuals on small outdoor tables or stools. Tuck these display stands here and there in the border. Or, if there is a fence or wall behind the border, use it as a support from which to hang half-baskets or window boxes full of flowering annuals.

Another good place to add annuals is in the vegetable patch. Not only will they enliven an area not normally expected to be colorful, they'll also provide an excellent source of cut flowers to bring indoors. Because the vegetable garden is not usually a display area, every flower can be picked if desired.

Plantings combining annuals with vegetables can be laid out in various ways. One approach would be to plant annuals around the outer edges of the garden, hiding or disguising the vegetable patch. Another alternative would be to plant rows of annuals here and there among the vegetables. Finally, a handsome combination design, especially where the total garden space is limited, would be a very formal geometric garden, laid out with some of the beds planted with annuals and others with vegetables. The final choice, of course, depends on your personal preferences as well as on the dictates of your garden site.

HANDSOME FOLIAGE AND FRUIT

Globe Amaranth	Dusty Miller
Alternanthera	Moses-in-a-Boat
Asparagus Fern	Nasturtium
Basil	Ornamental Corn
Rex Begonia	Ornamental Kale
Blood Leaf	Ornamental Pepper
Burning Bush	Perilla
Caladium	Polka-Dot Plant
Castor Bean	Purple Heart
Cockscomb	Scarlet Runner Bean
Coleus	Snow-in-Summer
Dracaena	

Livening up a Shrub Border

Most shrub borders have few blooms, if any, during the summer months. To liven up what is normally a dull area, add a few sweeps of colorful annuals, using the shrub border as a backdrop. This plan shows the way informal groupings can be inserted. Either plants of one kind and color or several different kinds of plants can be used. In the latter case, taller varieties should be located as indicated by the red-shaded areas.

☐ = Low-growing Annuals

☐ = Tall annual varieties

Annuals in a Perennials Border

This plan shows part of a perennial border, indicating where each grouping of perennials, biennials (plants that have a two-year life cycle, blooming and dying their second year), and bulbs is planted. Areas shaded in gray indicate sections that will be in bloom in spring months.

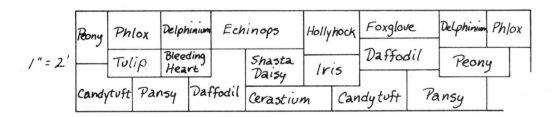

1" = 2'

This overlay of the above plan shows how annuals can add color in those sections of the perennial border where bulbs and early spring flowering biennials have died back or have been removed (shaded in gray). Red-shaded areas indicate where perennials will provide summer bloom. Note: When bedding plants are planted in bulb areas, care must be taken to place them between—rather than directly on top of—the bulbs in order to avoid damaging the bulbs while digging.

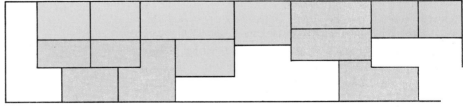

Selecting Annuals for Color & Characteristics

An eye-catching garden can be achieved by combining annuals of different colors and sizes.

Planting annuals can be as simple as selecting one favorite flower and flooding an entire planting area with it. When using this approach, you don't need to decide where to plant a particular variety; you don't need to be concerned about selecting colors and textures that blend well together; and there's no need to learn the cultural requirements for more than one kind of plant.

Most people, however, prefer to mix different annuals varieties in their gardens, even though it requires a bit more work and planning. Available colors, height of plants, shade or sun preference, soil requirements—all of these factors have to be taken into consideration.

Planning an annuals garden in advance is the only way to make sure that an annuals bed is color balanced and that the plants work well together in terms of sun or shade, height, and soil.

If you list your favorite plants on paper first, noting their available colors and cultural requirements, you're off to a good start. As you narrow down those that work well together, you can actually see a workable garden emerge in front of you. By taking this extra bit of time, you can save yourself from being disappointed later.

The charts that follow are a quick reference for selecting plants for your garden. However, it should be kept in mind that they give only a simplistic first screening. When scanning these lists, you may find many plants that seem appropriate for your garden. However, on further investigation, you'll find that some of them aren't appropriate after all. Use the charts to narrow down the choices; then refer to the more detailed description in the Encyclopedia section beginning on page 88, to identify those best-suited to your climate, soil, and light conditions.

These charts are very easy to use since they identify plants by color range (in most instances by flower color). However, those marked with an asterisk (*) and the "Grasses and Foliage" category have colorful foliage, fruits, or seedpods instead.

It's important to remember that the "Multicolor" category lists those plants that come in nearly every color range (any annual that comes in more than three color ranges has been put into this category). Because it contains the most universal and versatile annuals, be sure to use it often when making your selections.

Whether you are a novice or a gardener with many years of planting experience, using a chart with information on color, light, soil, and height can be the difference between a picture-perfect garden and one that just doesn't quite work.

MULTICOLOR

	Dry Soil	Average Soil	Moist Soil	Full Sun	Part Shade	Full Shade	Under 12 Inches	12-24 Inches	Over 24 Inches	Vining
Alternanthera	•	•		•			•			
Amaranth, Globe	•	•		•				•		
Begonia, Fibrous		•		•	•	•	•			
Begonia, Tuberous*		•	•		•	•	•			
Candytuft	•	•		•			•			
Chrysanthemum		•		•			•	•	•	
Coleus			•		•	•	•			
Cosmos		•		•				•	•	
Dahlia		•	•	•				•	•	
Daisy, African (Arctotis)	•			•			•			
Daisy, Livingstone	•	•		•			•			
Daisy, Swan River		•		•			•	•		
Daisy, Transvaal		•	•				•	•		
Everlastings	•	•		•			•			
Four O'Clock	•	•		•	•			•	•	
Foxglove			•	•	•	•			•	
Gazania	•						•	•		
Geranium, Ivy-Leaf		•		•	•		•	•		
Geranium, Other			•	•			•			
Geranium, Zonal			•	•			•			
Gladiolus		•		•				•	•	
Godetia (Clarkia)	•			•	•			•	•	
Hollyhock		•	•	•					•	
Impatiens		•	•		•	•	•	•		
Impatiens, New Guinea		•	•	•			•			
Lupine			•	•					•	
Marigold, Cape	•			•			•			
Nemesia		•		•	•			•		
Nicotiana		•	•	•	•			•	•	
Pansy		•	•	•	•		•			
Petunia		•		•				•		
Phlox		•		•			•	•		
Portulaca	•			•			•			
Primrose		•	•		•		•			
Salpiglossis		•	•	•					•	
Schizanthus		•	•	•	•				•	
Snapdragon		•		•			•	•	•	
Sweet Pea		•		•			•	•		•
Toadflax	•			•			•			
Verbena	•	•		•			•			
Zinnia		•		•			•	•	•	

BLUE TO PURPLE

	Dry Soil	Average Soil	Moist Soil	Full Sun	Part Shade	Full Shade	Under 12 Inches	12-24 Inches	Over 24 Inches	Vining
Alyssum, Sweet	•	•		•		•				
Aster		•		•			•	•	•	
Baby Blue Eyes	•	•		•	•		•			
Bachelor's Button		•	•	•				•	•	
Beard Tongue		•		•	•			•		
Blue Bells, California	•			•			•			
Blue Lace Flower		•		•					•	
Blue Marguerite		•	•	•	•		•			
Canterbury Bells		•		•					•	
Chilean Bell Flower	•			•			•			
Cup and Saucer Vine			•	•						•
Echium		•	•	•			•	•		
Floss Flower		•		•	•		•			
Forget-Me-Not		•	•	•			•			
Forget-Me-Not, Chinese		•			•			•		
Forget-Me-Not, Summer		•		•			•			
Fuchsia		•	•		•		•			
Heliotrope		•		•			•			
Lantana	•	•		•			•	•		
Larkspur		•		•				•	•	
Lisianthus		•	•	•				•	•	
Lobelia		•	•	•	•		•			
Love-in-a-Mist		•	•	•			•			
Morning Glory Vine	•	•		•						•
Moses-in-a-Boat*		•		•	•		•			
Nierembergia			•	•			•			
None So Pretty		•		•				•		
Perilla*	•	•		•					•	
Purple Heart		•		•	•	•				
Salvia		•		•	•		•	•		
Sapphire Flower		•		•	•		•			
Scabiosa		•		•				•	•	
Scarlet Flax	•	•		•				•		
Scarlet Pimpernel	•	•		•		•				
Southern Star		•		•				•		
Stock		•	•	•				•	•	
Torenia		•	•	•	•	•				
Violet, Persian			•	•			•			

* = foliage or fruits/pods this color
** = bulb

RED

	Dry Soil	Average Soil	Moist Soil	Full Sun	Part Shade	Full Shade	Under 12 Inches	12-24 Inches	Over 24 Inches	Vining
Abelmoschus		•	•	•				•		
Blanket Flower	•			•				•		
Blood Leaf*		•	•	•	•		•	•		
Calliopsis	•	•		•				•		
Canna**		•	•	•					•	
China Pink	•	•		•			•			
Cockscomb		•		•			•	•	•	
Daisy, English		•	•	•	•		•			
Firecracker Plant		•		•			•			
Hibiscus, Chinese			•	•					•	
Joseph's Coat*	•	•		•					•	
Lantana	•	•		•			•	•	•	
Lotus Vine		•		•					•	
Flowering Maple			•	•	•			•		
Marigold, Pot		•		•			•	•		
Monkey Flower			•		•	•				
Nasturtium	•	•		•		•				•
Ornamental Pepper*		•		•			•	•	•	
Poppy, Iceland		•		•				•		
Salvia		•		•	•		•	•	•	
Scarlet Flax	•	•		•				•		
Scarlet Pimpernel	•	•		•			•			
Scarlet Runner Bean		•		•						•
Stock		•		•				•	•	
Vinca		•	•	•			•	•		
Wallflower, English	•	•		•	•		•	•		

PINK TO FUCHSIA

	Dry Soil	Average Soil	Moist Soil	Full Sun	Part Shade	Full Shade	Under 12 Inches	12-24 Inches	Over 24 Inches	Vining
Abelmoschus		•	•	•				•		
Alyssum, Sweet	•	•		•			•			
Aster		•		•			•	•	•	
Baby's Breath		•		•				•		
Bachelor's Button		•	•	•				•	•	
Beard Tongue		•		•	•			•		
Caladium* **			•		•	•	•			
Calla**		•	•	•				•	•	
Canna**		•	•	•					•	
Canterbury Bells		•		•				•		
China Pink	•	•		•			•			
Cleome		•		•					•	
Cockscomb		•		•			•	•	•	
Corn Cockle		•		•					•	
Daisy, English		•	•	•			•			
Echium		•	•	•			•	•		
Forget-Me-Not		•	•	•	•		•			
Forget-Me-Not, Chinese		•		•			•			
Forget-Me-Not, Summer		•		•			•			
Fuchsia		•	•		•		•			
Hibiscus, Chinese			•	•					•	
Lantana	•	•		•			•	•	•	
Larkspur		•		•				•	•	
Lisianthus		•	•	•				•		
Lobelia		•	•	•	•		•			
Love-in-a-Mist		•	•	•			•			
Magic Carpet Plant		•		•	•		•			
Mallow		•		•				•		
Monkey Flower			•		•	•				
Morning Glory Vine	•	•		•						•
None So Pretty		•		•			•			
Ornamental Cabbage, Kale*		•		•			•			
Poppy, Iceland		•		•				•	•	
Rose Mallow	•	•		•					•	
Scarlet Flax	•	•		•			•			
Scotch Thistle		•		•					•	
Stock		•	•	•				•	•	
Torenia		•	•		•	•	•			
Vinca		•	•	•			•	•		
Violet, Persian			•		•	•	•			

These cultural recommendations are intended to suggest the average conditions over a wide geographical area. It is important to be aware of local requirements.

YELLOW TO ORANGE

	Dry Soil	Average Soil	Moist Soil	Full Sun	Part Shade	Full Shade	Under 12 Inches	12-24 Inches	Over 24 Inches	Vining
Black-Eyed Susan	•	•		•				•	•	
Blanket Flower	•			•				•		
Calla**			•	•	•			•	•	
Calliopsis	•	•		•			•			
Canna**		•	•	•					•	
Cockscomb		•		•			•	•	•	
Daisy, African (Golden Ageratum)	•			•			•			
Daisy, Dahlberg	•			•			•			
Hibiscus, Chinese			•	•					•	
Joseph's Coat*	•	•		•					•	
Lantana	•	•		•			•	•	•	
Flowering Maple			•	•	•		•			
Marigold, American			•	•				•	•	
Marigold, French			•	•			•			
Marigold, Pot		•					•	•		
Meadow Foam			•	•			•			
Melampodium		•		•			•			
Monkey Flower			•		•		•			
Nasturtium	•	•		•			•			•
Ornamental Pepper*		•		•			•	•	•	
Pocketbook Plant			•		•		•			
Poppy, California	•			•			•			
Poppy, Horned	•			•				•		
Poppy, Mexican Tulip	•			•				•		
Sanvitalia	•	•		•	•		•			
Scarlet Pimpernel	•	•		•			•			
Sundrop		•		•				•	•	
Sunflower		•		•					•	
Thunbergia		•		•						•
Tidy Tips	•			•			•	•		
Tithonia	•	•		•					•	
Venidium	•			•				•		
Wallflower, English	•	•		•	•		•	•		

GRASSES & FOLIAGE

	Dry Soil	Average Soil	Moist Soil	Full Sun	Part Shade	Full Shade	Under 12 Inches	12-24 Inches	Over 24 Inches	Vining
Alternanthera	•	•		•		•				
Amaranth, Globe	•	•		•					•	
Asparagus Fern		•		•	•			•		
Basil	•			•				•		
Begonia, Tuberous		•	•		•	•		•		
Burning Bush	•	•		•				•		
Caladium**			•		•	•		•		
Castor Bean		•	•	•					•	
Cloud Grass	•	•		•			•			
Coleus		•	•		•	•		•		
Dracaena		•		•					•	
Dusty Miller	•	•		•			•	•		
Geranium, Ivy-Leaf		•		•	•				•	
Geranium, Other			•	•				•		
Geranium, Zonal			•	•				•		
Golden Top	•	•		•		•				
Impatiens, New Guinea		•	•	•				•		
Job's Tears	•	•		•					•	
Gourds		•		•						•
Love-in-a-Mist		•	•	•				•	•	
Moses-in-a-Boat		•		•	•	•				
Ornamental Cabbage, Kale		•		•				•		
Ornamental Corn		•	•	•					•	
Ornamental Peppers		•		•			•	•		
Perilla	•	•		•					•	
Polka Dot Plant		•			•			•	•	
Quaking Grass	•	•		•			•			
Snow-in-Summer	•	•	•					•		
Wheat Grass	•	•		•					•	
Wild Oats		•		•			•			

* = foliage or fruits/pods this color
** = bulb

WHITE TO GREEN

	Dry Soil	Average Soil	Moist Soil	Full Sun	Part Shade	Full Shade	Under 12 Inches	12–24 Inches	Over 24 Inches	Vining
Alyssum, Sweet	•	•		•		•				
Angel's Trumpet		•	•	•					•	
Aster		•		•		•		•	•	
Baby's Breath		•		•			•			
Bachelor's Button		•	•	•			•	•		
Beard Tongue		•		•	•		•			
Bells of Ireland*		•	•	•	•				•	
Caladium* **		•			•	•	•			
Calla**		•	•	•				•	•	
Canterbury Bells		•		•	•				•	
Sweet False Chamomile		•		•					•	
China Pink	•	•		•		•				
Cleome		•		•					•	
Cup and Saucer Vine		•	•							•
Daisy, English		•	•	•	•		•			
Floss Flower		•		•	•		•			
Forget-Me-Not		•	•	•	•		•			
Forget-Me-Not, Chinese		•		•	•		•			
Forget-Me-Not, Summer		•		•	•		•			
Hibiscus, Chinese		•	•						•	
Larkspur		•		•				•	•	
Lisianthus		•	•	•				•	•	
Lobelia		•	•	•	•		•			
Love-in-a-Mist		•	•	•			•			
Flowering Maple			•	•	•		•			
Marigold, American			•	•				•	•	
Marigold, Pot		•		•		•	•			
Mignonette		•	•	•	•		•			
Morning Glory Vine	•	•		•						•
Ornamental Cabbage, Kale*		•		•			•			
Poppy, Iceland		•		•			•			
Rose Mallow	•	•		•					•	
Salvia		•		•	•		•	•	•	
Sapphire Flower		•		•	•		•			
Scabiosa		•		•				•	•	
Snow-in-Summer*	•	•	•	•				•		
Stock		•	•	•				•	•	
Torenia		•	•		•	•	•			
Tuberose		•		•				•		
Venidium	•			•				•		
Vinca		•	•	•		•		•		
Violet, Persian			•		•			•		
Wallflower, English	•	•		•	•		•	•		

These cultural recommendations are intended to suggest the average conditions over a wide geographical area. It is important to be aware of local requirements.

This waterside annuals border is filled with flowers in various shades of red and pink. Interspersed with foliage and surrounded by trees, this is truly an annuals oasis. Surprisingly little work is needed to create such beauty.

SECRETS TO SUCCESSFUL ANNUALS GARDENING

Many annuals are easy to start from seed, either indoors or directly in the garden. However, if they're given the extra boost of the best possible growing conditions, they're bound to thrive and bloom more abundantly than they would under less ideal circumstances. This chapter focuses on proper soil preparation, the supplies and tools needed to achieve good results, and selection and care of boxed bedding plants. Also included is information on starting seeds indoors and their planting in outdoor beds.

Included are tips on collecting seeds from your own plants for use the following season, along with information about why propagation from seeds works for some varieties and not for others. A list of those plants for which home seed collection is appropriate is an added feature. Similarly, you'll learn which annuals can readily be propagated from cuttings, as well as how to take cuttings, root them, and plant them out (transplant them outdoors).

For those who have the time and interest, starting your own plants from seeds and cuttings can be fun. For those who need quicker results, or don't have time to start their own plants, buying boxed plants is the perfect solution. Whatever your needs, there's much information here to help you grow annuals successfully.

Tools for Gardening Projects

Few tools are needed to successfully grow annuals.

I n any enterprise, the proper tools make the work much easier to accomplish. You don't necessarily need a large array of tools to garden successfully. The basic hand tools needed for annuals are: a hand trowel, a cultivator, a spading fork, a square-ended spade, an iron bow rake, a narrow-bladed hoe, a pair of small pruning shears, and a narrow-bladed paring knife or jackknife. Several additional tools worth considering are a hoe with a small blade that will fit into narrow spaces, a scuffle hoe, and a sprayer. Another piece of equipment that's handy, but not essential, is a large-wheeled garden cart for hauling. When selecting tools, it's worthwhile to invest in good quality at the outset. Buying cheap tools is false economy. Not only do they make the work harder to do, they're very likely to break as soon as stress is exerted on them. Thus, you save money by paying a higher price for one shovel every ten years than buying two or three at a slightly lower price over that same period.

At the same time, remember that higher price does not automatically *guarantee* higher quality. Check to see if the manufacturer provides a long-term or lifetime guarantee on the product. Willingness to stand behind a product is a good indication that the producer is conscientiously trying to make a well-made tool.

Carefully study the construction of several different brands of each tool you're buying to see which are most solidly built. Details to look for include wooden handles made of hickory or ash with the grain running straight along the full length of the handle; the metal portion fitted and securely attached to the wood portion—avoid those where a single rivet holds the entire tool together; a rolled edge along the top of the blade to allow more pushing surface for your foot; blade shanks that are reinforced rather than of a single thickness; and blade shanks extended along the wooden handle for added strength.

Consult garden center employees. Ask them to point out the comparative advantages and disadvantages of each brand they carry. Confer with experienced gardening friends about which features they've found to be important.

In addition to the basic tools listed here, many other garden tools and gadgets are available. Invest in them only after you own the basics and gain quite a bit of hands-on gardening experience. Over time, you may conclude that some of these specialty tools would make your work easier; more often than not, you'll find that the basic tools you have already do the job satisfactorily. Buy others only as you experience a need for them.

Keep tools in top condition by storing them carefully in an area protected from the weather. Remove dirt and mud after each use, wiping the metal parts with a lightly oiled cloth. Periodically sharpen the blades on shovels and hoes, as well as on knives and shears. Hanging tools for storage helps keep blades sharp longer, while also cutting down on storage area clutter.

Treat your tools well, and they'll give you many years of fine service.

Necessary Garden Tools

Illustrated here are the basic tools and gardening equipment needed to grow annuals. Start with these, adding others only if you find you need them. Items such as a garden cart, for example, may prove useful, but certainly are not essential.

trowel

rake   spade   fork   hoe   cultivator

Preparing the Soil

The fruit of your labors—a tiny hibiscus seedling grows.

As was mentioned in the section on soil and light in Chapter 1, soil characteristics vary widely. Naturally, then, there's also wide variation in the ways to amend and improve soil to achieve the best possible growing conditions.

If the results of your soil test indicate a lack of certain nutrients, you should follow the recommendations made by the testing company for supplementing the soil. If the imbalance is slight, organic fertilizers can be used. Because they generally contain a low percentage of nutrients that are slowly released into the soil, organic fertilizers are inadequate when fast results are needed, or if the imbalance of nutrients is great. In these situations, inorganic fertilizers are the better choice. A combination of both kinds may be a good compromise solution, using the quick-to-feed commercial plant foods first, then following up in subsequent years with the slow-feeding organic fertilizers.

Chemical fertilizer is formulated in a combination of the three major nutrients: nitrogen, phosphorous, and potassium—N, P, K. The numbers featured on each bag represent the percentage of each of these nutrients in the mix. For example, 5-10-5 contains 5 percent nitrogen (N), 10 percent phosphorous (P), and 5 percent potassium (K). 10-10-10 contains 10 percent of each. The NPK formula is also listed on each container of organic fertilizer. The percentages of each nutrient are lower in organic fertilizers than in inorganic fertilizers. Therefore, larger amounts of organic plant food are required to achieve the same results.

It's also possible to purchase fertilizers separately rather than in a three-nutrient mix. These are useful when there's a deficiency in a single nutrient. Consult with your Cooperative Extension office (there's one in every county) or garden center staff if you feel uncertain about solving nutrient deficiency problems.

Adjusting the nutrient and pH levels in your soil will not make any difference in its *consistency*. To improve soil texture will require the addition of one or several "soil conditioners." The most commonly used conditioners are leaf mold, compost, well-rotted cow manure, and peat moss. Vermiculite, perlite, and sand (coarse builder's sand, *never* use beach sand) can also be added, especially when the basic soil is heavy.

To properly prepare a planting bed, first remove any sod from the area, then rototill or hand dig the soil, turning it over thoroughly. (Rototillers can be rented by the day, and it's often possible to hire someone to come and till by the hour, if you don't have a tiller of your own.)

If the area is rocky, remove as many stones as possible as you till. Next, spread the necessary fertilizer, soil conditioners, and pH-adjusting chemicals over the area. Till again. You should be able to till more deeply the second time; ideally, you want to loosen and improve the soil to a depth of more than 6 inches. Turn and loosen soil by hand with a spade where the area is too small to require a rototiller. After this inital treatment, fertilizers, soil conditioners, and pH-adjusting chemicals will be added at different times of the year for best results.

If possible, allow the soil to stand unplanted for a week or more. Stir the surface inch or two every three to four days with a scuffle hoe or cultivator to eradicate fast-germinating weed seeds. This will make your weeding chores lighter during the rest of the season.

Now is the perfect time to install some kind of mowing strip around the garden bed. Patio squares or slate pieces laid end-to-end at ground level will keep grass and flowers from intermixing. Other options include landscape logs, poured concrete strips, or bricks laid side-by-side on a sand or concrete base. The mowing strip must be deep and wide enough so grass roots cannot tunnel underneath or travel across the top to reach the flower bed, and the top of the strip must not extend above the level of the adjacent lawn.

Over time, a mowing strip will save more gardening effort, to say nothing of the gardener's patience, than any other device. It's well worth the time and money invested at the beginning!

Planting Preparations

1 Mark the flower bed boundaries with pegs and string for straight edges and with a garden hose for curved lines. Cut through the sod along laid-out lines with a spade. Remove the sod from the entire bed. Till the area, removing rocks as you proceed. For a small planting area, dig and break up the soil by hand or with a spade.

2 Spread well-rotted manure, compost, or leaf mold onto the bed to provide organic matter and improve soil quality. If other soil conditioners are needed, perlite, sand, and moistened peat moss should be added at this time.

3 Rototill or hand dig the bed deeply a second time to thoroughly incorporate these additions. This second digging will allow the tiller to loosen soil to a greater depth than could be achieved by tilling only once.

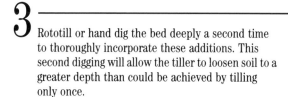

4 To keep the grass out of the flower bed and the annuals from overflowing onto the lawn, install an edging strip around the bed. This strip should be at least 2 inches deep and 6 inches wide. The top of the strip should be at ground level to allow the wheel of the lawnmower to run along it. Installation of an edging strip will save many hours of maintenance effort each year.

Bedding Plants by the Boxful

Boxed bedding impatiens are ready for your garden.

For those who want to have an almost instant show of annual bloom, boxed bedding plants are the answer. Every garden center and nursery, many roadside stands, and quite a few grocery and discount stores offer a selection of prestarted annuals. The main drawback to purchasing boxed bedding plants is the limited selection. There are many annuals that are unavailable from any commercial sources. A gardener who wants them will have to start them at home. Also, if large numbers of plants are needed, the cost of boxed plants can be prohibitive.

In these instances, or just for the pleasure of it, you may want to start your own bedding plants. It's quite possible for any gardener to succeed with only a small initial investment in equipment and supplies.

Light—The most essential ingredient for successful seed starting is adequate light. It's possible to start seeds on the sill of a sun-filled window, but plants often stretch out toward the light source and become leggy. A three-sided white or silver reflector shield set up behind the plant trays will reflect light back onto the plants to help combat this problem.

Where there is not enough light available naturally, an easy alternative is to raise seedlings under fluorescent growlamps. To provide maximum light from all sides, surround the area under the lights with a white or silver-painted reflector.

Heat—Along with light, another need is adequate heat. The bottom heat that warms the soil in which the seedlings are grown is very important. If the air temperature in the chosen growing area is colder than 70° F, bottom heat can be supplied by a heating cable installed under the growing medium.

Water—Water is a third requirement for plant growth. A rimmed watering tray will allow the seed trays and young plants to be watered from the bottom. Top watering can batter plants down, as well as increase the possibility of fungus problems.

The primary concern with bottom watering is overwatering. Water shouldn't continuously stand in the watering tray. Pour lukewarm water to a ¼ inch depth into the tray. Leave it for five to ten minutes. At the end of that time, observe how much water is left in the tray. Also, roll a small pinch of the planting soil between thumb and finger to test for moisture. What you want is soil that feels wet with very little or no water remaining in the tray.

Test the soil moisture once each day by rolling a small amount between your fingers. Water again when the soil feels more dry than wet. It's impossible to predict how many days will be needed between waterings. You'll be able to make a fairly accurate "guesstimate" of your own circumstances after a few weeks.

Soil—Planting soil for starting and growing young seedlings should be free of weeds and disease. This can be accomplished by sterilizing the planting mix. First, spread it in a thin layer on cookie sheets and bake at a low temperature (150 to 200° F) until it is completely dried out. Next, cool the soil and mix the water back into it until it's moist. Finally, pour the soil into sterile containers, allowing it to settle for a day before planting the seeds. A simpler approach is to purchase a specially formulated plant starter mix made up of inert materials. Fill the sterile containers with this mix, firm or tamp it lightly with your fingers, then sow the seeds.

Containers—Seeds can be started in a variety of containers: milk or egg cartons with holes punched in their bottoms or low on their sides, plastic or wooden boxes, clay or plastic pots, peat pots, or special seed starter cubes and trays are all equally acceptable. Virtually anything that will hold soil and allow easy passage of water through drainage holes in the bottom will work.

Containers designed to hold a single plant are the best choice for large plants, which tend to crowd each other out in six-packs; for plants that don't like to have their roots disturbed by transplanting; and for climbing vines. Most annuals do well in any container.

Equipment and Supplies for Starting Plants Indoors

The equipment needed for starting plants indoors includes:

1. A fluorescent light fixture with full-spectrum growlamp bulbs. Ideally, you should be able to easily raise and lower the fixture in order to maintain about 3 inches between the light bulbs and the plant tops at all times.

2. An automatic timer to turn the light fixture on and off each day is optional. However, it does take the worry out of trying to remember this twice-a-day chore. Since plants require between 16 to 18 hours of light daily, don't leave the lights on all of the time; darkness is also essential.

3. White or silver-colored reflectors placed around three, or all four, sides will bounce light onto plants from all angles. It will help keep them from leaning and stretching toward a single light source. A homemade reflector can be made of cardboard covered with aluminum foil.

4. If the seed starting setup is in a cool room, a thermostatically controlled heating cable should be laid under the seed boxes and pots. Bottom heat is more important than air temperature to encourage strong growth.

5. A drip tray allows watering of seedlings from the bottom. Water poured into the tray is absorbed upward into the soil.

27

Seed Sowing—Seeds can be sown individually in single pots. Plant two seeds in each, removing the weaker of the two seedlings when they grow their first real leaves (the very first leaves to unfold from a new seedling are called the seed leaves; the second set of leaves are their first real leaves).

When sowing a packet of seeds in a box or larger pot, they can either be broadcast over the surface in a scatter pattern or be planted in rows. If only a few plants of each kind are wanted, rows make more sense; when larger numbers of plants are desired, broadcasting is faster. If the seeds are very small, don't cover them with additional planting mix after sowing; medium to large seeds should have a layer of planting mix sprinkled on top. Lightly press the surface of the planting mix after sowing.

Label—Be sure to label each planting in some way. The system doesn't matter as long as you have one.

Once the seeds are sown, water the seed trays from the bottom until the mix feels moist. Allow excess water to drip out of the container bottom before placing the container in your growing setup.

Lay two sheets of newspaper over each seed tray. For the first few days, this provides the semi-darkness some seeds prefer for germination. Inspect each seed tray closely every day. As soon as you see seedlings pushing through, remove the newspaper layer. Germination time varies widely. Ideally, you should start the slower growers earlier than those that germinate rapidly in order to have them all at the same stage when planting time arrives. Study the descriptions of each plant to know when to get each of them started.

Damping Off—Probably the worst enemy of successful seed starting is a problem known as "damping off." It strikes within two weeks of germination when seedlings are very young. When it hits, the plants simply lie down and die, usually in less than a day's time. Damping off is a fungus infection that can best be avoided by making certain that both the soil and containers in which seeds are planted are sterile. The seeds themselves can be lightly dusted with fungicide powder prior to planting as an additional precaution. Young seedlings should be looked at morning and evening to check for any sign of a problem. Even if only two or three plants have lain down, take the precaution of immediately spraying the plants with a fungicide or, if none is available, try a mild vinegar solution.

Food—Prepared starter mixes usually have plant nutrients in them that feed the seedlings. If you make your own homemade starter from milled sphagnum, vermiculite, or sterilized sand, you'll need to fertilize in some way. The easiest method is to add a soluble fertilizer at a very weak rate to the regular waterings. (For details on various organic and inorganic fertilizers, read "Feeding Alternatives," Chapter 3, page 50.)

Pricking Off—Other than those that were planted individually, all seedlings should be transplanted from the seed trays when the first true leaves appear. This first transplanting is usually referred to as "pricking off." At this stage, seedlings should be planted into small individual peat pots, planting cubes, or partitioned growing boxes. They will remain in these containers until planting time.

Fill the boxes with a good potting soil or commercial growing mix. To make your own soil, mix equal amounts of garden soil or sterilized potting soil, moistened peat moss, and perlite or coarse builder's sand. Gently lift out and separate the young plants, holding them by their seed leaves.

Place the seedling in the new container so the soil line will be at the same level on the stem as it was in the seed tray. Gently firm the soil around the plant roots, bringing it to within ¼ inch of the container rim. Water from the top with a weak fertilizer solution. Place these pricked-off plants back by the window or under growlamps to continue their growth.

Hardening Off—By this time, plants should be stocky and strong, but they will need some toughening up. This process is referred to as "hardening off." It'll keep the plants from suffering shock, or trauma, when they are planted outside.

Carry the plants outdoors each day for a few hours, bringing them back inside overnight. Shade them with an old window screen to protect them from strong light and wind. Start with two or three hours, then increase the length of time they're outside by an additional hour each day. After a week, they can be outdoors all day, and only need to be brought in at night.

Planting Out—At this point, the plants are ready to plant out into the garden bed. Those in individual peat pots can be dropped into planting holes, the soil firmed around the pot, an earth dam formed around the stem to make a water-holding area, and a weak fertilizer solution poured in.

Plants in multi-plant containers will need to be turned out of the container and separated before planting. Water the plants well before removing them. If the soil is moist, they'll slide out easily, subjecting the plants to less shock. Some roots are bound to be broken off in this process; pinching out the top growth on the plant will help keep the top and root areas in balance. This pinching will also encourage side shoots to push out, helping to form a fuller flowering plant.

Shading—If possible, do your transplanting on an overcast and still day to cut down on wilting. If you must plant on a sunny and/or windy day, cover the transplants with a protective shield for a day or two. There are commercial blankets made of a nonwoven material that will do this and can also be used at night to protect against light frosts. A do-it-yourself way to provide shading is to form newspaper sheets into cones and place one over each plant, anchoring the edges with soil.

Although starting your own boxed plants takes a bit of time and effort, it can be a very enjoyable activity. Best of all, you can have as many plants as you want of exactly the species and varieties you prefer.

Sowing Seeds

2

For a small number of seeds, plant two seeds per starting cube, then remove the weaker seedling when they grow their second true leaves. Or plant seeds in rows—one or two rows per variety—in a seed tray. For larger quantities, sprinkle a packet of seeds over the entire seed tray. *Be sure to label* each row or tray; otherwise, seedlings can be difficult to identify by sight.

3 Transplanting Seedlings

Except when planted in individual cubes, seedlings should be transplanted from seed starter trays when they grow their first set of true leaves. Hold a seed leaf (*never* hold by the stem at this stage) and lift the soil from underneath it with a fork or similar tool, gently removing the seedling. Insert it in a hole already poked in the soil of a six-pack or peat pot. The soil level on the plant stem should be the same in the new planter as it was in the seed tray. Firm the soil around the roots with your fingers. Water to firm the soil more. Plants remain in these containers until they're planted outdoors or into planters for the summer.

PLANTS TO START INDOORS

Globe Amaranth	Lisianthus
Asparagus Fern	Lobelia
Aster	Nicotiana
Fibrous Begonia	Ornamental Pepper
Tuberous Begonia	Pansy
Candytuft	Petunia
Cleome	Polka-Dot Plant
Coleus	Salpiglossis
Dahlia	Salvia
African Daisy	Sapphire Flower
Dahlberg Daisy	Snapdragon
Dracaena	Stock
Dusty Miller	Verbena
Floss Flower	Vinca
Geranium	Persian Violet
Impatiens	

(Note: Some plants will be found on both this list and the list of plants to sow directly in the garden. Either option will work; you may want to start those with short growing seasons indoors in order to enjoy the longest possible period of bloom.)

Planting Bedding Plants

Water bedding plants just before transplanting them into garden beds or planters to ensure that they slip out and separate easily. Pinch out the center growth bud to encourage bushiness. Turn the plants out of the pack and divide by pulling gently apart. Avoid excess damage to tender roots. Place the plant in a hole at the same depth or slightly deeper than it was in the pack. Firm the soil around the root with your fingers. Form a shallow dam around the plant to hold water—this is especially helpful if a flower bed is on a slope. Fill each dam with water that contains a weak fertilizer solution. This will get rid of air pockets around the roots and provide food to encourage quick growth.

Selecting Quality Plants & Seeds

Healthy flats of colorful impatiens are available at most nurseries and garden centers.

Seeds and boxed bedding plants available in the United States are generally of high quality. Whether you make your purchases through a local greenhouse or nursery, a chain store, or a roadside stand, you'll usually find fresh, high-quality seeds and vigorous, insect- and disease-free plants. What's more, with very rare exceptions, these offerings can be relied upon to be correctly labeled.

Because of this consistently good quality, it's possible to buy plants wherever you find the best price on the variety you want. However, before buying, be sure that it really *is* the lowest price. That is, one retailer may sell a "box" for $1.25 and another sell a "box" of the same variety for only $1.00. But if the first box contains eight plants and the second contains six, the higher-priced box is the better buy.

When possible, purchase boxed plants early in the season, especially if the store you buy them from is not a nursery or garden shop. Too often, the plants arrive at the store in vigorous condition, but then are tended by personnel who know nothing about plants. As a result, watering is frequently haphazard and inadequate. Added to the problem is the fact that boxed plants are usually displayed in a hot and brightly sunlit outdoor location where the sun and wind dry them out. Unfortunately, each time the plants wilt down some of their strength is lost. Bedding plants that suffer from these conditions will be slow to recover when they're put in the garden.

If the last frost date isn't yet past, or your planting bed isn't fully prepared, it still makes sense to buy plants when they first arrive at the retailer's. Bring them home where you can care for them properly until you can plant them out.

When purchasing packets of seeds, there are two things to check on. First, be sure the seeds are fresh. Somewhere on the label it should read "Packed for sale in 19☐☐." Make sure it's the current year. Second, when deciding between several sources for the same kind of seed, look at the number of seeds each company offers in its packet. As with the boxed plants, the lower-priced packet is not always the best buy.

All of the large seed houses supply reliable, fresh, high-quality seeds. In addition, you'll find there are many small specialty seed companies sending out catalogs. Little is known about these suppliers; they may or may not be reputable. When dealing with a seed company you haven't ordered from before, it's a good idea to buy only two or three packets the first season. How well those seeds perform will determine whether or not you want to order more from that company in the future.

Over time, you'll develop your own list of reliable garden supply sources. The list below is intended to introduce a few well-known, reputable mail-order seed companies that offer a large selection of annual seeds. Start with these, then add others after trying them personally or receiving recommendations from experienced gardeners in your area.

Park Seed Company
Cokesbury Rd.
Greenwood, SC 29647-0001

W. Atlee Burpee & Co.
Warminster, PA 18974

Comstock, Ferre & Co.
Box 125
Wethersfield, CT 06109

Stokes Seeds Inc.
Box 548
Buffalo, NY 14240

What to Look for in Container-Grown Plants

Look for these signals when selecting plants grown in containers. They'll go a long way toward indicating how long the plant has been in the container and how it's been cared for during that time. Strong, vital plants that have been given good care have a far better chance of surviving when transplanted into the garden.

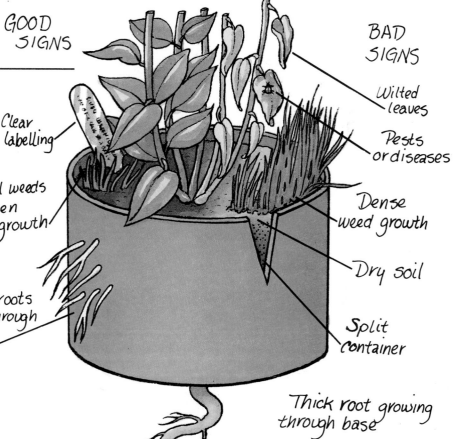

CONTAINER-GROWN PLANT

GOOD SIGNS

BAD SIGNS

Wilted leaves

Pests or diseases

Dense weed growth

Dry soil

Split container

Thick root growing through base

Clear labelling

Small weeds of green signal growth

Small roots peeping through container

Sowing Seeds

Seeds sown in the garden can reward you with these stunning marigolds.

Sowing seeds directly into the garden is the simplest method of growing annuals. For those who have neither the extra money nor the inclination to buy boxed plants, sowing directly into the garden in springtime is the answer. Once the ground is warm and the planting bed properly prepared, it's amazing how quickly most annuals sprout and grow to the flowering stage!

There are some plants that grow better when planted directly in the garden rather than started ahead as boxed plants. For example, both Shirley poppies and zinnias experience difficulty surviving transplanting. You'll also find that trailing and vining plants can't be started very much ahead of planting out time or they become hopelessly entangled. As a result, most vines don't gain enough of a head start to make the extra effort worthwhile.

There are several ways to approach direct seeding. For a somewhat structured but still informal cottage garden look, use a stick to mark out flowing sweeps on the prepared bed. Plant each sweep with a different kind of seed. If the garden is large enough to allow it, repeat the same variety in several sections. Place taller varieties toward the rear of the bed and the lower ones at the front. There is really no reason to precisely plan in advance where each kind will go.

Broadcast the seeds in each section and rake lightly, then briefly sprinkle a fine spray of water over the bed to settle the soil a bit. When the young seedlings sprout, they'll need to be thinned to prevent overcrowding. When thinning, adjust the space you leave between the plants according to their growth characteristics: Tall upright-growing plants such as plumed cockscomb, bachelor's buttons, and larkspur can be left much closer together than wide-spreading plants such as sweet alyssum, petunias, cosmos, and baby's breath. Surplus seedlings can be discarded, passed on to friends, or moved to grow in planters or other garden areas.

For a more formal garden design, make a precise plan on paper beforehand. Then carefully copy the layout onto the prepared seedbed. With this approach, each preselected variety is planted in rows or clumps in the appointed order—two or three seeds to a cluster, spaced 4 to 12 inches apart depending on their growth habits. When the plants are 1 to 2 inches tall, thin out all but the strongest one from each cluster. The resulting beds will have a neat, organized, well-planned look that will enhance any formally laid-out garden design.

Another approach to flower bed layout is simply to mark off rows the length of the bed and plant each one with a different annual favorite. By planting the tallest kind in the back row and increasingly shorter ones in each row in front of it, it's possible to effectively display all varieties. Take into account the width to which each type grows when spacing the rows. Maintenance of this garden is easy because you always work along straight rows.

To decide which design style to use, consider what is best suited to your own tastes and talents, as well as to the style of your house and the already existing garden.

PLANTS TO START OUTDOORS

Sweet Alyssum*	Morning Glory
Baby's Breath	Nasturtium
Blanket Flower	Nierembergia*
Castor Bean*	Ornamental Corn, Kale
Coleus*	Petunia
Cosmos*	Phlox*
Cup and Saucer Vine	California Poppy
Dahlia*	Horned Poppy
Forget-Me-Not	Portulaca
Four O'Clock	Scabiosa
Gazania	Sunflower
Ornamental Grasses	Zinnia*
Marigold*	

*Those plants that might be started ahead indoors or bought as boxed bedding plants in Zone 5 and colder.
(Note: Some plants on this list also appear on the list of those that can be started ahead as boxed plants. Either option is acceptable.)

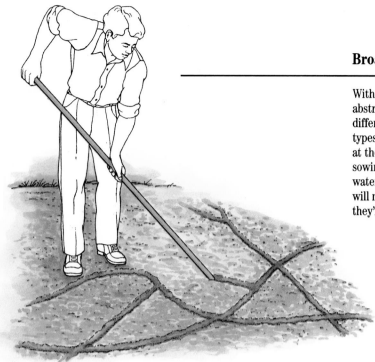

Broadcasting Seeds

With a stick or rake handle, mark out flowing abstract sweeps on the prepared bed. Broadcast a different variety of plant in each section, with taller types located toward the back and low-growing ones at the front. Rake the soil surface lightly after sowing, then briefly sprinkle with a fine spray of water after the entire bed is seeded. Seedlings will need to be thinned to appropriate spacing when they're 2 to 3 inches tall.

Planting Seeds over Mulch

For large plants that need to be spaced a foot or more apart, it's easiest to lay mulch over the bed prior to planting. Cut 3-inch holes at proper intervals in the mulch sheet. (If an organic mulch is used, push mulching aside for appropriate spacing.) Plant three seeds in a triangular pattern in each hole. Pat soil gently over each group. When seedlings grow their second set of true leaves, thin out the weaker plants, leaving just the strongest one to continue growing.

Planting Seeds in Rows

Flower seeds planted in rows are easily cared for. If varieties are arranged so the tallest is in the back row with each row forward planted with a shorter variety, all of them will be visible from the front of the bed. Mulch can be laid in place before or after seed rows are sown. Thinning of seedlings for proper spacing should be done when plants are 2 to 3 inches high.

Propagating Stem Cuttings

Most annuals are grown from seeds. However, impatiens, fibrous begonias, coleus, and geraniums can be grown from stem cuttings.

Select a mature plant that is in a stage of active midsummer growth. Prepare a container filled with rooting medium. It should be at least 3 to 4 inches deep, filled with 2½ inches or more of rooting medium. Clean, coarse builder's sand, a mixture of half perlite and half peat moss, or half perlite and half vermiculite are good choices. Fill the container with the moistened medium, then let it settle and drain for a half hour.

Take cuttings in the morning. Using a sharp knife, cut off growth tips just above the node, or the point where a leaf or side shoot attaches to the main stem. Each of the cuttings should be between 3 and 6 inches in length and have 4 to 6 nodes. The stem tissue should be easy to cut through.

Don't spend more than five minutes taking cuttings from the parent plants. To prepare a cutting for rooting, remove the leafless piece of stem at the bottom. Cut it off about ⅛ inch below the first node with a clean knife or razor cut, leaving no torn or dangling pieces of tissue hanging from the stem. Remove *all* of the leaves from the lower half of the cutting. These can be cut off with a knife or manually snapped off.

If there are any flower buds on the cutting, cut these off as well. Cut back the tips of any large leaves remaining on the cutting so that one-third to one-half of their surface remains. To help stimulate root formation, it's helpful to coat the lower one-third of each stem cutting with rooting hormone powder. Just dip each stem in the rooting powder and shake off any excess. Poke a hole in the dampened rooting medium, insert the cutting in the hole to one-third of its length, and press the medium firmly around the stem with your fingers. When all of the cuttings are set in the medium, water the surface.

Place a plastic bag over the cuttings to form a tent, using bamboo stakes or wooden dowels as supports. This will serve as a mini-greenhouse, which should be kept out of direct sunlight. If the bottom edge of the plastic tent is left a bit loose, some fresh outside air will be able to circulate up inside. This will help reduce the possibility of mildew and mold problems. Some growers prefer to hold the plastic tightly against the container with an elastic band. In this case, it's necessary to remove the elastic and lift up the tent sides for a short period each day or else to poke holes in the plastic bag in order to supply the cutting with necessary fresh air. With a plastic tent there will be little need for watering the cuttings.

Certain annuals such as these New Guinea impatiens can be propagated by stem cuttings.

Annual cuttings will root quickly. They should be checked in a week to ten days. Insert a narrow knife blade or a fork beneath one of the cuttings and gently lift it out. When the longest roots are ¼ inch long, remove cuttings from the rooting medium and transfer each to a 1–1½-inch pot filled with planting mix.

Propagating Healthy Plants from Stem Cuttings

1 Cut 3- to 6-inch growth tips from the parent plant with a small, sharp paring knife. Make a clean, slanted cut just above a leaf node, side shoot, or growth bud. The plant should be in a stage of active growth with young and succulent stems. If stems are woody and difficult to cut, try recutting closer to the tip.

2 Bring the cutting indoors immediately. Recut the stems just below the bottom node. Use a single-edged razor blade or a sharp paring knife to give the cleanest possible cut. Crushed stem cells and hanging strands of tissue cause problems that you want to avoid.

3 A cutting is ready to plant after the side shoots and leaves have been removed from the lower half of the stem. Any flowers or flower buds should also be removed, and large leaves trimmed back to about half their original size. Dip the lower one-third to one-half of the stem in rooting powder. Tap off any excess powder.

4

Poke a hole in the rooting medium and insert a cutting to between one-third and one-half of its length. Firm the rooting medium around the stem with your fingers. When all the cuttings are inserted, water them in place. A large, clear plastic bag forms a mini-greenhouse over the cuttings. The bag is held several inches above the tops of the cutting by sticks or stakes inserted around the edge of the container.

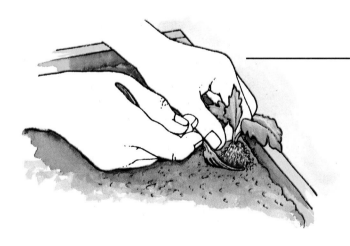

5

Annual cuttings root quickly. After seven to ten days, check for roots by gently lifting one of the cuttings out. When the longest roots are ¼ inch long, transplant them into 1½-inch pots. After several weeks, replant them into larger pots when a good strong root system has formed.

Collecting Seeds from Your Garden

Picking and planting seeds you collect from sunflowers can result in this beautiful flower.

How legitimate is the impulse to collect your own seeds? Will these seeds germinate? If they do, will the resulting plants look exactly like or differ greatly from the parent plant? How much and what kind of care do collected seeds require?

The results from collecting your own seeds will vary widely. Seeds from pure species, or nonhybrid plants, produce plants very similar to the parent plant. Flower color may vary more if there was cross-pollination between the parent plant and other nearby plants of the same kind but of different colors. For example, if you pick a seedpod from a deep purple foxglove but there are white foxgloves nearby, some of the resulting seedlings will have white flowers and some will have purple ones.

Least successful are seeds collected from hybrid plants. These are varieties developed by seedsmen who deliberately cross-pollinate specific parents. Seedlings from these plants will revert back; they'll look like their respective "grandparents" rather than the hybrid parent plant.

Annuals generally produce seeds abundantly—one or two seed heads are likely to provide enough plants for the average home garden. And the germination rate is usually very high if the seeds are planted within a year. So there is a good chance of success with collecting your own seeds.

Here's what you need to know before you start. Seedpods vary in design. Some are challenging to collect because they fling or spill the seeds out when they're ripe. To avoid losing these seeds, attach paper bags or squares of panty hose over the seed heads after pollination but before maturity. *Never* use plastic bags for this purpose, as destructive molds will develop.

Other pod types hold the seeds or sprinkle or spill them out a few at a time. Some retain their seeds tenaciously. These seed heads can be allowed to mature undisturbed, then harvested when ready. Label each kind as you collect it, or you may easily lose track of which is which.

After harvesting, separate the seeds from the pods and spread them out in a dry place away from the sun. Allow them to dry out for a couple of weeks. Then store in airtight containers in a cool, dry place until planting time. Seeds stored in the refrigerator may retain a high germination rate even when planted several years later.

Collecting and growing your own seeds can be fun, especially if you like an informal mixed garden. But when you want a particular plant of a certain color in a specific location, the only sure way to get it is by buying seeds or bedding plants of the proper variety from a reputable dealer.

Catapulting Seedpods

Some seedpods catapult or spray seeds when they're ripe. After they've been pollinated, but before they dry out, a small paper bag or squares of panty hose (*never* plastic) should be secured over the seed head in order to catch the seeds. Examples: pansy, impatiens, cleome, geranium, sweet pea, and lupine.

Seed Heads That Drop Seeds

Other seedpods hold the seeds until they dry completely; then their tops open and allow seeds to drop out. To harvest, shake the newly ripe seed heads over a bowl. Examples: larkspur, poppy, sweet William, petunia, nicotiana, calliopsis, and pot marigold.

Seed Heads to be Torn Apart by Hand

This group of seed heads remains tightly packed to maturity, often well into winter. These can be torn apart by hand when they're well-dried to release the seeds. Examples: marigold, zinnia, morning glory, scabiosa, and hollyhock.

Seedpods Requiring Protection

Some seed heads are especially appealing to birds and animals. The trick is to harvest them before the competition! Protect these seed heads by covering them with brown paper bags as they near maturity and then pick promptly. Examples: sunflower, cosmos, and sweet pea.

This well-maintained annuals border features zinnias and marigolds against an evergreen hedge. Basic care techniques are not difficult for these flowers and certainly result in beautiful seasonal color.

CARING FOR ANNUALS

Most gardeners ramble around their yard regularly, stopping to admire a healthy plant here, snapping off a few dead flower heads there, then pulling out some weeds in another area.

At the same time, they're noticing clues that signal possible problems. If some of the plants have limp-hanging leaves, the gardener will check how dry the soil is and turn on the soaker hose if needed. If some leaves or flowers are peppered with holes or totally eaten away, a closer inspection will be made to discover whether a caterpillar or bug has invaded. This, in turn, will lead to spraying or powdering with the appropriate insecticide or hand removal of the insect.

There are tips included that will help make your summer's work easier: ways to minimize weeding and watering chores, feeding and plant staking alternatives, followed by suggestions on how to prepare for winter and the next growing season.

An illustrated section that allows easy identification of garden pests and diseases contains recommendations for dealing with each problem. Also included are two handy charts. One outlines the proper time of year to perform specific activities, the other indicates how easy or difficult various annuals are to grow.

By selecting those plants that are easiest to grow and are best-suited to your garden site, then following gardening techniques that reduce the need for maintenance, your summer can be both carefree and color-filled.

Quenching a Plant's Thirst

Dew supplies this blossom with necessary water.

Along with soil and light, water is an essential ingredient for plant growth. The soil and light requirements of annuals have been dealt with in Chapter 1; the ways to take care of their water needs will now be considered.

It's not easy, especially at first, to gauge exactly when plants require water—so much depends upon current weather and soil conditions. For example, if good soaking rains fall frequently, it's obvious additional watering is unnecessary. However, when there's a light rainfall every few days, it's possible that only the soil surface has been dampened without much water actually reaching plant roots, necessitating the addition of water. Plants subjected to bright sun and wind also lose a lot of water that needs to be replenished. Similarly, because trees continually pull large quantities of moisture from the surrounding soil, annuals planted near or under them need more frequent watering than those in the open. All of these factors affect the rate at which soil dries out.

So how do you judge when to water and how much water to give? The one sure way to test is by poking your finger 2 to 3 inches into the soil and feeling how moist or dry it is. Taking a pinch from the surface isn't good enough; you need to know what it's like down in the root zone. Inexperienced gardeners should check soil moisture any day that there is little or no rainfall. Over time, you'll develop a feel for the overall conditions and check only when you suspect the soil may be turning dry. Remember, it's always better to check too often rather than not often enough. Don't wait until drooping plants indicate that the soil is parched.

When you do water, water deeply. Many people briefly spray a thirsty flower bed with a hand-held hose. When they tire of holding it, become bored, or think they have watered enough because the water has stopped soaking into the soil as rapidly as it did at first, the watering session is ended. Always pause to check how deeply the water has penetrated. Guessing usually results in reaching only the top ½ inch leaving the soil beneath it still dry.

A better approach is to use an automatic sprinkler, letting it gently "rain" for an extended period of time. Check at half-hour intervals to see how deeply the water has penetrated. Turn the water off when the soil is moistened to a 2-inch depth. Don't water again until your testing indicates the need.

One problem with sprinkler water is that the foliage becomes very wet, creating an ideal environment for the spread of fungus diseases. In addition, flower clusters heavy with water are more likely to bend and break or to become mildewed.

The best way to water is with a soaker hose. The water slowly oozes from the hose's many tiny holes for several hours—even overnight. All of the water soaks directly on the soil and down to the plant roots without any waste or damage.

Drip irrigation is another excellent slow-soaking system, but it's more expensive than a soaker hose. Thus it's probably a sensible alternative only for those who have large plant beds or who garden in climates where irrigation is constantly needed in order for cultivated plants to survive. Once the system is laid out, it can remain in place year after year; in areas that freeze, however, it must be drained for the winter.

There are two additional factors that will help conserve moisture and thus reduce the frequency of need for watering. One is the incorporation of peat moss into the planting area; this causes the soil to be able to soak up and hold water longer. (This is true when peat is added to light and sandy soils; conversely, when it's added to heavy soils, it helps to lighten and aerate them.)

The second technique that helps retain moisture is the use of mulch. Laid on the soil surface between the plants, a mulch protects the soil from sun and wind drying. (More on the benefits of mulch, as well as descriptions of various mulch alternatives, can be found in the following section, "Keeping Weeds at Bay.")

By using these two ideas, you can cut down on the time needed to care for your garden, and even more importantly, help conserve water, nature's precious resource.

Soaker Hose Watering

An easy way to handle deep watering of an annual bed is to lay a soaker hose in place when plants are small and leave it there for the season. Mulch can be laid on top of the soaker hose without disruption. A quick connector on the soaker hose allows speedy attachment to the regular garden hose whenever watering is needed. When the soil is well-soaked, the garden hose can easily be disconnected and stored out of the way until it's needed again.

Plants with Water Dams

A dam of soil ringed around each plant when it's transplanted into the garden helps to keep the water from settling in and early rains from running off immediately. This gives the water time to soak in around the plant's roots. Where flower beds are level, this isn't essential, but when planting on a slope, a dam is a great help. The dam disappears after a week or two and is no longer needed.

The Benefits of Deep Watering

When plants are watered infrequently but heavily, they'll develop large and deep root networks. Frequent light waterings cause plants to develop shallow root systems just below the soil surface. This causes plants to be poorly anchored and therefore subject to toppling in heavy wind or rain, as well as liable to wilting unless they're watered daily. Therefore, slow, deep-soak watering produces stronger and hardier plants. Whenever possible, water in the evening or overnight rather than in the morning or the heat of the day.

Watering with a Drip Irrigation System

For very large planting beds or in very dry or sandy conditions, a drip irrigation system may be the best watering solution. It allows slow, deep watering directly into each plant's roots. This helps keep foliage dry, thus reducing the possibility of the spread of diseases. Use this system in conjunction with a mulch for greatest water conservation. An on-off timer and a soluble fertilizer feeder are optional parts of a drip-irrigation system for those wanting additional ease of maintenance.

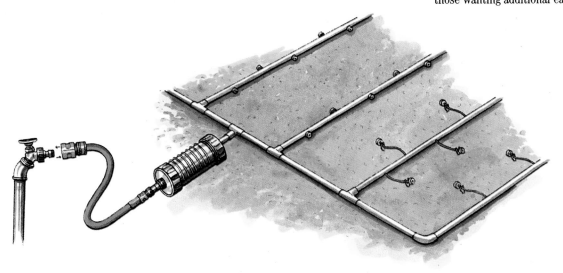

Keeping Weeds at Bay

Weed seeds are quick to germinate and grow rapidly. As soon as they're brought to within an inch of the soil surface (through digging), they'll begin to sprout. After digging deeply in early spring to ready the bed for planting, wait a week or more before doing any planting or seed sowing. Every three days, stir up the top 1 inch of soil with a scuffle hoe or cultivator, leaving the lower soil undisturbed. This will expose several cycles of young sprouted weeds to dry out and die in the sun and air.

This approach can be used when seeds are going to be planted either in addition to, or instead of, bedding plants. But in places where *only* bedding plants will be used, the use of a pre-emergent chemical is recommended. This is sprinkled on the soil around the already planted annuals. It's important that the annuals be at least 3 to 4 inches tall before the chemical, triluralin, is applied. In the case of seedlings, this same chemical can be applied once the young plants have grown to this 3- to 4-inch size.

Finally, the most popular way of dramatically reducing weed problems is by using some kind of mulch. Mulch is a layer of organic or inorganic material laid on the soil surface to shade out weeds, retain soil moisture, and have a moderating effect on soil temperature.

Many materials can achieve these results, but some are more practical, less expensive, easier to handle, and more attractive than others. The list of organic mulches includes: pine needles, leaves, straw, dried seaweed, tree bark strips, bark chunks, peat moss, old newspapers, sawdust, wood chips, cocoa bean hulls, and cotton seed hulls. Inorganic mulches include "blankets" made from solid sheets of black plastic (**Caution:** These can become very slippery when wet); black plastic made porous with thousands of small holes; porous, nonwoven fiberglass landscape fabric; and pieces of new or used carpets.

Perhaps the choice of which kind of mulch to use isn't as important as the decision to use *some* kind of mulch. Mulching cuts down dramatically on weed problems, conserves soil moisture, keeps soil warmer in cool weather and cooler on hot days, and, if it's an organic mulch, will improve the quality of the soil as it breaks down and adds to what gardeners call "soil tilth."

Some mulches are not very attractive-looking. Other organic mulches may alter the soil chemistry as they break down (annual soil tests will detect these changes so you can adjust fertilizer applications to compensate). Still other types have an odor when they're fresh or may prove too expensive for use in large quantities.

Mulching crested cockscomb reduces weed problems.

Still, there must be at least one among all of the alternatives that will satisfy your needs. The use of a mulch will dramatically reduce weed problems in any garden.

Using a Pre-Emergent Chemical

Granules of a pre-emergent chemical can be scattered on the soil between the already planted bedding plants. It will prevent weed seeds from sprouting in these open areas. Because it kills *all* seeds—weeds, annuals, and perennials—do *not* use a pre-emergent in any area where you have recently planted, or plan to plant, flower seeds. A pre-emergent can be used once seedlings have germinated and grown to bedding plant size or larger.

Boxed Plants and Mulching

Mulch, whether organic or inorganic, can be laid before planting of boxed plants. Holes can be cut through sheeting or dug through organic mulches at proper spacing for the plants.

Seedlings and Mulch

Where seeds are to be planted instead of bedding plants, wait to lay in organic mulches until seeds have germinated and the seedlings are 3 inches or taller. This reduces possible smothering of vulnerable, young seedlings by mulch that the wind may blow over them. Watering down of organic mulches after they're laid helps settle and hold them in place.

Cultivation of Nonmulched Areas

In beds where no mulch is used, frequent cultivation of the top 1 to 2 inches of soil is the best way to control weeds. Newly germinated weed seedlings die quickly when stirred up this way. Larger weeds should be hand-pulled and removed from the bed, since they can easily reroot if left in the garden.

Feeding Alternatives

Healthy marigolds and floss flowers provide color enjoyment.

As mentioned in Chapter 1, the best course to follow is to have your garden soil tested each year, then follow the recommendations given with your test results. Knowing what nutrients are needed helps cut down on the number of choices, but still leaves the decision of whether to use an organic or inorganic source up to you. If you're able to obtain the nutrients you need from organic fertilizers, you reduce the risk of possibly harming the environment. However, if the nutrients you require cannot realistically be obtained from such sources, there's little danger in using inorganic fertilizers as long as you apply only as much as is needed.

As you study the NPK formula on each plant food, you'll notice that organic fertilizers contain much lower percentages of nutrients per pound than do inorganic fertilizers. For the most part, this doesn't matter when feeding annuals. Where this *can* become a problem is when you're trying to adjust a large garden bed's nutrient content at the beginning of the growing season. You may find that, in order to raise the nutrients to the recommended level, you'll have to add 4 inches of the organic material. This can be done if the area to be covered is small, but for large areas, it could become unwieldy. In these cases it's more practical to make major adjustments with inorganics, then proceed with organics for minor adjustments in future years.

Fertilizers are applied in a dry granular or powder form, or mixed with water for a liquid application. The granular or powder foods should be broadcast over the soil surface and dug in; liquid applications can be made with a hand sprayer or a special mixing attachment for your garden hose.

To supply food for immediate use by bedding annuals that are newly planted out, a weak solution of water soluble fertilizer—either fish emulsion or an inorganic type—can be poured from a watering can directly around each plant. Thereafter, a couple of sidedressings of granular plant food sprinkled around each plant at two-week intervals should carry them through the rest of the summer.

For best absorption, fertilize when the soil is moist. Take care to apply it on the soil rather than on the plant leaves. The plants, your hands, and the fertilizer should be dry when you fertilize. **Caution:** Always wash your hands after handling fertilizer.

A final word regarding two homemade soil amenders: compost and liquid manure. Compost is made by combining plant wastes with soil and fertilizer, allowing them to decompose for several months, then mixing them back into the garden. Liquid manure is made by combining animal wastes and water, allowing them to decompose, then watering the garden with the resultant liquid. Both are good organic nutrient sources, even though their level of nutrients is low. However, neither is especially practical for the average, small home garden.

Making Organic Fertilizer

Gardeners preferring organic fertilizers can make their own liquid manure by fermenting animal and vegetable wastes in water for several weeks. An easy and reliable source of soluble organic fertilizer is fish emulsion, which can be purchased at any garden center. When adding this concentrate to water, there is a strong fish odor. Therefore, it's best to do this job outdoors or in a well-ventilated area. Fortunately, the odor is very short-lived.

Composting

Making your own compost from plant wastes, soil, and nutrients takes several months. Many gardeners find it easier to purchase bagged compost instead. Either way, compost is a good additive for soils low in organic materials.

Sidedressing

Granular and powdered commercial fertilizers release nutrients more quickly than organic fertilizers. Sprinkling a small handful of 5-10-5 or 10-10-10 around each plant (known as sidedressing) in late spring and again in midsummer will give annuals a feeding boost that will keep them in top growing and flowering condition through the summer.

Liquid Fertilizer Solution

Another fast source of nutrients is a liquid fertilizer solution. This comes in a concentrated form that is diluted by mixing it with water according to the manufacturer's directions. Use a mild solution in water on newly planted bedding plants or recently thinned seedlings to help them quickly recover from the shock. Liquid fertilizer can also be applied in place of powdered or granular sidedressings, if preferred.

Ways to Increase/Control Growth

Zinnias and vincas benefit from proper growth care.

Annuals will flourish when provided with the best possible growing conditions. However, there are a few simple care techniques that will help increase and control their growth.

Pinching Back—To encourage plants to fill out, remove the growth bud at the end of the main stem when the plant is in its rapid growth stage that precedes first flower bud formation. For bedding plants, the best time to do this is when you're planting them out in the garden. They're at a good stage of growth and, in addition, the removal of some of their foliage will help balance any root damage they may suffer in the transplanting process. Plants grown from seeds sown directly in the garden should be pinched back when they're 3 to 4 inches tall.

Simply pinch out or snap off the last inch or so of the main growing tip. This will redirect the plant's energy from this single shoot to numerous latent side buds—there is a latent growth bud located at the point on the stem where each leaf is attached. Several days after pinching, you'll see several small shoots pushing from the remaining stem. These will grow into a cluster of stems to replace the original single stem. The plant will be shorter, stockier, and fuller than if no pinching had been done. It will also be neater-looking, more compact, and have many more branches on which to produce flowers. A second pinching can be done two weeks after the first one if an even fuller plant is desired.

Deadheading—Once annuals begin to bloom, it's important to remove spent flowers promptly for several reasons. First, once the flower dies, it detracts from the good looks of the garden. Second, even though we say it's dead, it's actually very much alive and continues with its growth toward seed production. This process pulls plant energy that would otherwise be available for new foliage and flower production into the seed head. Third, removal of spent flowers helps to quickly redirect plant energy to side shoots for smooth and speedy transfer to new growth.

To make this rerouting most efficient, always cut back to just above the first side bud that is already beginning to grow. If there is no active side bud below the bloom, cut back either to a side branch or immediately above a leaf node where a latent bud will be likely to push out new growth. Make a clean cut with a sharp-bladed knife, since ragged cuts take much longer to heal and are likely sites for entry of rot and disease. These rules for cutting apply to the removal of cutting flowers as well.

Occasionally it becomes necessary to cut back growth in order to keep a plant from becoming leggy or from drowning out neighboring plants. Cutting back should be approached in the same way as removing dead flower heads. Always cut back to a side growth shoot or branch that is headed in the direction you want future growth to go. This way you can steer and control growth as you see fit.

Pinching out Growth Tips

Pinching out the plant growth tip helps encourage multiple branching. This, in turn, causes production of more flower buds along these additional branches. At the same time, pinching produces a more sturdy, compact plant that not only looks nice but is also less subject to breakage due to wind, rain, or heavy bloom weight.

Deadheading Flower Heads

Deadheading, or removing dead flower heads, should be done soon after the flower dies, so no plant energy is wasted on seed formation. Cluster flowers will look fresh and attractive longer if the individual florets are snapped out of the group as they die. Single flowers should be cut back to the place on the stem where a side shoot is already pushing out. If none is evident, then cut back to above a leaf, a node, or a side branch. Cut on a slant to allow water to run off of the wound.

Staking Garden Plants

Larkspur grow better if staked properly.

Most healthy annuals are sturdy and self-supporting. They often don't require any special staking to keep them looking good. However, plants with heavy flower clusters, especially those on tall, slender stems such as snapdragons and dahlias, may flop over when exposed to strong winds or heavy rains. Another group that sometimes requires support to keep their flower heads visible are those with stems that will either bend over or break off when the weight of their leaves and blooms becomes too great. Asters, baby's breath, salpiglossis, and some zinnias are known to have these problems.

Often plants gain enough support when a kind of corral is placed around them. The plant stems lean out against the metal or string sides of the corral instead of flopping down to the ground. Another simple type of support consists of poking many-branched pieces of brush into the ground beside the plants. These form a network of twigs through which the plants can grow and against which they can lean for support. The tops of these branches can be bent over to form an even more interlaced network if needed.

These two support systems work well with plants that have a spreading growth habit. For those that produce tall, single spikes, a third staking method is more suitable. Poke a wooden or bamboo stake into the ground 2 to 3 inches from the plant stem. It should be pushed deeply enough into the soil to be solidly secure. Loosely tie each plant stem to this central stake every 6 inches along the stem's height. A final tie should be made just below the flower bud cluster. To keep the ties from sliding downward, first form a half-granny knot around the stake, then a full granny knot around the plant stem.

Although tying plants seems a nuisance, it really only takes a few minutes to do and is only necessary for a few varieties. If those that need it aren't tied, however, they'll either bend over, becoming impossible to see, become mud covered, or snap off and die. Either way, there's little sense in growing these kinds of plants if you aren't willing to stake them. Select easier care annuals instead. Or, if they happen to be your favorites, make up your mind to give them this little extra care that will make it possible for them to look their best.

Single Staking

Tie stems to a stake that is firmly anchored in the soil. First tie the string around the stake with a half-granny knot, allowing an inch or more of slack between the stake and the plant stem. Then tie a full-granny knot around the stem. As the plant grows taller, add ties further up on the stake 6 to 8 inches apart. The topmost tie should be located at the base of the flower spike. All of the branches can be tied to a single stake in the center of the plant.

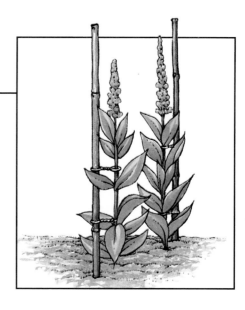

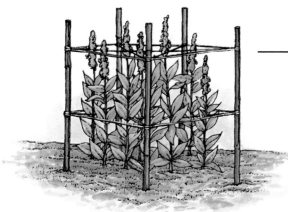

Stake Corrals

A better way to hold clumps of fine stems upright is by inserting four or more stakes around the plant. Tie a string to the first stake, then wrap it one turn around each of the other stakes along the perimeter and back to the starter stake. For a large clump, run string diagonally across within this corral for more support. Several tiers of string may be needed for tall plants—space tiers 4 to 6 inches apart. Flower heads should float 4 to 6 inches above the top tier of string.

"L" Shaped Metal Stakes

A more expensive, but easier to install, corral can be made from "L" shaped metal stakes specially designed and sold for this purpose. They hook together quickly to make whatever size is needed. These can be used year after year once the initial investment is made. String can be diagonally cross-woven between these stakes if more support is needed.

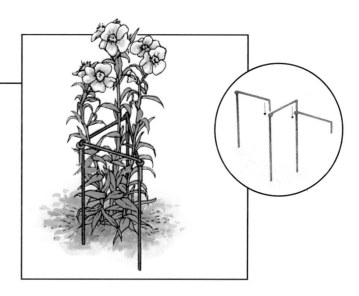

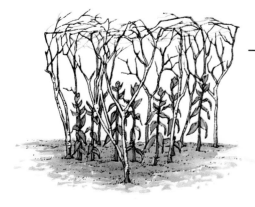

Brush Thicket Staking

A simple no-cost plant support for fine-stemmed annuals can be made by poking the stems of well-branched brush into the ground next to the young plants. The plants' stems simply lean against the twigs for support without any tying. This brush thicket will give even more support if the tops are bent over and interwoven. Plant stems will grow up through the resulting tangle and hide it from view.

Pests & Other Problems

Healthy flowers and foliage make this all-white garden especially attractive.

The following lists are designed to help you identify the most common garden pests and diseases. However, if you feel uncertain about what is causing damage to your plants, it is advisable that you take a specimen to your local garden shop or your county Cooperative Extension office to have it identified.

Once you know what your problem is, you'll need to decide how to control it. When an infestation is slight, it's often possible to simply remove the sick plants or individual insects. For a heavy infestation, you'll probably need to turn to chemical insecticides or fungicides.

Just remember to follow the manufacturer's instructions precisely, and to read and follow any cautions on the package label. Apply these chemicals as directed and only when they're absolutely necessary. It's when people spray and dust with the attitude that "more is better"—whether the plants need it or not—that excessive poisons become a possibility.

One final note: new biological and chemical controls are continually being developed. Those listed here are current at the time of this writing, but more effective new ones may well be discovered in the future. Therefore, it is very important to correctly identify your pest or disease problem and to consult with your local nursery or garden shop. They can recommend the best available product for controlling that particular problem.

INSECTS AND ANIMALS

SYMPTOM	CAUSE	CURE	PLANTS
Cluster of small, soft-bodied insects on buds and growth tips (gray, black, pink, or green in color); sticky secretions may be evident	*Aphids*	Spray with rotenone or malathion[1] in evening.	Pot Marigold Nasturtium Primrose Sweet Pea
Leaves chewed away; hard-shelled beetles on plant and burrowed into flowers	*Beetles of various kinds*	Spray with rotenone or Sevin*[1]; pick by hand and destroy.	Gourds Hollyhock American/French Marigold Zinnia

SYMPTOM	CAUSE	CURE	PLANTS
Growth tips wilted; small hole in plant stem at point where wilting begins	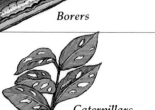 *Borers*	Snap off at level of hole, dig out borer and destroy; spray with endosulfan[1], pyrethrum, or rotenone.	Gourds American/French Marigold Ornamental Corn Zinnia
Leaves and flowers chewed away; caterpillars on plant	 *Caterpillars of various kinds & sizes*	Pick off by hand and destroy; spray with pyrethrum, malathion[1], or *Bacillus thuringiensis.*	Nicotiana Ornamental or Flowering Cabbage Petunia
Entire young plants wilted; partially or entirely chewed through at ground level	 *Cutworms*	Dig in soil around plant base, find rolled up caterpillars and destroy; circle plant with cardboard collar on edge (1″ below ground and 1″ above ground).	China Pink Nicotiana Ornamental or Flowering Cabbage Petunia
Leaves and stems chewed; insects seen hopping and flying	 *Grasshoppers*	Spray with Sevin*[1]; pick off by hand.	Ornamental Corn Ornamental Grasses Petunia
Leaves peppered with small, round holes; small, triangular-shaped bugs seen when disturbed	 *Leaf Hoppers*	Spray with malathion[1] or methoxychlor[1]; dust with diatomaceous earth.	Aster Dahlia Pot Marigold
Leaves "painted" with whitish, curling trails	 *Leaf Miners*	Spray with malathion[1]; remove and destroy badly infested leaves.	China Pink Hollyhock
White or pinkish fuzzy clumps on stems and at base of leaves; sticky to the touch	 *Mealybugs*	Spray with malathion[1] or pyrethrum; hand kill by painting each bug with alcohol on cotton swab.	Asparagus Fern Transvaal Daisy Moses-in-a-Boat

[1] = Inorganic treatment
* = Copyrighted brand name

SYMPTOM	CAUSE	CURE	PLANTS
Plants entirely gone or eaten down to small stubs; evidence of footprints or droppings	*Rabbits or Deer*	Spray with Hinder*[1]; fence out rabbits with 3′ high chicken wire or other close-woven fencing.	Impatiens Ornamental or Flowering Cabbage Ornamental or Flowering Kale Pansy Scarlet Runner Bean
Silvery slime trails on plants; soft sticky slugs on plants after dark (check with flashlight); holes eaten in leaves	*Slugs and Snails*	Set out shallow containers of beer; set out metaldehyde slug bait[1]; pick by hand after dark or on dark days.	Hollyhock Nicotiana Petunia Primrose
Leaves yellowing with speckled look; fine spider webs on backs of leaves and at point where leaves attach to stem; very tiny bugs on backs of leaves	*Spider Mites*	Spray with a miticide[1] from underneath to hit backs of leaves; wash or spray with soapy water.	Impatiens Flowering Maple Primrose
Small glob of white bubbles on plant stem or leaves; small insect hidden inside	*Spittlebugs*	Ignore unless very pervasive; spray with malathion[1]; wash off repeatedly with water from hose.	Bachelor's Button Four O'Clock
Brown or white flecks on plant leaves	*Thrips*	Spray with malathion[1] or dust with sulfur.	Gladiolus
Cloud of tiny white flies fluttering around plant	*White Flies*	Spray with malathion[1] or diazinon[1]; use yellow sticky traps.	Heliotrope Lantana Morning Glory Vine

[1] = Inorganic treatment
* = Copyrighted brand name

DISEASES

SYMPTOM	CAUSE	CURE	PLANTS
Leaves become mottled, curl, and shrivel; plants become deformed	*Blights and Viruses*	Remove and destroy plants; buy blight-resistant strains; do not smoke; wash hands before handling plants.	Aster Snapdragon
Newly sprouted seedlings fall over and die	*Damping Off*	Start seeds in sterile soil mix. Dust seeds with Captan*[1] before planting.	All plants
Round, dusty brown or black spots on leaves; leaves drop from plant	*Leaf Spot*	Remove badly diseased leaves and destroy; spray with benomyl[1] or zineb[1].	Aster Chrysanthemum Foxglove Phlox
Lower leaves and stems turn grayish and look slightly wilted	*Powdery Mildew*	Increase air circulation; spray with benomyl[1] or sulfur.	Bachelor's Button Floss Flower Phlox Sweet Pea Zinnia
Orange or reddish-brown raised dots form on backs of leaves; leaves look wilted	*Rust*	Increase air circulation; keep foliage dry; buy rust-resistant varieties; spray with ferbam[1] or zineb[1]; spray leaves with sulfur or benomyl.	Cleome Hollyhock Snapdragon
Leaves wilt and turn yellow; entire plant shuts down and dies	*Wilt*	Remove infected plants and destroy; buy wilt-resistant varieties.	Aster Dahlia Snapdragon

[1] = Inorganic treatment
* = Copyrighted brand name

Preparing for Winter & Another Year

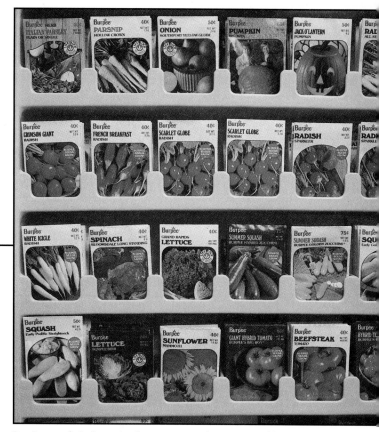

Sowing seeds indoors in the winter can be an enjoyable experience.

Most gardeners find they begin preparing for another growing season while still in the midst of the present one. Certainly, this is the best time to study your yard and to plan for next spring. It's also the best time to note down your conclusions.

In addition to making future plans, there are also some basic gardening preparations you'll want to consider. For instance, if you wish to carry some annuals indoors over winter—many people bring in geraniums, impatiens, and fibrous begonias as potted plants to use as the source of rooted cuttings for the following summer—late summer is when you'll transplant them into pots, cut them back, and move them inside.

An even better approach for carrying such plants over winter is to take cuttings from them in midsummer when they're still in a very active growing phase, then root and pot them up to grow through the winter. By late winter, they'll be mature plants from which to take cuttings for next summer's garden.

Dahlias, tuberous begonias, cannas, callas, caladiums, and gladiolas are treated as annuals in colder climates. Many people simply discard them each fall and buy new ones each spring. However, it's possible to dig and store them for replanting the following season after the first frost when the tops die back. Remove the dead tops along with any loose soil and feeder roots from the swollen tubers (or corms) and store them loosely in brown paper sacks or open-weave bags in a dark, cool area. Packing material around them will help keep them from drying out.

Later in the fall, there are other chores to do. Soaker hoses should be rolled up and stored, drip irrigation systems should be drained, and the dead plants should be removed and disposed of. Where an organic mulch has been used, an additional layer should be laid over the existing mulch. The new layer added in the fall will replenish any soil that has been lost, cover bare areas, protect the soil from wind or water erosion over winter, and help discourage weed growth during late fall and early spring.

Inorganic mulch sheeting should be rolled up and stored for the winter. In its place, either spread an organic mulch or seed in annual ryegrass or buckwheat to provide a winter cover crop that will need to be turned under in early spring as a source of organic nutrients (referred to as a "green manure").

Autumn is a good time to take soil samples and have them tested. If slow-working nutrients such as lime are needed, they can be spread over the area during the fall or winter. The faster-releasing fertilizers should be applied when the beds are readied for planting the following spring.

Some annual enthusiasts like to sow seeds in containers each autumn for winter display indoors. Select those annuals that require only a short day length for blooming. Otherwise, grow those that have attractive foliage and enjoy them as houseplants all winter. You can even add a few annual herbs to spice up your winter cooking!

ANNUALS SUITED TO OVERWINTERING	
Asparagus Fern	Geranium*
Fibrous Begonia*	Impatiens*
Tuberous Begonia	Ornamental Pepper
Coleus*	Polka-Dot Plant
Dracaena	Vinca
Flowering Maple	Persian Violet
Fuchsia*	

* = Those that can be propagated from stem cuttings.

Preparing Garden Plants for Winter

Bringing full grown garden plants inside for the winter should be done several weeks before frost. Dig them up with a large ball of soil so that as few roots as possible are lost. Set in the ground so that the plant is at the same level in the pot as it was in the garden. Fill in around the plant roots with good soil mix and firm with fingers to eliminate air pockets. Cut back plant tops by 40 to 50 percent to reduce wilting. Water with a mild liquid fertilizer solution. Keep in a cool location out of direct sunlight for at least a day before moving indoors.

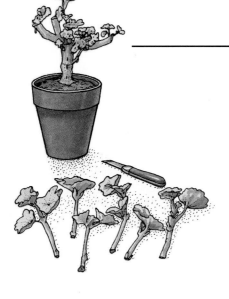

Raising Cuttings over Winter

An alternative to bringing large garden plants inside for the winter is to take cuttings from them and raise the resulting plants instead. Cuttings should be made in midsummer while plants are still in an active stage of growth, since plant growth slows down when night temperatures cool.

Starting Annuals from Seed

A third alternative for raising annuals in the winter is to start them from seed. Coleus and annual herbs such as parsley and basil do well treated this way, as do flowering annuals that bloom with short day lengths.

Keeping Notes

A helpful end-of-season task is to jot down thoughts for use in future years: which plants did well and which poorly, where to add plants to brighten dull spots, how many plants it took to fill a particular area, and names of plants you've admired in other people's gardens. Also make a note of where you've planted bulbs this fall so you don't dig into them next spring.

Zone Map: The Last Frost in Your Area

T he United States Department of Agriculture Plant Hardiness Zone Map is a guide designed to link frost dates with regions. It divides the United States into 10 zones based on average minimum winter temperatures, with Zone 1 being the coldest in North America and Zone 10 the warmest. Each zone is further divided into sections that represent 5 degree differences within the 10-degree zone.

This map should only be used as a general guideline, since the lines of separation between zones are not as clear-cut as they appear. Plants recommended for one zone might do well in the southern part of the adjoining colder zone, as well as in the neighboring warmer zone. Factors such as altitude, exposure to wind, and amount of available sunlight also contribute to a plant's winter hardiness. Also note that the indicated temperatures are average minimums—some winters will be colder and others warmer than this figure.

Even though the USDA Plant Hardiness Zone Map is not perfect, it is *the* most useful single guide for determining which plants are likely to survive in your garden and which ones are not.

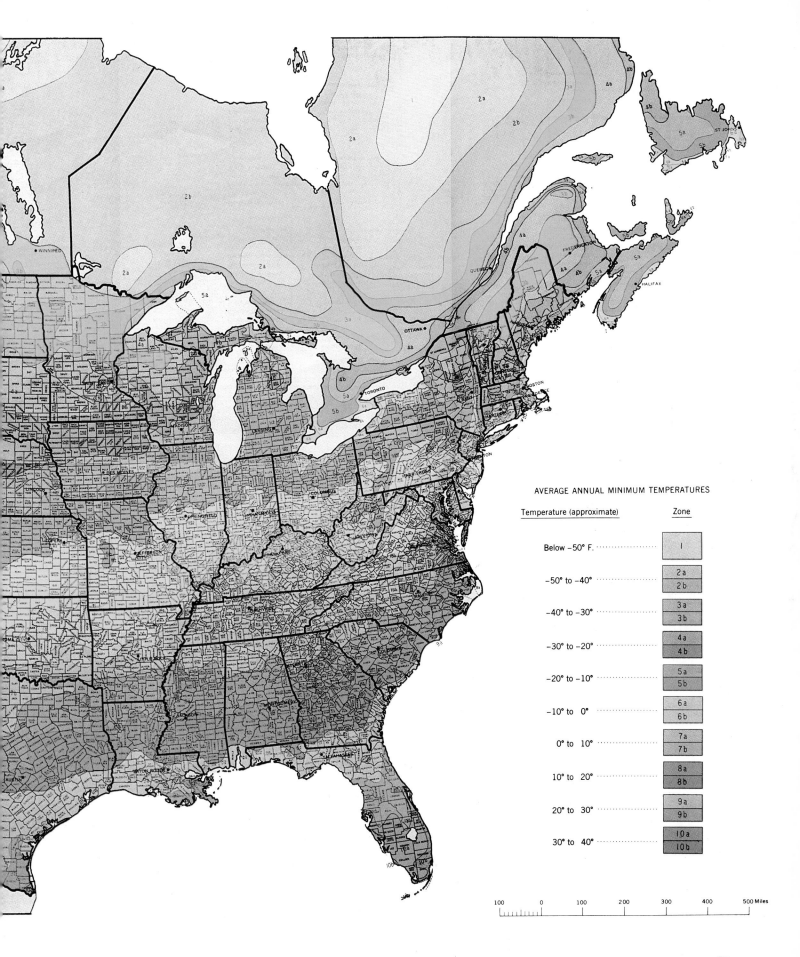

AVERAGE ANNUAL MINIMUM TEMPERATURES

Temperature (approximate)	Zone
Below −50° F.	1
−50° to −40°	2a
	2b
−40° to −30°	3a
	3b
−30° to −20°	4a
	4b
−20° to −10°	5a
	5b
−10° to 0°	6a
	6b
0° to 10°	7a
	7b
10° to 20°	8a
	8b
20° to 30°	9a
	9b
30° to 40°	10a
	10b

100   0   100   200   300   400   500 Miles

Maintaining Annuals Month by Month

T he following list includes the various gardening tasks to be done each year. *When* they should be done depends on the climate in your area. Our month-by-month chart indicates when each task should be performed in the different hardiness zones in North America. Because conditions can differ within a zone and dates of first and last freezes of the season vary each year, these are only approximate guides. But they will provide you with a general outline for your garden year. One additional task—that of making notes for future years—should actually be carried out throughout the season. Be sure not to forget it just because it isn't on the list!

Careful preparation rewards a gardener with colorful blooms.

Tasks to be Done	Zones 1–3	Zones 4–5	Zones 6–7	Zones 8–10
1—Plan garden for coming season*	NOV/DEC/JAN	DEC/JAN	JAN	JAN/AUG
2—Order seeds*	FEB	FEB	JAN	JAN/AUG
3—Buy seed starting supplies*	FEB	FEB	JAN	JAN
4—Take cuttings*	MAR	MAR	FEB	JAN
5—Start slower-growing seeds indoors*	APR	MAR	MAR	
6—Prick off seedlings*	APR	APR	MAR	
7—Start faster-growing seeds indoors*	MAY	APR	APR	
8—Prick off later seedlings*	MAY	APR	APR	
9—Lay out new beds	APR	APR	APR	FEB
10—Take soil samples if not done in the fall	APR/MAY	MAR/APR	MAR	JAN
11—Adjust pH if not done during the winter	MAY	APR	APR	FEB
12—Add conditioners to soil	MAY	APR	APR	FEB
13—Add fertilizers to soil as recommended by testing lab	MAY	APR	APR	FEB
14—Till soil	MAY	APR	APR	FEB/SEPT
15—Purchase and plant nontender bedding plants	MAY	APR/MAY	APR	FEB
16—Harden off home-grown bedding plants*	MAY	MAY	APR	
17—Lay mulch on beds for bedding plants. (See step 24 for direct seed sowing.)	MAY	MAY	APR	MAR/SEPT

Tasks to be Done	Zones 1–3	Zones 4–5	Zones 6–7	Zones 8–10
18—Sow seeds directly in outdoor beds. Feed as needed until seeds sprout. (Do not allow them to become dry.)*	JUNE	MAY	APR	MAR/SEPT/OCT
19—Purchase tender bedding plants	JUNE	MAY	ARP	MAR
20—Pinch and plant tender bedding plants	JUNE	MAY	APR	MAR
21—Plant out tender bulbs	JUNE	JUNE	MAY	APR
22—Sprinkle pre-emergent weed killer on soil between bedding plants (**Caution:** Do not use with direct-sown seeds or young plants.)	JUNE	JUNE	MAY	APR
23—Thin seedlings from direct-sown seeds*	JUNE	JUNE	MAY	APR/OCT
24—Lay mulch when seedlings reach 4 to 6 inches*	JUNE	JUNE	MAY	APR/OCT
25—Put in plant supports	JUNE	JUNE	MAY	APR/OCT
26—Deep water as needed	JULY	JULY/AUG	JUNE/JULY/AUG	MAY/JUNE/JULY/OCT/NOV/DEC
27—Fertilize with general plant food (sidedress or water on)	JULY	JULY/AUG	JUNE/JULY/AUG	MAY/JUNE/JULY/OCT/NOV/DEC
28—Weed as needed	JULY	JULY/AUG	JUNE/JULY/AUG	MAY/JUNE/JULY/OCT/NOV/DEC
29—Remove dead flowers, as needed	JULY	JULY/AUG	JUNE/JULY/AUG	MAY/JUNE/JULY/OCT/NOV/DEC
30—Control pests and diseases, as needed	JULY	JULY/AUG	JUNE/JULY/AUG	MAY/JUNE/JULY/OCT/NOV/DEC
31—Plant biennial seeds for next year*	JULY	AUG	AUG	JULY
32—Take cuttings	JULY	AUG	AUG	JULY
33—Pick flowers for drying	AUG	SEPT	SEPT	JULY
34—Harvest mature seeds	AUG	SEPT	SEPT	JULY
35—Pot plants to bring indoors for the winter	AUG	SEPT	SEPT	
36—Protect beds from early frosts	AUG	SEPT	SEPT	
37—Dig and store tender bulbs	SEPT	SEPT	OCT	JAN
38—Pull out dead plants; destroy or compost	SEPT	OCT	OCT	
39—Make notes for next year's garden	SEPT	OCT	OCT	
40—Apply mulch to depleted and bare spots for winter	SEPT	OCT	NOV	
41—Take soil samples	SEPT	OCT	NOV	
42—Clean and sharpen tools; store for winter	OCT	NOV	DEC	DEC
43—Adjust pH according to soil test recommendations	OCT	NOV	DEC	

* Applies only to those plants that are started from seed. Does *not* apply to purchased bedding plants.

Ease of Care

	Ease	Comments
Abelmoschus moschatus	E	Needs abundant water
Alternanthera species	E	Frost-tender
Alyssum, Sweet	E	Survives light frosts
Amaranth, Globe	E	
Angel's Trumpet; Trumpet Flower; Horn of Plenty	E	Frost-tender
Asparagus Fern	E	Gross feeder
Aster; China Aster	MD	Prone to disease carried by insects
Baby Blue Eyes	E	Reseeds vigorously
Baby's Breath	E	Lime-loving
Bachelor's Button; Cornflower	E	
Basil	E	Poor soil makes leaves more pungent
Beard Tongue	E	Needs acid soil
Begonia, Fibrous, Wax, Everblooming	E	
Begonia, Tuberous	MD	Prone to mildew, brittleness
Bells of Ireland; Shell Flower; Molucca Balm	E	Reseeds vigorously
Black-Eyed Susan; Gloriosa Daisy	E	
Blanket Flower	E	May need fungicide
Blood Leaf	E	Frost-tender
Blue Bells, California	E	Heat-sensitive
Blue Lace Flower	E	Heat-sensitive
Blue Marguerite	E	Heat-sensitive
Burning Bush; Summer Cypress; Belvedere	E	Reseeds vigorously
Caladium hortulanum	E	
Calla; Calla Lily	E	
Calliopsis; Tickseed	E	Reseeds vigorously

	Ease	Comments
Candytuft	E	Lime-loving
Canna	E	
Canterbury Bells	E	Shade makes stems weak
Castor Bean	E	
Sweet False Chamomile	E	Reseeds vigorously
Chilean Bell Flower	E	
China Pink	E	Needs alkaline soil
Chrysanthemum	E	
Cleome; Spider Flower	E	Reseeds vigorously
Cockscomb, Plumed	E	
Coleus	E	
Corn Cockle	E	Reseeds vigorously
Cosmos	E	Reseeds vigorously
Cup and Saucer Vine; Cathedral Bells	E	Frost-tender
Dahlia	E	Needs air circulation
Daisy, African (Arctotis)	E	
Daisy, African (Golden Ageratum)	E	
Daisy, Dahlberg; Golden Fleece	E	Reseeds vigorously
Daisy, English	E	
Daisy, Livingstone	E	Resistant to salt spray
Daisy, Swan River	E	
Daisy, Transvaal; Barberton Daisy	E	
Dusty Miller	E	
Echium	E	Avoid too much fertility
Everlasting; Strawflower	E	
Firecracker Plant	E	Frost-tender
Floss Flower	E	
Foliage Plants	E	
Forget-Me-Not	E	Reseeds vigorously
Forget-Me-Not, Chinese; Hound's Tongue	E	
Forget-Me-Not, Summer; Cape Forget-Me-Not	E	Do not fertilize
Four O'Clock; Marvel of Peru	E	Reseeds vigorously
Foxglove	E	Reseeds vigorously
Fuchsia; Lady's Ear Drops	E	Gross feeder
Gazania; Treasure Flower	E	Heat-sensitive
Geranium, Ivy Leaf	E	Heat-sensitive
Geranium, Regal	E	
Geranium, Zonal	E	Frost-tender
Gladiolus; Glad	E	
Godetia; Farewell-to-Spring; Clarkia	E	

	Ease	Comments		Ease	Comments
Gourds, Ornamental	E	Frost-tender	Poppy, California	E	Hard to transplant
Grasses, Ornamental	E		Poppy, Horned; Sea Poppy	E	
Heliotrope; Cherry Pie	E	Tolerates high humidity	Poppy, Iceland	E	
			Poppy, Mexican Tulip	E	Drought-tolerant
Hibiscus, Chinese; Hawaiian Hibiscus; Rose of China	E		Portulaca; Moss Rose	E	Reseeds vigorously
			Primrose	E	
Hollyhock	MD	Prone to rust	Rock Purslane	E	
Impatiens; Busy Lizzie; Patience	E		Rose Mallow	E	
Impatiens, New Guinea	E		Rose-of-Heaven	E	
Variegated Ground Ivy	E		Salpiglossis; Painted Tongue	E	Frost-tender
Joseph's Coat; Love Lies Bleeding; Prince's Feather	E	Avoid root rot	Salvia; Scarlet Sage	E	
Lantana	E	Frost-sensitive	Sanvitalia; Creeping Zinnia	E	
Larkspur; Annual Delphinium	E		Sapphire Flower	E	
Lisianthus; Prairie Gentian	E		Scabiosa; Pincushion Flower; Mourning Bride	E	Sensitive to water
Lobelia	E	May need fungicide	Scarlet Flax	E	
Lotus Vine; Parrot's Beak	E		Scarlet Pimpernel; Poor-Man's Weather Glass	E	
Love-in-a-Mist; Devil in a Bush	E		Scarlet Runner Bean	E	
Lupine	E		Schizanthus; Butterfly Flower; Poor Man's Orchid	E	Blooms best with root restriction
Magic Carpet Plant	E				
Mallow; Cheese	E		Scotch Thistle	E	Reseeds vigorously
Flowering Maple	E		Snapdragon	E	
Marigold, Cape; African Daisy; Star-of-the-Veldt	E	Heat-sensitive	Snow-In-Summer; Ghost Weed	E	Reseeds vigorously
Marigold, American; Marigold, French	E		Southern Star; Star of the Argentine	E	
Marigold, Pot; Field Marigold	E		Stock	E	Survives light frost
Meadow Foam; Fried Eggs	E	Reseeds vigorously	Sundrop	E	
Melampodium	E		Sunflower	E	
Mignonette	E	Reseeds vigorously	Sweet Pea	E	
Monkey Flower	E	Tolerates wet soil	Thunbergia; Black-Eyed Susan Vine; Clock Vine	E	
Morning Glory Vine	E		Tidy Tips	E	Drought-resistant
Nasturtium	E	Reseeds vigorously	Tithonia; Mexican Sunflower	E	
Nemesia	E		Toadflax	E	
Nicotiana; Flowering Tobacco	E		Torenia; Wishbone Flower	E	Tolerates high humidity
Nierembergia; Cup Flower	E				
None So Pretty	E		Tuberose	E	Frost-tender
Ornamental Corn	E	Frost-tender	Venidium; Monarch of the Veldt; Cape Daisy	E	Heat-sensitive
Ornamental Cabbage; Ornamental Kale	E		Verbena	MD	Prone to mildew
Ornamental Peppers	E	Drought-tolerant	Vinca; Madagascar Periwinkle	E	Needs air circulation
Pansy	E				
Perilla; Beefsteak Plant	E	Frost-tender	Violet, Persian	E	
Petunia	E		Wallflower, English	E	
Phlox, Annual; Texas Pride	MD	Prone to mildew	Zinnia	MD	Prone to mildew
Pocketbook Plant	E				

E = Easy   MD = Moderately Difficult

This beautiful border of marigolds, cosmos, zinnias, dusty miller, and snapdragons illustrates the versatility of annuals. They brighten up this porch splendidly, adding seasonal color to an otherwise stark location.

68

GARDENING WITH ANNUALS

Any visitor to commercial public gardens such as Disney World or Busch Gardens can tell you just what a fantastic display annuals provide. Bare walls are decorated with half-baskets full of flowers; large massed plantings line sidewalks and fill sitting areas; huge planters are jammed with color; baskets of blooms hang from tree limbs and archways; and window boxes decorate balconies.

The versatility of annuals makes them the perfect choice in many planting situations. After all, they bloom for a long time and come in a wonderful variety of colors, sizes, and forms—all producing an abundance of blossoms or decorative leaves. Most of them thrive with minimal care. And they're inexpensive to grow.

Whether you plan to tuck annuals into a few blank spots to brighten the summer yard or to plant them in containers for use both indoors and outside, there is information in this chapter to help you. Likewise, if you feature them in large planting beds, use them to mask an ugly wall, or grow them as a source of blooms to cut and bring inside as decorations, the following pages will show you how to do so with ease and success.

Whether you have a large yard, a small one, or just a balcony, you'll find ideas here for ways to appreciate the beauty of annuals. Above all, you can enjoy the experience of planning your own garden, keeping in mind that there is no "right way" or "wrong way," there's just *your way*. If you're happy with the garden you create, that's what's important.

Laying Out an Annuals Garden

Colorful marigolds bring added life to this Japanese-style bridge.

It is seldom possible to create an attractive annuals garden simply by planting out boxed plants or flower seeds without any plan. More often than not, this approach will produce unsatisfactory results. You need advance planning. Without it, it's easy to slip up and be disappointed.

The best way to plan is with a simple sketch. Draw a quick outline of your garden bed, noting down its approximate dimensions and the amount of sun the area receives each day. Also list the names of your favorite annuals so you'll be sure to include most, if not all, of them in your plan.

The next step is to look up your favorites and to note the colors they come in and their growth habits. Mark down whether they prefer full sun, partial shade, or full shade. Also specify how tall they grow (T=tall, I=intermediate, L=low, V=vining). Check to see if any of your favorites prefer a different amount of sun than your site has available; cross out those that aren't suitable. In other words, if you love impatiens, but your bed is in full sun, only New Guinea impatiens will succeed there. (Since other varieties of impatiens do not tolerate full sun, you may want to see if there's a shady location elsewhere in the yard or on a covered porch where you can enjoy a few instead.)

If you have very few favorites and a large space to fill, add a second list of annuals that you find attractive and that fit the light and color limitations of your site. Use seed catalogs to help choose the variety of petunia, marigold, snapdragon, or whatever, with the color and height you want. Be sure to note down several variety names and sources if a plant comes in more than one desirable color.

Use colored pencils to color in planting sections within your bed outline. A more informal and interesting design will result if you vary the size and shape of these sections. Then decide which plants should go into what sections of your plan. Remember to keep tall plants in the back and low plants up front, filling in with intermediate heights. That way none of the plants will be blocked from view. If a bed is going to be in an area where it will be seen from all sides, the tallest plants should be in the center of the bed with low ones around the outer edges.

As you plan, be sure flower colors in adjacent sections vary but don't clash. Maintain a balance of color in the bed—avoid placing all the same-colored flowered plants on one side. In large beds, repeat the same variety in several sections, making the sections much larger than you would in smaller beds. Once you've decided what will go in each section, double-check to be sure you haven't inadvertently made a mistake—such as putting a tall plant up front or all the marigolds in one area. If you have, it's easy to change on paper.

Once the plan is in its final form, you can then figure out approximately how many plants you'll need of each kind to fill the allotted space. This will help in ordering seeds for sowing or starting ahead and in buying boxed bedding plants. **Caution:** If you plan to buy bedding plants rather than grow your own, remember that the variety of plants available will be limited. It might be best to visit suppliers and make a list of what colors and kinds of plants they have available *before* making your garden plan. That way you won't have to settle for substitutions or totally redo your garden plan.

Annuals Garden Against a Wall or Fence

This plan shows how to lay out a garden bed so all of the plants will be well displayed against the backdrop of a wall, fence, or building. Note that space has been left between the wall and the rear of the flower bed so gardening work—weeding, watering, spraying, etc.—can be done from both sides of the bed.

☐ = Tall

▨ = Intermediate

☐ = Low

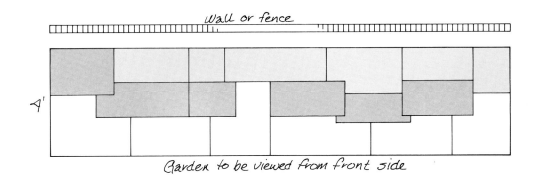

Garden to be viewed from front side

Annuals Garden Displayed From All Sides

☐ = Tall

▨ = Intermediate

☐ = Low

When planting a flower bed that is to be on display from all sides, the plants should be placed as illustrated in this plan. A pathway through the middle of the bed allows easy access for plant care if a bed is wider than 3 to 4 feet.

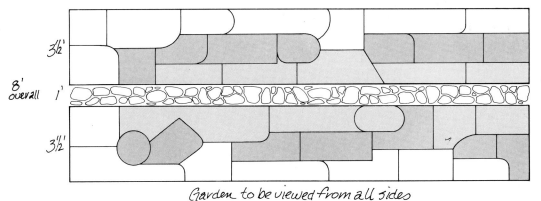

Garden to be viewed from all sides

Path for Gardener Access

Planning an Annuals Garden

3 To plan a flower bed, sketch its shape, noting its dimensions and the amount of sun available to it (full sun, partial shade, or full shade). Make a list of your personal plant favorites with notes about their height and colors. Cross off any that are inappropriate for the amount of light available beforehand. Once you've found niches for all of your favorites, make a second list of other plants you'd like to try—use some of these to fill any empty slots in your plan.

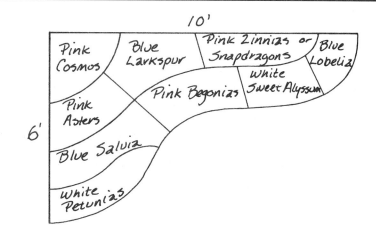

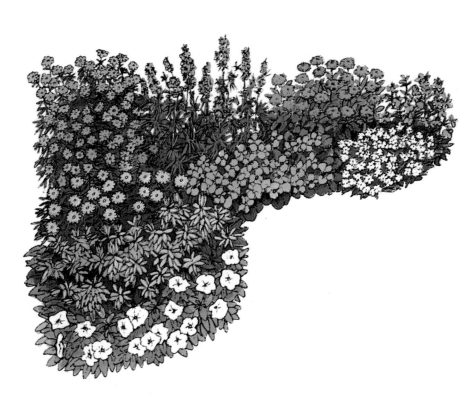

√ = Those actually used in plan.

Scale
1" = 2'

Colors	Height
blue = B	low = L
pink = P	Intermediate = I
white = W	Tall = T

Favorites - _must_ have:

√ Sweet Alyssum	W; L
√ Asters	B, P, W; I
√ Larkspur	B, P, W; I
√ Lobelia	B, W; L
√ Petunia	B, P, W; L
√ Salvia	B, P, W; I

Other possibilities :

√ Begonia	B, W; L
√ Cosmos	P, W; T
√ Geranium	P, W; I
Lantana	P, W, B; L
√ Snapdragon	P, W; L, I, T
√ Zinnia	W, P; L, I, T

Mixed Gardens

Multicolored snapdragons and petunias give this garden an informal look.

Many of us recall the old-fashioned gardens of our grandparents or other elderly relatives and neighbors. These were usually a hodge-podge of annuals, perennials, and shrubs. Frequently, there were also trees, vegetables, and small fruits—strawberries, raspberries, or currants—mixed in.

It seemed that gardens, rather than being planned, more or less "happened." More likely, they evolved. As the gardener fancied something new or was given a plant by a friend, it was inserted into an available blank spot. Where yards were small and space was limited, these mixed gardens combined whatever was at hand. The end result often had an individual charm that was undeniable and delightful.

There's no reason, of course, why we can't create a similarly informal effect in a modern garden. For those with limited garden space, a mixed garden makes especially good sense. It allows us to have some of our personal favorites, rather than limiting us to only a few kinds of plants—as is the case of massed garden designs.

A mixed garden is a very personal one that truly reflects the individual taste of the homeowners. Rather than being a garden for show, it's a garden designed for the pleasure of those who own it. If others who visit it also find it enjoyable, so much the better.

Some uniquely charming mixed gardens are possible. Fruit trees, such as peach, pear, or apple, can supply partial shade to flower beds filled with combinations of different-colored annuals and perennials. Clumps of favorite vegetables can also be placed among these flowering plants. The casual visitor might never notice these, since so many vegetables have attractive foliage to add to the garden scene. Feathery carrot tops; purplish beet greens; the bold and interesting foliage of parsnips; smooth, blue-green onion spikes; and large rhubarb leaves all make attractive additions to any flower bed.

If you don't want to be limited to only a few kinds and colors of flowers in your garden, consider planting a mixed garden. With the wonderful array of annuals at your disposal, it's even possible to have an entirely different and unique garden every growing season.

ANNUALS FOR MIXED GARDENS

Sweet Alyssum	Nasturtium
Aster	Nicotiana
Baby's Breath	Pansy
Bachelor's Button	Petunia
Cockscomb	Phlox
Coleus	Shirley Poppy
Cosmos	Portulaca
Dahlia	Blue Salvia
Forget-Me-Not	Scabiosa
Heliotrope	Snapdragon
Hollyhock	Sweet Pea
Impatiens	Torenia
Larkspur	Verbena
Lisianthus	Vinca
American/French	Xeranthemum
Marigold	Zinnia

Combining Annuals, Fruits, and Vegetables

This small garden contains a mixture of annuals, fruits, and vegetables. This plan could easily be modified to include your own food favorites.

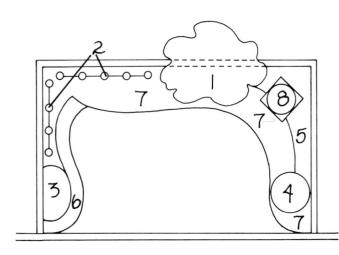

1. Favorite flowering tree
2. Pole beans, snap peas, or raspberries on trellis
3. Rhubarb
4. Blueberry (2 different varieties for cross-pollination)
5. Beets or Swiss chard
6. Herbs and other vegetable favorites
7. Flowering annuals
8. Fountain, statue, or other garden feature

The same small space is packed full of color while providing a private, vine-covered sitting area. The birdbath might be replaced with a piece of garden sculpture or an unusual accent plant—perhaps a tree lantana, topiary evergreen, or rosemary.

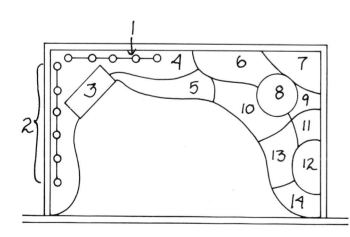

3. Garden seat or other garden feature with impatiens planted around and behind it.
4. Marigold
5. Lobelia - blue
6. Cosmos - mixed
7. Hollyhock - mixed
8. Birdbath
9. Marigold
10. Red salvia or red peppers
11. Perilla
12. Pot marigold - yellow
13. Sweet alyssum - white
14. Swan River daisy

1. Morning Glory } over trellis
2. Moon Vine

Container Gardening

Probably no form of gardening allows more versatility than container gardening. Growing plants in containers makes it possible to garden in situations where there is no yard or soil available: on a rooftop, a high-rise balcony, a deck, a fire escape, or even in an area that's covered with concrete.

The containers themselves can be as plain or elaborate as you wish. Clay or plastic pots; wood, plastic, or metal window boxes; decorator pots of ceramic, terra cotta, alabaster, or wrought iron; recycled plastic or metal pails; wire frames lined with sphagnum moss; a child's cast-off metal wagon; hanging planters; a plastic-lined bushel basket—any of these can be used. Here's a chance to give your imagination free rein!

All that's essential is that the container be capable of holding soil as well as allowing excess water to drain away. Keep in mind that plants thrive more readily in larger amounts of soil, because the soil temperature and moisture level fluctuate less as soil volume increases. Unless the gardener is extremely vigilant, plants are more likely to suffer frequent drying out and overheating when planted in small pots.

Annuals are particularly well-suited for use in container plantings. They quickly fill and overflow the planters. You can also plant them in masses of a single species or in a mixture of different kinds and colors.

Another advantage to growing plants in containers is their portability. You can move them from one area to another at will, as long as you remember that shade-loving plants can quickly burn if shifted into brilliant sun. Conversely, sun lovers won't flourish if shaded for more than a few days.

Planters full of annuals can be used singly or in groups. They can be mixed with houseplants brought outdoors for summer or inserted here and there in between shrubbery. Container plants can be hung from a garden fence, a low-hanging tree limb, or a porch rail. Even a small apartment balcony can be turned into a colorful garden by filling it with annuals.

Care of container plantings takes little total time, but it does require daily attention. Soil moisture needs to be checked every evening. When the weather is dry and windy, you may even need to check soil moisture morning and evening. Rub a small amount of the surface soil from each pot between your thumb and finger to test the moisture level. Ideally, you want to rewater each planter *before* the soil becomes bone dry. On the other hand, the soil should not be constantly soaking wet or the plants will drown. Therefore, it's necessary to keep track of the moisture level very conscientiously.

Geraniums are excellent choices for all sorts of containers.

To be sure that water reaches all of the soil in the container, fill the planter to the rim with water, allowing it to soak in completely. If no water comes out of the drainage holes, fill again. Repeat this process until water starts to drip from the bottom of the container.

To keep the plantings looking full and to encourage abundant blooming, remove dead flower heads promptly. At the same time, check for any signs of insect or disease problems. Once every ten days to two weeks, water with a mild fertilizer solution. That's all it takes to keep container gardens in peak condition.

Container gardening can be an ideal solution for people with physical limitations that prevent them from working down at ground level. It can also be the answer for those with soil problems. For anyone, growing annuals in containers can provide an extra dimension of gardening pleasure, both outdoors in summer and indoors in winter.

Drainage in Container Gardening

To grow plants successfully in containers, good drainage is essential. Drainage holes need to be covered to keep soil in place: Pieces of broken pottery, fine screening, or a coffee filter are all good choices. You can also add a layer of small stones, perlite, or coarse sand in the bottom of the container. Indoors, or on a porch where dripping water would do damage, place a drip tray under the container to catch excess water.

Gardening in Decorative Containers

When using a decorative container with no drainage holes, place a well-drained pot inside of it in which to actually grow plants. Raise the inner pot on a layer of pebbles to keep it above water level. Peat moss in the space between the inner and outer pots would provide insulation to help stabilize soil temperatures.

ANNUALS THAT DO WELL IN CONTAINERS

Fibrous Begonia	Nasturtium
Coleus	Pansy
Dracaena	Ornamental Pepper
Geranium	Perilla
Impatiens	Petunia
Lobelia	Phlox
American/French Marigold	Sweet Pea
	Verbena
Pot Marigold	Vinca
Morning Glory Vine	

The Versatility of Window Boxes

Window boxes are versatile planters that are not just useful on window ledges. They can also hang from porch rails or fences, perch along the tops of walls, mark the edge of a deck, or line a walk or driveway. Add them wherever you want color without creating a flower bed.

The Many Uses of Hanging Baskets

Hanging baskets provide another almost endless source of color. You can group them at different levels on a porch; hang them from tree limbs; or add half-baskets to brighten a blank wall or bare fence. You can even create tall pillars of color by hanging baskets from an old coat rack or other suitable recycled stand.

Cutting Garden

A cutting garden full of marigolds, zinnias, daisies, and baby's breath can bring annual color into a home.

If you'd like to have containers full of flowers brightening your home, a perfect source is a cutting garden filled with annuals. Most gardeners are unwilling to cut many blooms from their regular flower beds because they want as full and colorful a display as possible. Therefore, a garden specially set aside to supply flowers for cutting is a good solution. This can be a separate flower bed, or you can devote a row or two of your vegetable patch to a flower crop.

Most seed companies offer packets of "Cutting Flower Mix" that contain a variety of flowering annuals. The mixture varies, but it will always include seeds that are easy to grow and produce nice, bouquet-type flowers. Mixes usually include some, but not all, of the following plants: marigolds, zinnias, plumed cockscomb, baby's breath, bachelor's buttons, pot marigolds, cosmos, asters, blanket flowers, and seedling dahlias.

The major disadvantage to buying such a mix is that you don't know in advance what colors the flowers will be. If you want to key the flower colors to the colors in your home or if you only want specific kinds of cut flowers, then you'll need to purchase those varieties separately.

When cutting for indoor use, select flowers that are in bud or in early stages of bloom. Those in later stages of bloom should be cut from the plant and discarded. If they're left, plant strength will be wasted on the formation of seeds. To obtain the longest period of enjoyment possible from cut flowers, pick them in the early morning. Use a sharp knife and make a slanted cut. Cut just above the point where another flower bud or a side shoot is beginning to grow. This way, plant energy will quickly shift to production of additional blooms.

As you cut, place the flowers in a container of water and bring them indoors promptly. Remove the leaves from the lower portion of each stem, immediately putting the flowers back into a tall container of fresh water. You can either arrange bouquets right away or keep cut flowers in a cool location to arrange later.

Each time you recut a stem, always use a sharp knife and cut on a slant. This keeps all available stem cells open to the transfer of water up into the cut flower. Scissors and shears can pinch some of these water channels closed. Also, remember to remove all leaves that will be under water once the flower is in a container. If left on, they'll rot, which not only causes a terrible odor, but also shortens flower life by clogging stem cells needed for water transfer.

Annuals are lovely in both elaborate formal arrangements and in simple, informal bouquets. It's easy to quickly make attractive bouquets if you keep these hints in mind as you pick and arrange flowers:

- Select flowers in bud as well as in early bloom.
- Select colors that blend well.
- Separate clashing colors with gray foliage or white flowers.
- Cut flowers at different lengths. Leave longer stems on smaller flowers; shorter stems on larger ones.
- Mix flowers of varying sizes and forms.
- Use containers that are narrower at the top than at the bottom for an easy, informal bouquet. If a different effect is desired, use cylindrical vases or containers with flared mouths.
- Match container size to bouquet size.

ANNUALS FOR THE CUTTING GARDEN

Canna	Pansy
Chrysanthemum	Poppy (sear stems)
Coleus	Salpiglossis
African Daisy	Blue Salvia
Transvaal Daisy	Scabiosa
Ornamental Grasses	Snapdragon
Larkspur	Stock
Pot Marigold	Sweet Pea
Nasturtium	Vinca
Nicotiana	Zinnia

Elements of Attractive Bouquets

1. Stems of different lengths make bouquets more interesting.

2. Flowers in different stages of bloom provide more variety of form than when they're all at the same stage.

3. Matching vase size to bouquet size keeps a good balance between flowers and container.

4. Daisy-type flowers are fresh when all of the buds in the flower center are closed or when only the outermost ring is blooming. When the entire center shows pollen, the flower is finished blooming and ready to die.

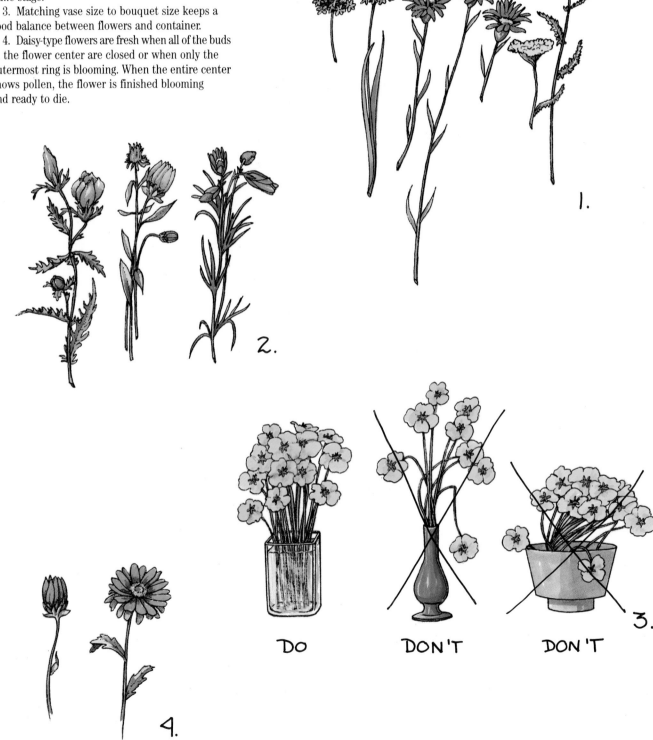

DO   DON'T   DON'T

Drying & Pressing Annuals

A basket of dried annuals is a year-round treat.

There are several different drying techniques for annuals. The easiest is hang drying. After picking, all leaves should be removed, and flowers grouped in bunches of 6 to 8 stems. Wind an elastic band tightly around the stems.

Hang bundles upside-down out of the light in a well-ventilated, dry area. Leave enough space between bundles to allow for good air circulation and protect the bundles by enclosing them in large paper bags. The flowers will dry in two to three weeks. They can then be laid in covered boxes or left hanging.

Some flowers are too thick and others too delicate to successfully hang dry. Instead they can be dried with a desiccant—a material that will draw moisture into itself. Floral desiccant is sold commercially. Or you can make it yourself by mixing equal parts of fine, dry sand and borax powder.

To use, pour an inch or more of desiccant in the bottom of a box, then lay the flowers on top. Very carefully spoon more desiccant up and around each flower head. Once all of the flowers are mounded over, an additional inch or two of desiccant should be gently poured on top. Use a large, shallow box for long spikes of bloom such as larkspur. For single, dense blooms, like roses and marigolds, remove the flower stem first and replace it with a stiff wire stem. Lay the flowers flat on the surface of the desiccant, then mound more dessicant around and over them.

Drying will take several weeks, depending on the density of the flowers. When they're dry, carefully unbury them, gently brush away any adhering desiccant with a soft artist's brush, and store them in covered boxes in a dry place until ready to use.

A third drying method is to press flowers and leaves between layers of absorbent blotting paper or paper towels. The drawback to this method is that everything comes out flat. But for use in pictures, notepaper, or as a frame around a motto or wedding announcement, flowers dried this way can be very effective.

This technique works best with small flowers that are not very thick, such as pansies, petunias, and baby's breath. It is also suited for parts of flowers, such as single petals of sweet peas, poppies, and cosmos. To dry, start with a piece of heavy cardboard at the base; then lay a sheet of drying paper on top. Carefully arrange flowers and leaves, making sure that there is space between them. Lay one or two more layers of drying paper on top. Arrange another layer of leaves and flowers. Keep alternating until there are a half dozen layers of plant materials. Top these with more drying paper and a final piece of cardboard. Finally,

place a heavy weight on top of the stack. Moisture will be squeezed out of the flowers into the paper. Check after a week to see how drying is progressing. If any mold has formed, remove and replace the drying paper. After several weeks, the plant materials will be ready to use or store.

FLOWERS TO AIR DRY

Globe Amaranth	Ornamental Grasses
Baby's Breath*	Love-in-a-Mist pods
Bells of Ireland	Pansy*
Cockscomb	Single Pink*
Dusty Miller foliage*	Strawflower
Forget-Me-Not*	Zinnia

*=Press

Air Drying Flowers

Hang small bunches of flowers upside-down in a dry, well-ventilated area away from direct sun. Brown bags protect them against dust.

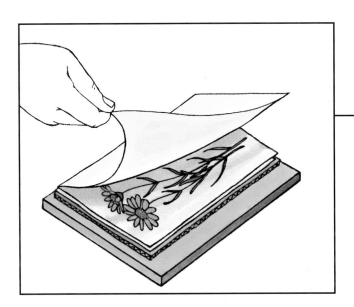

Drying Flowers with Weights

Alternate layers of absorbent paper and flowers, applying steady pressure on the stack to flatten and dry them.

FLOWERS TO DRY IN DESICCANT	
Dahlia*	Nasturtium
Gladiolus	Petunia
Hollyhock	Double Pink
Lantana	Snapdragon
Larkspur	Verbena
Marigold*	Zinnia*

*=Use wire stem

1 Drying Flowers in Desiccant

Replace natural stems with wire ones before laying
large, individual flowers (such as marigolds, zinnias,
asters, pot marigolds, and dahlias) in desiccant.

2

Lay tall flowers (such as larkspur, Canterbury bells, salvia, and gladiolus) horizontally on a layer of desiccant and gently sprinkle more desiccant around and over them.

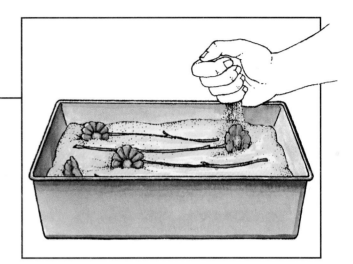

3

When flowers are dry, carefully remove them from the desiccant. Use a soft artist's brush to gently brush away any desiccant adhering to the blooms.

Vines & Other Climbers

Morning glory vine is effective as a window decoration.

To cover a bare wall, fence, or trellis, annual vines are the perfect choice. During the summer months, you'll have an abundant green cloak over the bare surface as well as a continuous show of colorful blooms. Where you need attractive year-round coverage, perennial vines are the better choice. But you may also want to use annual vines to fill in areas that the perennials have not yet reached.

You may like this mixture so much that you'll even continue to intermix annual and perennial vines once the perennial vines have reached full size, letting the annual vines provide flower color during the perennials' nonblooming periods. As long as you prune back the annual vines if they threaten to overwhelm the perennials, the two can be very effective together.

Annual vines require some kind of support to climb. The support can be made of wire or string woven into netting or stretched vertically between the top and bottom of the outer frame. It can also be a trellis constructed from plastic or wood. The vines will hold on to a support by simply twisting their stems or leaf tendrils around it.

For a single season, the most inexpensive and sensible choice would be to run strands of sturdy twine or plastic clothesline up and down between two horizonal pieces of wood—one no higher than 6 inches from the ground; the other 6 feet or so above the ground. Other comparatively inexpensive supports are woven polyester string netting or Ross garden netting—both can be found at most garden shops. If you plan to grow vines year after year, a more solid and permanent support, such as a wood, plastic, or metal trellis, is the best choice.

Whatever kind of support you choose, the most important factor to keep in mind is that vines become surprisingly heavy with foliage as the season progresses. The support should be solidly built and strong enough to hold up the vine weight. A flimsy support will sag or even buckle and break partway through the season, leaving an ugly and unmanageable tangle.

Annual vines require very little special care. When they first begin to vine, you may need to steer them toward the bottom of the support if they start to run along the ground rather than upward. But once they start their climb, they're all set. If you want to encourage multiple stems, pinch back the growing tip when the plants are 10 to 12 inches high.

Some annual vines have certain limitations in the hours during which they bloom. The moon vine begins blooming late in the day and flowers overnight (hence its name); it has a lovely perfume and is ideal for a porch or patio that is used mostly in the evening. Morning glories, on the other hand, open early in the morning and bloom until about noontime. Most other annual vines bloom around the clock. Keep these factors in mind when you make your selection.

Vine foliage varies from the very light and fernlike cypress vine to the large, round nasturtium pads and the heart-shaped morning glory and moon vine leaves. The foliage of dolichos has a purplish tinge, and its flower clusters are an interesting lavender and purple blend. This plant's most dramatic and comment-gathering feature, however, is the clusters of shiny, bright purple bean pods it abundantly produces.

Annual vines are also effective when grown in window boxes or large pots on a house deck or apartment balcony. They'll twine up existing railings or supports specially constructed for them. With some imagination, it's possible to create an unexpected and delightful garden retreat far above ground level!

CLIMBING ANNUALS	
Canary Creeper	Moon Vine
Cup and Saucer Vine	Morning Glory Vine
Cypress Vine	Sweet Pea
Gourds	Scarlet Runner Bean
Dolichos	Thunbergia

Tips on Vining Plants

1 As vines become heavy with leaves and flowers, a sturdy frame is needed to support them. Alternatives to the polyester netting shown here include wire fencing, plastic clothesline, sturdy twine, or lath strips. Once young growing tips are guided to the support, they'll wind and weave their way upward without further help.

2 Plant 2 to 3 seeds per hole, spacing the holes 6 to 10 inches apart. Several seeds will push through the soil surface better than a single one, and there's also a backup if some seeds don't germinate. When the plants are 3 to 4 inches high, thin each group leaving the strongest seedling to continue to grow.

3 Pinching vines once when they're 10 to 12 inches high will encourage branching and result in a more solid coverage of greenery and blooms.

This colorful garden uses only a few of the hundreds of annual species and varieties that are available. Even this simple planting of marigolds, salvia, and floss flowers is visual proof of the versatility of these lovely flowers.

ENCYCLOPEDIA OF ANNUAL DELIGHTS

The plants selected for this directory cover a wide base—some are annuals, others are biennials, still others are perennials in some parts of the world. A few can even be recognized as houseplants. But they can all be used successfully to provide seasonal color outdoors as annuals. Names, descriptions, how-to-grow techniques, propagation, uses, and related species and varieties are all dealt with in depth. Photos are included for each entry.

Whether you live in a suburban home with a large yard or in a condominium 14 stories above the ground with only a windy balcony to plant in, you will find annuals here that will work for you. Given their extensive variety, there are types that can be used to beautify your particular living space, allowing you the opportunity to make entirely different planting choices each year.

Many of the plants listed in the directory are everywhere—a relatively reliable guide to their success rate. Some can be found as started plants at garden centers. Others you will have to start yourself from seed, either from seed packets found on racks locally or from mail order catalogs that offer the greatest selection available. You will be able to familiarize yourself with enough annuals so that you can decide for yourself what will work best for you, depending on your location and the amount of time and effort you want to put into starting and maintaining an annuals garden.

Abelmoschus moschatus

Abelmoschus moschatus

Newly introduced to ornamental gardens in the United States, this brightly colored flower is the same genus as the vegetable okra. Hibiscus is also a close relative and their resemblance is striking. Three- to 4-inch flowers appear in July from an early start indoors. Each flower lasts only a day, but the profusion of buds provides a continuous show of color.

Description: Plants grow 15 to 20 inches high and wide. Flowers are pink or red with white centers appearing above the arrowhead-shaped leaves.

How to grow: As with other members of the genus, it thrives in heat in full sun. Abundant water and a rich soil are also important for its best performance.

Propagation: By seed. Seeds take at least 15 days to germinate at 70° F. For husky plants, start at least 8 weeks prior to planting in the garden. First bloom is approximately 100 days after sowing. Plant 1 foot apart when the soil has warmed and nights remain above 50° F.

Uses: This bright plant can be used for a sunny garden ground cover. Plant it mid-border or as an edging for borders in front of taller plants. Use it as a container plant where its mounding, flowing habit combines well with taller plants. Its tropical appearance looks attractive with cannas, caladiums (in shade only), callas, and other exotic-appearing plants. Abelmoschus can also be grown on sunny windowsills indoors.

Related varieties: New varieties include *A. moschatus* 'Mischief,' bearing cherry-red flowers with white centers; 'Oriental Red,' similar in appearance; and 'Pink,' a bright pink. The Pacific series includes 'Pacific Pink' and 'Pacific Scarlet,' an orange-scarlet variety.

Alternanthera species

Alternanthera species

Alternantheras, of which there are possibly 200 species, are brilliantly colored foliage plants used for their leaves. Different species and varieties are strongly marked with yellow, pink, red, and coppery red.

Description: *A. ficoidea* forms a bushy plant up to 1 foot tall with leaves veined with brownish-red, carmine, and orange. Varieties include *A. f. amoena,* a compact form with red-splashed leaves and *A. f. rosea-nana,* with rosy pink leaves. *A. f. bettzickiana* is taller with olive-green to red leaves; *A. f. aurea-nana* has yellow leaves; and *A. f. brilliantissima* bears bright red leaves. *A. f. versicolor* has dark green or red leaves with pink veins and leaf margins of white and pink.

How to grow: High temperatures in full sun bring out the brightest coloring in alternantheras. They do best in well-drained soil that is not excessively moist. They are very frost-tender and should not be planted out until all danger of frost has passed and the soil is warm. They are usually kept sheared to induce uniformity in formal bedding situations. Plant small varieties 8 inches apart and tall ones every 12 inches.

Propagation: By cuttings or by division. Cuttings root easily and quickly.

Uses: Alternantheras are at their best combined in patterns of color in formal bedding situations, but they also make handsome container and hanging basket specimens. They can also be planted in design combinations with flowering annuals, the brightly colored leaves being especially effective with light-colored flowers. In areas without frost, they are often used for bed and walkway edgings.

Related species: *A. dentata rubinginosa* is a red- or purple-leaved form of a species that is normally green-leaved. It will normally grow from 1 to 2 feet tall.

Sweet Alyssum

Lobularia maritima

Alyssum is covered with thimblelike flowers for months on end, even through the winter in milder climates. A member of the mustard family, alyssum has a pervasive fragrance.

Description: Alyssum grows only a few inches high but spreads as much as 1 foot in diameter. The tiny flowers are closely packed around the small racemes that grow upward as the lower flowers fade. Although white is the most planted color, pink, lavender, and darker shades of violet are also available.

How to grow: Alyssum grows best in full sun in cool weather, but it will tolerate partial shade. Plants will survive light frosts. Space 6 to 8 inches apart. Alyssum will reseed vigorously.

Propagation: By seed. In mildest climates, it can be planted in the fall for cool season display. Otherwise, sow seeds outdoors as soon as the ground can be worked. For earliest bloom, sow seeds indoors 4 to 6 weeks earlier and transplant to the garden while plants are still small. Seeds germinate in 7 to 14 days at 65 to 70° F.

Uses: Alyssum is traditionally used for edging beds and borders. However, it can also tumble over the rocks in a rock garden or be planted in niches between paving stones. Place it where the scent can perfume the air for passersby. It makes a good, sunny ground cover for large or small areas. It is good in containers.

Related varieties: 'New Carpet of Snow' is the most planted, but the newer 'Wonderland' series has three distinctive colors: 'White,' 'Rosy-Red,' and 'Deep Purple,' the darkest alyssum color so far. Medal-winning 'Rosie O'Day' is a rose color. 'Snow Crystal' is a new, award-winning white variety.

Globe Amaranth

Gomphrena globosa

Here's a weather- and soil-tolerant plant. This tropical native has small, cloverlike flowers that continue coming through the whole summer season. It's a member of the amaranth family.

Description: Globe amaranth can grow up to 2 feet with newer, smaller varieties that are bushy dwarfs. The flowers are about 1 inch in diameter and have a papery texture. The flowers nestle in two large, modified leaves called bracts. The basic color is violet, but varieties have red, orange, pink, and creamy white flowers. The flowers are small, but there are many of them.

How to grow: The only demand for good performance is sun. Plant in the garden after the last frost and, depending on variety, space from 10 to 15 inches apart.

Propagation: By seed. Soak seeds in water for 3 to 4 days before sowing. Sow seeds in place in the garden after last frost. For earlier bloom, start transplants 6 to 8 weeks earlier. Seeds germinate in 14 to 21 days at 65 to 75° F.

Uses: The tall varieties are ideal for mid-border. Use dwarf varieties for edging beds, borders, or for a colorful ground cover. Combine them with other plants for container plantings. The tall varieties are especially good for cutting and drying.

Related species: *Gomphrena haageana* has yellow to orange, pinecone-shaped flowers, each about 1 inch in diameter. It also dries well.

Related varieties: 'Buddy' is a compact variety, growing only 9 to 12 inches tall. Flowers are deep purple in color. 'Strawberry Fields' is bright red and grows to 2 feet with long stems. It is splendid for cutting. Several mixtures are offered including white, pink, rose, and reddish-purple flowers.

Angel's Trumpet, Trumpet Flower, Horn of Plenty

Datura metel

A tropical native, the angel's trumpet has long flowers (up to 10 inches and 4 inches across the face). It is related to Jimson weed, and, like its cousin, contains a poisonous alkaloid called hyoscyamine.

Description: Angel's trumpet will grow 3 to 5 feet tall and has oval leaves up to 8 inches long with toothed margins. The flowers have 5 large lobes with pointed tips. Flowers are mostly white; but there are yellow, blue, and red forms too. Double-flowered varieties that contain duplicates of the flowers inside the spreading face are also available.

How to grow: Angel's trumpet grows well in any good, moist garden soil in full sun. They're very tender—so plant them out after all danger of frost has passed and the ground is warm. Prune freely to shape plants. To prolong bloom, remove the flowers as soon as they finish blooming to prevent seed formation. In frost-free areas of Zones 9 and 10, they can be overwintered outdoors. For overwintering indoors, move container plants to a cool but frost-free location and keep barely moist until spring. In late spring, cut back the plant and resume feeding and watering.

Propagation: By seed. Start seeds indoors 8 to 12 weeks before planting out. They germinate in 8 to 15 days at 70 to 85° F. Seeds may be saved from blooming plants for replanting the following season.

Uses: Because the trumpets hang down, it is of great advantage to plant them where they can be seen at eye level—on slopes, beside upward-leading paths, or as raised container plants.

Related species: *Datura sauveolens* has richly scented, white, lilylike trumpets that hang down. *Datura sanguinea* produces the same type of flowers in orange-red. It is perennial, sometimes producing flowers the first year.

Asparagus Fern

Asparagus densiflorus

Asparagus fern, of which there are many kinds, is related to the favorite springtime vegetable, and you'll notice that new shoots look like skinny asparagus spears. The most frequently used ornamental one is called *A. sprengeri*.

Description: New asparagus growth expands to form feathery, branched shoots 1 to 2 feet long. From a small plant in spring with 3 to 4 stems, at summer's end up to 10 or more billowing stalks emerge from pots or containers.

How to grow: Key factors to good growth include moderate water, a rich, well-drained soil, and full sunlight. Asparagus fern will tolerate low light (even existing satisfactorily as a house-plant), but growth will be diminished. Asparagus fern is a gross feeder; at planting use a slow-release fertilizer lasting summer long or feed weekly with a water-soluble fertilizer mixed at half the recommended strength.

Propagation: By seed (must be fresh) or by division. It's most readily available as started plants.

Uses: Asparagus fern is primarily used as a filler plant in containers of mixed flowers growing during the summer. It works in wall boxes, hanging baskets, window boxes, and planters of all kinds. Asparagus fern also grows well in partially shaded ground beds, alone, or intermixed with larger, shade-tolerant flowers such as tuberous begonias. Because asparagus fern is a vigorous plant, combine with plants of some stature so they are not overpowered.

Related varieties: Several other asparagus relatives are also used as ornamentals. *A. densiflorus* 'Myers' is a selection with stiff, upright growth like foxtails. *A. asparagoides*, the florist's smilax, is sometimes planted in flowering containers. Leaves are coarser, and it is a definite trailer.

Aster, China Aster

Callistephus chinensis

From one highly variable species has come a whole range of China asters—singles, semi-doubles, and doubles as well as tall, medium, and dwarf—all in a wide range of colors that includes white, pink, yellow, blue, and red.

Description: China asters are available from petite varieties that form compact mounds at 1 foot all the way to tall ones that grow to 2½ feet tall. Bloom times differ too, with early summer, midsummer, and late summer varieties. For a continuous show, you'll need to pick different varieties and/or stagger sowing dates.

How to grow: China asters grow best in full sun in rich soil. Two disease problems have plagued them in the past: aster yellows, carried by leafhoppers, and fusarium wilt, a soil-borne disease. Select disease-resistant varieties when you buy seeds or plants. Spray to control insects. Don't plant them in the same ground two years in a row. Sow seeds indoors 6 to 7 weeks before planting outside. They germinate in 10 to 20 days at 70° F. Otherwise, sow them into the ground outside after the last frost. Each variety blooms only 3 to 4 weeks, so for a continuous show, successive plantings must be two weeks apart.

Propagation: By seed.

Uses: Use China asters in beds and borders. Alternate a space and a plant, then fill the spaces with young plants that bloom later. Tall varieties make superb cut flowers.

Related varieties: 'Pinocchio' is a dwarf strain of mixed colors with a garden mum flower form and garden habit. 'Perfection Mixed' plants grow to 2 feet with 4-inch fully double flowers. 'Super Giants Mixture' grows to 2½ feet with 5-inch double spidery flowers.

Baby Blue Eyes

Nemophila menziesii

Baby blue eyes is a California native found in woodland sites. It blooms well all summer in full sun as long as it is kept well watered and night temperatures drop below 65° F.

Description: Baby blue eyes is a small plant, rarely growing over 10 inches high. The mounding plants are covered with flowers that are up to 1½ inches in diameter. Most commonly, the flowers are sky-blue centered with white; some forms are spotted or veined with deeper colors.

How to grow: Nemophila does best in cool, dry climates where it will grow well in full sun as long as it is kept moist. In warmer regions, it will benefit from partial or dappled shade. In the warmest areas, it should be planted for a spring display. Baby blue eyes must have good drainage; a light, sandy loam is best. Transplant plants into the garden after the last frost. Space 6 to 9 inches apart. Nemophila readily reseeds itself in the garden.

Propagation: By seed. To get a jump on warm weather in hot summer areas, sow seeds indoors 4 to 6 weeks prior to planting out. Seeds germinate in 7 to 12 days at 55° F. In cool summer areas, seeds can be sown in place outdoors in the spring as soon as the ground can be worked. Thin seedlings to a 6-to 9-inch spacing.

Uses: This low-growing plant is wonderful in front of borders and as an edging for beds, walkways, and paths. Try it tucked between the paving stones in a patio. Plant it in rock gardens. It's a natural for containers.

Related species: *Nemophila maculata* is commonly called "Five Spot." Very similar in growth habit, it's so named because the white, open-faced flowers have a purple spot at the tip of each petal.

Related varieties: Most seed houses offer their own selection of the species. Sometimes available is 'Insignis Blue.'

Baby's Breath

Gypsophila elegans

Their light, airy texture and petite white or pink flowers make baby's breath a wonderful addition to the garden. This annual is native to the Caucasus and is related to carnations. Because they bloom for only 6 weeks, new seedlings should be started to replace those that have finished blooming.

Description: Annual baby's breath grows to 1½ feet tall, forming an airy bush with many forked branches covered with flowers. Although the flowers, up to ½ inch in diameter, are usually white, there are pink, rose, and carmine forms.

How to grow: Grow in full sun in average, lime-rich garden soil. They grow rapidly and will come into bloom about 8 weeks after germination. Sow new baby's breath every 2 to 4 weeks to assure continuous bloom for the summer.

Propagation: By seed. Sow seeds outdoors in place after the danger of frost has passed. For earlier bloom, sow indoors in peat pots 2 to 3 weeks before planting out, then plant—pot and all. (They grow so rapidly, it is difficult to separate the seedlings, so plant them in a clump.) Germination takes 10 to 15 days at 70° F.

Uses: Baby's breath is effective in borders or cottage gardens. Baby's breath also makes a superb cut flower. It is used primarily as a filler to give unity to arrangements with strong vertical or horizontal lines.

Related species: *Gypsophila paniculata* is a perennial and widely planted. Both single- and double-flowers are found, with 'Bristol Fairy' the most popular species.

Related varieties: The favorite white is 'Covent Garden,' which is also the favorite cut flower strain. 'Kermesina' is a deep rose. 'Red Cloud' has shades ranging from pink to carmine. Mixtures of rose, white, and red are also available.

Bachelor's Button, Cornflower

Centaurea cyanus

The boutonniere flower is reputedly where this favorite got its name. And "cornflower blue" has frequently been used in the fashion trade to merchandise that particular shade. The flowers also come in soft shades of pink, lavender, maroon, red, and white.

Description: Bachelor's buttons grow 1 to 3 feet tall with innumerable round flowers held above the rather sparse, long and narrow gray-green leaves. The habit of growth is relatively loose.

How to grow: Full sun in average soil is good. For earliest bloom, sow seeds outdoors in the fall so they will start to grow before the first frost and bloom the next spring. They may also be started indoors and transplanted. Otherwise, sow seeds outdoors as early in the spring as the soil can be worked. Thin to 8 to 12 inches apart. Early bloom is heavy and prolific; it tapers off later. Repeat sowings will maintain a lush bloom.

Propagation: By seed. To grow seedlings indoors, germinate at 65° F four weeks before planting out. Germination time is 7 to 14 days.

Uses: Bachelor's buttons lend themselves to informal planting, especially with other annuals and perennials in beds and borders. When planting in containers, the gardener should take into consideration their informal growth habit. The flowers dry well, but stems are weak and must be wired for arrangements.

Related species: *C. moschata,* commonly called "sweet sultan," bears sweetly scented, fuzzy, 3- to 4-inch yellow, pink, lavender, or white blossoms. Growing to 2 feet, sweet sultans are good for cutting.

Related varieties: 'Blue Boy' grows to 2½ feet. Award-winning 'Jubilee Gem' is shorter at 12 inches. 'Polka Dot Mixed' and 'Frosty Mixed' have white or pastel contrasts at petal tips.

Basil

Ocimum basilicum

Basil is one of the world's favorite flavorings, used in all kinds of meat, fish, and vegetable dishes. The purple-leaved varieties can stand on their own in any ornamental garden, a feast for both the eye and the stomach.

Description: Basil is an herb that grows rapidly to form a bright green (or purple) bush. Standard varieties will grow 12 to 18 inches high with a 12-inch spread. Dwarf varieties may only grow 6 inches high and as wide. The arrow-shaped leaves are used for flavoring. The inconsequential flowers are best cut off when they appear, for they diminish foliage production. Plants should be sheared back hard to 6 inches to force young, new growth.

How to grow: Full sun and hot weather suit basil perfectly. Grown in poor soil, the flavoring oils will intensify, making the leaves more pungent. However, for ornamental use, moderate water and fertility (feed once a month) will increase basil's succulence and good looks.

Propagation: Sow seeds indoors 4 weeks prior to the last frost date. They'll germinate in 5 to 7 days at 70° F. Or sow seeds outdoors when the soil is warm and danger of frost has passed. Depending on the variety, plant 8 to 12 inches apart for ornamental use.

Uses: Compact, mounding varieties such as 'Spicy Globe' make ideal edging plants, while tall plants such as 'Green Ruffles' add a bright chartreuse note to borders. 'Purple Ruffles,' the best dark-leaved variety, is an admirable contrast to whites, pinks, and shades of green. Any of these also grow well in containers on decks and patios. For crisp overtones of extra flavor, look for other basils reminiscent of cinnamon or camphor.

Related varieties: 'Spicy Globe' (small, compact), 'Dark Opal,' and 'Purple Ruffles' (purple).

Beard Tongue

Penstemon heterophyllis

All but one of the 250 species of penstemon are American natives, although they vary greatly. Virtually all of them are perennial, but some are grown as summer annuals. The name "beard tongue" alludes to the fuzzy, insect-attracting stamens protruding from the open-faced flowers.

Description: *P. heterophyllis* is a shrub that grows up to 2 feet tall. A native of California, it has many flowers of dark blue, purple, or lilac. The long, narrow flowers are slightly over 1 inch long.

How to grow: Penstemons will grow in full sun or light shade in hot summer areas, needing slightly acid soil enriched with compost or leaf mold. They grow best in cool, mild winter climates. Set plants 12 to 18 inches apart. In Zones 8, 9, and 10, plants may be started in summer to bloom the next season. Elsewhere, seeds should be sown in mid-winter 12 to 14 weeks before flowering the same season.

Propagation: By seeds, cuttings, or division. Seed germination takes 10 to 15 days at a temperature of 55° F. Cuttings or division are often used for choice, named varieties. Cuttings may be taken in the spring and root readily.

Uses: Penstemons can be used at mid-border and are beautiful in mixed plantings or cottage gardens. They can be planted in beds combined with other flowers. Use them at the transition point between garden and woodlands. They make attractive cut flowers.

Related species: *Penstemon gloxinioides* is a cross between *P. gentianoides* and *P. Hartwegii,* with large flowers resembling gloxinias. 'Skyline' is a mix of large-flowered penstemons on bushy, compact plants. Colors are scarlet, rose, pink, violet, and deep gentian blue.

Related variety: 'True Blue' has deep blue, tubular flowers that contrast nicely with the gray-green leaves.

Fibrous Begonia, Wax Begonia, Everblooming Begonia

Begonia semperflorens

The brightly colored bedding begonias are equally at home in full sun (except where temperatures stay above 90° F for days on end) or dappled shade and will even bloom moderately well in full but bright shade (where trees are pruned high). From first setting them out until laid low by frost, they'll be packed with white, pink, rose, or red blossoms (some even have white petals edged in red), each flower centered by a cheery yellow eye. Virtually untouched by bugs or blight, their only shortcoming is a relatively narrow color range.

Description: Uniformity is the trademark of most tight mounds of closely packed leaves covered with blossoms. All four flower colors are available with your choice of leaf color: chocolaty-red or shades of green. The deeper-colored or bronze-leaved varieties offer especially eye-catching contrast with flowers. Though not as well known, there are also varieties with double flowers that resemble fat, little rosebuds and others with variegated foliage.

How to grow: Begonias perform well in rich, well-drained soil, but the soil must be allowed to dry between waterings. They'll form tight, compact plants in full sun, with increasingly looser form and fewer flowers as you move them deeper into the shade. Most hybrids will grow 6 to 9 inches high and spread as wide.

Propagation: By seed or cuttings. Most hybrids are grown from seed, but great patience is required. Dustlike seeds (2 million per ounce) must be sown in December or January for large, husky plants by May. Seeds need light to germinate. The seeds should be covered with glass in starting containers to maintain high humidity during germination. Germination temperature is 70 to 85° F and requires 14 to 21 days. Cuttings also root readily. A good way to start plants is on a sunny windowsill during winter.

Uses: Wax begonias lend themselves to large, formal plantings because of their uniform size and shapeliness. They're also suitable in front of summer annual borders and combine well with other cool-colored (blue and green) flowers in mixed plantings and containers. (They tend to be overwhelmed by hot colors.) Even a small planting of begonias in a small pot by a window or door will bloom lustily all summer.

Related varieties: The most popular, dark-leaved kinds are the 'Cocktail' series: 'Brandy,' 'Vodka,' 'Whiskey,' and 'Gin.' Good green-leaved varieties are found in the 'Olympia' and 'Prelude' series. 'Avalanche' begonias in pink or white are rangier, suited for containers and hanging baskets where their arching growth habit is handsome. 'Charm' begonias, grown only from cuttings, have green foliage marked with white. Calla lily begonias, which can be grown from seed, have green and white variegated foliage and pink flowers. 'Lady Frances' is one of the several double-flowered varieties you'll be able to find at garden centers.

Tuberous Begonia

Begonia tuberhybrida

A triumph of the breeder's art, tuberous begonias at their biggest have flowers of salad-plate size in fanciful forms and bright colors, even with petal edges tipped in a contrasting color (picotee). These beautiful flowers that grow well in morning sun and light shade have been joined in recent years by new varieties with altogether more modest flowers but many more of them.

Description: The large-flowered tuberous begonias come with many flower types, both upright and pendulous, single or double-flowered, and with frilled or plain petals. Unlike their *semperflorens* cousins, tuberous begonias offer wide color choices: white, pink, rose, red, orange, and yellow. They grow upright with large, arrow-shaped leaves. Both the large- and small-flowered tuberous begonias alternately bear male (ravishingly beautiful) and female (single and smaller) flowers. The smaller-flowered tuberous begonias bear many flowers up to 3 inches in diameter.

How to grow: Tuberous begonias grow best in midday and afternoon shade; otherwise the foliage will scorch. They need rich, well-drained soil with high organic matter. Allow soil to dry between waterings. The large-flowered varieties easily become top-heavy and require judicious staking, while the smaller-flowered ones can usually support their own growth. Powdery mildew is frequently a problem with tuberous begonias, especially if they are grown where the air around leaves and stems is stagnant. At the first signs of a white powder on leaves, spray with a fungicide.

Bells of Ireland, Shell Flower, Molucca Balm

Molucella laevis

Propagation: By seed, tubers, or cuttings. Most of the big-flowered tuberous begonias are sold as named-variety tubers. When tiny, pink growth appears on the upper side (with a depression where last year's stem was attached), place the tuber with the hollow side up at soil level in a pot filled with packaged soil mix. Water well once to firm the tuber in the pot and provide a temperature of 65° F. As the top swells and grows, roots will be forming below the surface. Do not allow the soil to dry out, but avoid drenching until the leaves expand. Provide high light until time for planting outside (after all danger of frost has passed, the weather has settled, and the soil has warmed). Carefully plant at the same level as the begonia was growing in the pot.

Uses: Grow the large-flowered kinds as specimen plants in semi-shady locations. Pendulous varieties make good container plants. The new, small-flowered kinds (varieties include 'Memory,' 'Non Stop,' and 'Clips,' all with separate colors) can be used for larger beds, in containers, and in hanging baskets. Watch container plantings to prevent drying out.

Related species: The iron cross begonia (*Begonia masoniana*), a widely grown indoor plant, makes a handsome foliage specimen for shade in summer planted directly into the ground or plunged in its own pot. The chartreuse leaves strongly marked with a chocolate-brown iron cross make a bold statement. Be sure to take this plant inside before cool weather starts because it is very frost-sensitive. *Begonia richmondensis* exhibits a graceful, flowing habit, vigorous growth, handsome, glossy leaves, and copious flowers, making it a very popular hanging basket plant in many parts of the country. Flower buds are cherry-red opening to a bright pink. It is easily rooted from cuttings. Morning sun and afternoon shade are ideal. Rex begonias (*Begonia rex*) are foliage plants colored in every conceivable combination: steel-gray, red, pink, green, and with splashes of white. They do well outdoors in the summer in shady spots. Elatior begonia (*Begonia hiemalis*) are hybrid begonias produced by crossing several species. One series is upright, good for planters, while the other has a flowing character and is ideal for hanging baskets and other containers to be viewed at eye level or above. Because much of the early development work was done by the Rieger firm in Germany, they are frequently known by this name. Flowers are 1 to 1½ inches in diameter, single, semi-double, and double. Colors are red, orange, pink, and a luscious white that looks green when the light shines through it.

Related varieties: Tubers of large-flowered varieties in separate colors and flower forms are usually available at garden centers and from specialists as named varieties. Smaller-flowered types are available as seed or started plants in garden centers.

Bells of Ireland form dramatic spires of green in the garden, the tiny white or pinkish flowers being almost hidden within the large, green bells (or calyxes). Native to western Asia, the name "Molucca balm" and "Molucella" were applied mistakenly, for at one time they were thought to be natives of the Molucca Islands.

Description: Bells of Ireland at their best grow in spires to 3 feet, surrounded by the netted, green, bell-like calyxes. The flowers are fragrant.

How to grow: Grow bells of Ireland in full sun or partial shade in an average garden loam with good drainage. They can be sown outdoors in spring as soon as the ground can be worked. Space them 12 inches apart. To prevent their toppling, plant them in areas protected from high wind; they may also be staked. They mature fairly rapidly and do not rebloom. For a longer show, start plants at different intervals. They reseed themselves readily. After maturity, plants are not especially attractive, so they should be planted where the residual foliage is out of sight.

Propagation: By seed. Sow in place. For earlier flowers, start 8 to 10 weeks prior to planting out. Seeds germinate in 25 to 35 days at 55° F. Don't cover the seeds; they need light to germinate.

Uses: Plant at the rear of the border for a vertical thrust. The chartreuse color of the bells combines nicely with lemon-yellows, sky-blues, and pinks. Especially revered by flower arrangers, the light green flowers hold unfaded for a long time in arrangements. For drying, hang them upside down in a dark place. They'll mute to a warm tan when dry and will last well in winter arrangements. They are especially attractive with other warm-toned components such as ornamental grasses and seedpods.

Related varieties: Seed companies offer their own selections.

Black-Eyed Susan, Gloriosa Daisy

Rudbeckia hirta

This widespread native of the prairie states has been turned into a horticultural delight. The name "gloriosa daisy" has been applied to the multitude of varieties that have grown out of this prairie weed. Although they're short-lived perennials, they'll bloom the first year and are often grown as annuals.

Description: Varieties of black-eyed Susan grow from 1 to 3 feet tall and are relatively erect. The flowers are available in many warm-toned colors: yellow, gold, orange, russet, and mahogany. Many of them have bands of color intermixed. The single varieties all have a large black or brown center, contrasting with the color surrounding it. Double flowers may reach 6 inches in diameter.

How to grow: Bright sun is the gloriosa daisy's main requirement. It will tolerate poor soil and erratic watering, although it does flourish with better care. Transplant it into the garden in the spring after the last frost. Space plants 10 to 15 inches apart. The taller varieties may need protection from strong winds or staking to keep them from toppling. Cutting the flowers encourages increased blooming.

Propagation: By seed. Treated as biennials or perennials, the seeds can be sown in the garden the preceding summer or fall. For bloom the same season, start seeds indoors 8 to 10 weeks prior to transplanting. Seeds germinate in 5 to 10 days at 70 to 75° F.

Uses: Any sunny location is ideal. Beds, borders, and planting strips will benefit from them. Plant them with ornamental grasses. They'll do well in large containers and are good cut flowers.

Related varieties: 'Goldsturm' has black-centered, single yellow flowers up to 5 inches in diameter. 'Rustic Colors' is composed of many gold, bronze, and mahogany shades. 'Irish Eyes' has golden flowers with green eyes.

Blanket Flower

Gaillardia pulchella

The annual gaillardia is a native of the Plains states to the East Coast. The name "blanket flower" comes from its resemblance to Indian blankets, blooming in yellow, orange, red, and their combinations.

Description: The annual gaillardia grows erect, 1 to 2 feet tall, with narrow leaves 2 inches long and flowers on long stems. In addition to single-flowered varieties, there are doubles with numerous quilled petals. In these, the original orange, red, and yellow colors have been extended to bronze and cream colors.

How to grow: The annual gaillardia will grow well in full sun in any well-drained soil. It does not like clay, excess water, or fertilizer. A fungicide may be needed in areas with high humidity. It continues to perform admirably under dry conditions. Space it from 9 to 15 inches apart.

Propagation: By seed. Barely cover, since gaillardia needs light to germinate. Sow seeds outdoors after the danger of frost has passed. For earlier bloom, sow indoors 4 to 6 weeks prior to planting out. Seeds germinate in 4 to 10 days at 75 to 85° F.

Uses: Plant gaillardias in groups. Grow them in meadows, in the cottage garden, at the edge of lawns, or near woodlands. The flowers are good for cutting.

Related species: Hybrids under the name *G. grandiflora* behave as perennials. Two dwarf forms are 'Goblin,' with flowers of deep red edged in yellow, and 'Yellow Goblin,' a pure yellow. 'Portola Giants,' growing 2½ feet tall, have bronze-colored flowers with yellow tips. The long flower stems are good for cutting.

Related varieties: 'Gaiety' is a mixture of heavily quilled, double flowers in bright yellow, orange, rose, maroon, and bicolors, many tipped with yellow. 'Double Mixed' flowers are 3 inches in diameter in cream, gold, crimson, and bicolors.

Blood Leaf

Iresine herbstii

These plants are grown for their colorful foliage, especially the purple-red color that brings the name "blood leaf." Originally from tropical South America, blood leaves are very easy to grow. They're from the amaranth family.

Description: Although in the tropics they can reach 5 to 6 feet, summer planting here tops out at 1 foot, usually less. The leaves are round, somewhat puckered, and colored red—except for yellowish midribs and veins. There are variants with green leaves, yellow veining, and bright red stalks and veins. Their white or yellow flowers are tiny and insignificant.

How to grow: Blood leaf tolerates no frost, so plant outside after all danger has passed and the soil is warm. They thrive in any well-drained, moist soil. Full sun is most desirable to develop the strongest foliage color, but they will grow in partial shade or shade. Pinch out the tips of shoots to promote bushiness. Space 6 to 9 inches apart. They can be sheared periodically for a neater appearance.

Propagation: By cuttings. Keep them misted during rooting to prevent wilting. Take cuttings 4 to 6 weeks in advance for husky plants to be set out after frost.

Uses: They're favorites for edging beds, borders, and for formal plantings. Blood leaf is also good in containers, especially mixed with other flowering plants. Given a sunny window sill, they are nice indoor plants, especially if they are trimmed.

Related species: *Iresine lindenii* has narrow, sharp-pointed leaves of deep red. Another variant, *I. l. formosa*, has green leaves with yellow veining. The leaf stalks and stems of both are red.

California Blue Bells

Phacelia campanularia

This native of southern California adapts to gardens or wildflower plantings with equal ease. The name *Phacelia* comes from the Greek word *phakelos* for "cluster," referring to the groups of flowers the plants bear.

Description: California blue bells grow about 8 inches tall with a branched, open form. They have triangular-shaped leaves and blue, bell-like flowers. The stamens stick out beyond the flower, resembling the clapper of a bell.

How to grow: Phacelias grow best in full sun in dryish, sandy soil, although they will tolerate other conditions if they have good drainage. They bloom best given cool, dry, sunny weather in the spring and diminish in the hot, humid weather of summer. Space plants 6 to 8 inches apart. Plant in areas protected from high winds or stake them. Brushwood stakes inserted in the ground when plants are small will be concealed when foliage grows around them.

Propagation: By seed. In mild winter climates, seeds can be sown outdoors in the fall for earliest bloom. Elsewhere, sow as early in the spring as the ground can be worked. Thin them to the proper spacing shortly after they emerge. For earliest bloom, start plants indoors 6 to 8 weeks prior to planting outside as soon as the danger of frost has passed. Seeds germinate in 8 to 15 days at 60 to 70° F. Growing them in peat pots will facilitate transplanting.

Uses: California blue bells are good in informal situations. Plant them in masses for the dominant blue tones they provide. Grow phacelias in natural gardens and wildflower meadows.

Related species: *Phacelia viscida* has deep blue flowers with white- and blue-speckled throats. It grows up to 2 feet tall. *P. tanacetifolia*, sometimes called "wild heliotrope," bears clusters of purple-to-violet flowers with lighter centers.

Blue Lace Flower

Trachymene coerulea

You might think of this as a glorified version of Queen Anne's lace in sky blue. Although a relative, this one is from Australia. The plant has the same, flat-headed flower form with tiny flowers. It's also fragrant—an extra bonus for discerning gardeners.

Description: The grayish, feathery leaves cover tall stems that grow 24 to 30 inches in height. They bloom in July and August with quantities of light blue flowers in large flower heads. Tiny, white stamens stick up above the flowers adding to their charm.

How to grow: Blue lace flowers need full sun in light, sandy, well-drained soil. They're best under cool-to-moderate temperatures. They do not tolerate heat well. Plant in the garden after the last frost. Space 12 inches apart. Protect them from high winds. As a precaution, brushwood stakes can be pushed into the ground among them when they are young. The foliage will cover the stakes as they grow.

Propagation: By seed. Sow in the garden outdoors after all danger of frost has passed. For earlier plants, sow seeds indoors 6 to 8 weeks prior to planting out. Cover seeds thoroughly; they need darkness to germinate. Seeds germinate in 20 to 25 days at 70° F.

Uses: Blue lace flower shines in the mixed border where its cool color tones down hot shades and mixes well with pastels. It's also recommended for cottage gardens where the old-fashioned look and informality blend together. Mix it with yarrows and other flowers for meadow plantings. Blue lace flower is good for arrangements where its airiness lightens up heavier flowers.

Blue Marguerite

Felicia amelloides

The blue marguerite's sky-blue color contrasts nicely with each flower's bright yellow center. Although perennial, this is a tender plant, so except for Zones 9, 10, and occasionally 8, it will not live over winter. It is a native of South Africa.

Description: Blue marguerite is normally an erect subshrub growing from 1 to 2 feet tall. It has glossy, deep green leaves with flowers on relatively short stems in sky-blue to darker shades, centered with a yellow eye.

How to grow: Felicias thrive in moist but well-drained soil, in full sun to partial shade. Truly hot weather causes their decline, making them best as a summer plant for maritime or mountain climates, as a spring and autumn plant elsewhere, and as a year-round plant for mild winter regions. At the young stage, pinching out tips will induce bushiness. Plant outside after all danger of frost has passed, spacing them 9 to 12 inches apart.

Propagation: By seed or by cuttings. Trailing forms are available only by cuttings; seed-grown plants are mostly upright. Sow seeds 6 to 8 weeks prior to planting out after all danger of frost has passed. Germination rate and speed is improved by refrigerating seeds in a moistened medium for 3 weeks prior to sowing. Germination takes up to 30 days at 70° F. Cuttings root quickly and easily.

Uses: Group them in beds and borders or use them in moist rock gardens. They combine well in containers with other flowers.

Related species: *Felicia bergerana* is called the "kingfisher daisy." It is smaller than *F. amelloides* and leaves are longer and narrower. The kingfisher daisy grows to about 8 inches tall with bright blue flowers with yellow centers.

Related varieties: Selections that trail will be found at garden centers.

Burning Bush, Summer Cypress, Belvedere

Kochia scoparia trichophylla

A native of Europe and Asia, kochia is named for a German botanist, Wilhelm Koch. "Summer cypress" refers to its mimicry of the true cypress in form and shape. "Burning bush," of course, refers to its brilliant autumn color.

Description: Kochia develops into an egg-shaped bush, reaching about 2 feet tall. Best in hot climates, it develops slowly in cooler regions. Foliage is finely textured, bright green, and dense. This becomes purplish by the end of summer, finally turning a brilliant red. The tiny, green flowers are inconspicuous.

How to grow: Give kochia full sun and avoid overwatering; otherwise it tolerates virtually all other conditions. Early season growth in cool weather is slow, but it rapidly develops when heat arrives. For individual specimens, plant 15 to 24 inches apart. For use as a summer hedge, space 12 inches apart. Kochia can be sheared easily for a more formal shape. It reseeds prolifically.

Propagation: By seed. Sow outdoors after all danger of frost has passed. For earlier development, plant indoors 4 to 6 weeks before outdoor planting. Do not cover the seeds, since they need light to germinate; keep them moist. Seeds germinate in 10 to 15 days at 70 to 75° F.

Uses: Kochia is a good hedge or background for summer flowers. In formal beds, individual plants can be used to define corners. Kochia is good for defining paths or walkways. It can also be used as a planting around other garden features. Tolerant of wind, kochia is often used in containers in balconies and other high-rise plantings.

Related variety: The only readily available selection is 'Childsii.'

Caladium hortulanum

Caladium hortulanum

Tropical caladiums are grown entirely for their brightly colored and wildly patterned foliage. Gardeners can choose from many combinations of green, pink, red, white, and creamy yellow.

Description: Large, spear- or arrowhead-shaped leaves rise on long stems directly from the tuber buried in the ground below. Depending on weather and soil, each leaf can grow up to 12 inches in length on 1-foot stems.

How to grow: In hot sections of Zones 9 and 10, caladium tubers are planted directly in the ground 1 inch deep, but in the rest of the country, it's usual to start them in pots indoors and plant them outside when the weather is warm. Plant tubers in pots 1 inch deep in soil high in organic matter. Kept moist, they grow at 70 to 85° F. Caladiums thrive in high temperature and humidity. Outdoors, grow in moist, rich soil, and protect them from intense sun. High, overhead shade or eastern exposures will provide maximum growth and color development of the leaves. Feed weekly with a diluted water-soluble fertilizer to assure continued growth of new leaves. A slow-release fertilizer may also be mixed into the soil before planting. In the fall, dig tubers before frost, allowing them to gradually dry off. Store in a frost-free location.

Propagation: By cutting tubers in pieces similar to potatoes, being sure each piece retains growing "eyes."

Uses: Caladiums are unexcelled for foliage color in bright, shady beds or borders, window boxes or containers. Grow in moist areas to reduce water needs.

Related varieties: 'Candidum' is primarily white with green ribs and leaves. 'Pink Beauty' has patterns of pink overlaid on a green background. Leaves of 'Frieda Hemple' are solid red with a green border.

Calla, Calla Lily

Zantesdeschia aethiopica

The great, white, waxy flowers so often seen at florists are nearly weeds in their native South Africa. They're actually perennials in Zones 8, 9, and 10, but since they are not tolerant of frost, they are grown as annuals in other parts of the United States. Gardeners throughout the country can enjoy their lush, green leaves and bright flowers in summer by planting the tuber each spring.

Description: Glistening, white flowers grow to 2½ feet above the arrowhead-shaped leaves that arise from the rhizome planted below ground. By summer's end, a large clump of leaves displays a more or less continuous succession of flowers.

How to grow: For maximum enjoyment, start rhizomes indoors 8 weeks prior to warm weather. Plant the large tubers in a soil mix high in peat or other organic matter and grow at 70° F. Keep uniformly moist and fertilize weekly with a water-soluble fertilizer. Plant outside in a rich soil high in organic matter that retains moisture. Incorporate a slow-release fertilizer before planting. Grow in full sun for maximum growth. In the fall, lift before frost, drying off foliage and rhizomes. Store in a frost-free place until spring.

Propagation: Buy rhizomes at garden centers in the spring. Check to make sure they are firm and moist.

Uses: Plant callas anywhere you want to achieve a tropical look. They also make dramatic container plants and superb cut flowers.

Related species: *Z. rehmannii* is the pink calla, although it shows much variation in spathe color from wine-red to nearly white. It is smaller, growing to 18 inches. *Z. elliotiana* is a species with white, spotted foliage, and a golden-yellow spathe.

Calliopsis, Tickseed

Coreopsis tinctoria

Native to many parts of the United States, calliopsis have bright, daisylike flowers. The name "tickseed" comes from the resemblance to an insect, as does the name *coreopsis*, which is derived from the Greek.

Description: Growing 1 to 3 feet tall, coreopsis plants are sparsely branched with bright, toothed, daisy flowers. Some have extra layers of petals and include double varieties. Colors range from yellow through orange and cinnamon-red to burnished mahogany. Many varieties are bicolored with sharply contrasting colors in the petals.

How to grow: Any sunny site with good drainage will grow coreopsis. They will even tolerate poor or dry soils after seedlings are well established. They will reseed year after year if not deadheaded.

Propagation: By seed. Seedlings grow quickly; sow them outdoors after final frost, covering them with ¼ inch of soil. Seeds may also be sown indoors 6 to 8 weeks prior to planting out. Germination takes 5 to 7 days at 70° F.

Uses: The dwarf forms make good bed edgings, while the taller varieties are effective at mid-border. Coreopsis also makes good cut flowers and can be dried for arrangements.

Related species: Some perennial coreopsis can be grown as summer annuals. Medal-winning varieties of *Coreopsis grandiflora* are: 'Sunray,' with bright, double-yellow flowers and 'Early Sunrise,' with glowing, yellow, semi-double flowers.

Related varieties: Most annual coreopsis is found in mixed colors, separated into dwarf and taller varieties. 'Tiger Flower Improved' is a dwarf mixture with bicolored flowers. 'Finest Mixed' is a taller selection with a full range of colors.

Annual Candytuft

Iberis hybridus

Candytufts have flowers in white, pink, lilac, red, and purple. Where *Iberis amara* "blood" predominates, they're called rocket candytufts, since their growth is upright. Globe candytufts, with a more mounding form, emphasize the *I. umbellata* parentage.

Description: Rocket candytufts have compact clusters of flowers on top of short, erect stems. In globe candytufts, the flower clusters are flat with a more bushlike appearance. Neither will grow more than 1 foot tall and usually remains compact.

How to grow: Candytuft needs full sun and good drainage. The addition of lime to acid soils will improve the growth of candytufts. Plant as soon as the danger of frost is over. Space 6 inches apart.

Propagation: By seed. In mild climates, seeds can be sown in the ground in the fall for earlier bloom. Elsewhere, sow in the spring after the last frost. For earlier bloom, start candytuft indoors 6 to 8 weeks before planting out. Germination takes 15 to 20 days at 68 to 85° F.

Uses: Candytuft naturally grows as an informal plant. However, with shearing, it can be tamed to a more formal appearance. Plant candytuft in the front of borders or as edging of beds and borders. Grow it along sidewalks and pathways; tuck it into pockets in rock gardens; and display it in containers. The rocket kinds will have an erect growth habit, while the globe candytuft will drape over the edges. They combine effectively with other flowers in mixed plantings. The rocket candytuft can be used for cut flowers. Seed heads can be used for everlasting arrangements.

Related varieties: 'Dwarf Fairy Mixed' mixes lilac, pink, maroon, red, and white. 'Flash' is a mixture that includes several shades of pink, bright red, maroon, purple, lilac, and white. 'Hyacinth Mixed' is a rocket type with large, white, fragrant blooms.

Canna

Canna species

The name *canna* comes from the Greek word for "reed," referring to the stems. The parentage of garden hybrids is very mixed, but breeders have provided many sturdy and colorful kinds.

Description: Cannas grow from fleshy roots with erect stalks from which broad, long leaves emerge. Flower stalks rising in the center bear large flowers. Foliage may be green, bronze, or purplish in hue.

How to grow: Cannas need full sun and grow best in a deep, rich, moist but well-drained soil. Incorporate extra organic matter and a slow-release fertilizer in the soil before planting. For earliest bloom, start in pots indoors. Otherwise plant roots directly into the ground after soil is warm and all danger of frost has passed. Use pieces of rootstock with 2 or 3 large eyes and plant 2 inches deep. Space 1½ to 2 feet apart. Remove spent flower heads for more prolific bloom. In fall after the first light frost, cut back stems to 6 inches, dig roots with soil attached, and store in a cool, frost-free place. While in storage, water sparingly.

Propagation: By seed or by division of roots. Seed propagation is slow; cut roots into pieces, each with 2 to 3 eyes, in the spring just prior to planting.

Uses: Use cannas in the center of island beds, at the sides or back of brightly colored borders, or near pools and ponds. They also dominate large containers.

Related varieties: Tall ones that grow up to 4 feet include: 'Yellow King Humbert,' yellow with scarlet flecks; 'The President,' bright crimson; and 'City of Portland,' a deep pink. Dwarf kinds growing to 2½ feet tall are known as "Pfitzers" for their German breeder: 'Chinese Coral,' a soft coral-pink; 'Primrose Yellow,' a sunny yellow; and 'Salmon-Pink.'

Canterbury Bells

Campanula medium

The name comes from *campanula* meaning "little bells," an accurate term, since the flowers are bell-shaped. Although biennials, they can be grown to bloom the first year by sowing seeds indoors early.

Description: Plants grow 2½ feet to 4 feet tall, with roughly the top two-thirds covered with pink, rose, lavender, blue, or white flowers. The plant shape is pyramidal and leaves are long and narrow.

How to grow: Canterbury bells need rich, moist, well-drained soil and full sun. Although partial shade is tolerated, stems may grow weak under these conditions. Planting a group together will help plants support each other without staking, although in windy locations stakes may be needed. Plant 8 to 12 inches apart.

Propagation: By seed. To grow for first year bloom, sow seeds 10 weeks prior to the last frost. Do not cover the seeds, since they require light to germinate. Germination time is 6 to 12 days at 70° F. To grow as a biennial, sow seeds outdoors in July or August. The small plants will bloom late the next spring.

Uses: Canterbury bells are ideal for the informal, cottage garden look, where they can be inter-mixed with a variety of other plants. They're also useful for planting at the center of island beds, where they're viewed from all sides.

Related species: *Campanula isophylla,* a tender perennial, is a species with a many-branched trailing habit, smothered in powder-blue or white flowers. 'Stella' is available both in blue and white. *Campanula ramosissima* grows 6 inches to 1 foot high. Its most prevalent form has violet-blue flowers, but also appears in pink, rose, and lavender.

Related varieties: *Campanula medium caly-canthema,* called "cup and saucer," has double bells, one inside the other.

Castor Bean

Ricinus communis

This plant brings great distinction to the garden quickly, growing to a large shrub of treelike proportions in a single season. The seeds yield an oil that is used commercially. The coats of the seeds contain ricin, a deadly poison. If there is any chance of their being eaten, break off the flowers. This native of Africa is naturalized in tropical parts of the world.

Description: In the tropics, castor bean becomes a small tree. In areas with long growing seasons in the United States, it will reach 10 feet. The distinctive tropical character comes from the large, hand-shaped leaves that are up to 3 feet wide. Each one has from 5 to 12 deeply cut lobes.

How to grow: Castor beans are indifferent to soil if they receive full sun, adequate heat, and plenty of moisture. In areas with long growing seasons, plant them directly in the ground after all danger of frost has passed and the ground is warm enough to germinate the seeds. In frost-free areas of Zones 9 and 10, they will live through the winter. Plant them at least 3 feet apart.

Propagation: By seed. Before sowing the seeds, soak them for 24 hours in water or nick the seed coat with a file. Start seeds indoors 6 to 8 weeks prior to planting in the garden. Start them in individual pots for transplanting.

Uses: Castor beans are one of the most useful plants for shielding eyesores or providing temporary screens in the garden. They need lots of room; this plant is not modest in size. Side branches with flowers are cut to make attractive floral arrangements; the spiny seed-pods are used in dried arrangements. Some people have a skin reaction to the foliage and seedpods.

Related varieties: 'Impala' has maroon-to-carmine young growth and sulfur-yellow blooms. 'Carmencita' has deep brown leaves.

Sweet False Chamomile

Matricaria recutita

White, daisy flowers with bright yellow button centers make this annual a pleasant sight in the garden. Originally from Europe and Western Asia, it is naturalized now in parts of the United States. The foliage is scented, releasing a pleasant, sweet fragrance when leaves are crushed.

Description: Sweet false chamomile grows up to 2½ feet tall. It's a many-branched plant, with numerous small flower heads. Flowers are up to 1 inch in diameter, with about 25 white petals surrounding a golden-yellow disc. Finely cut leaves are 2 to 3 inches long.

How to grow: Sweet false chamomile will grow easily in any average garden soil. It needs full sun to flower its best. Continuous moisture will ensure larger, more vigorous plants. Apply a balanced fertilizer at planting to develop good plants. Plant in the spring when frost danger has passed. Space 6 to 10 inches apart. It is a prolific reseeder.

Propagation: By seed. Sow in the ground in the spring as soon as the ground can be worked. For an earlier start, sow seeds indoors 6 to 8 weeks prior to planting out. Seeds germinate in 20 to 25 days at 70° F. Do not cover seeds; they need light to germinate.

Uses: Grow them in the front of beds and borders, grouping a number of plants together for a mass effect. Because they grow informally, sweet false chamomile also look good in cottage garden plantings and in containers. Grow them in herb gardens for their scent. Plants and foliage are often dried for sachets.

Related species: Four species from South Africa are sometimes grown: *M. globifera, M. grandiflora, M. suffruticosa,* and *M. africana,* although it is suspected that plants cultivated under these names may really be *Chrysan-themum parthenium.*

 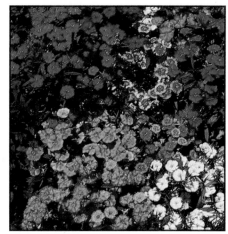 

Chilean Bell Flower

Nolana paradoxa

Natives of South America, they're tender perennials that are grown like annuals in the garden. The name *Nolana* comes from the Latin *nola* or "little bell," an apt description of the flower shape.

Description: The Chilean bell flower is a prostrate, spreading plant growing 6 to 8 inches tall and spreading a foot or more by summer's end. The leaves and stems are somewhat succulent. Flowers resemble morning glories, a twilight-sky-blue with white centers, shading to yellow in the throats. There are also forms with white- or violet-colored flowers. Bloom is continuous over a long season.

How to grow: Chilean bell flowers thrive in light, poor soils and tolerate drought, although they will grow under a wide range of conditions, including high humidity. They must have good drainage and full sun. With adequate moisture, the plants grow more vigorously. Plant them in the garden as soon as all danger of frost has passed. Space them 10 to 15 inches apart for full coverage. In frost-free areas, nolana will be perennial, but should be cut back halfway in the spring to induce new growth and tidiness.

Propagation: By seed. Start seeds indoors 6 to 8 weeks prior to planting in the garden after the last frost date and when the soil is warm. Seeds germinate in 10 to 20 days at 70° F.

Uses: This is a versatile plant. Use it for trailing over rock walls or rock gardens. Try it as a sunny ground cover for difficult sites. It's a good edging plant for hot pockets by houses and fences. Plant nolana in containers, too.

Related varieties: 'Blue Bird' has dark sky-blue flowers with white and yellow throats. The bell-shaped flowers are slightly ruffled, enhancing the light and shadow patterns. 'Sky Blue' is similar.

China Pink

Dianthus chinensis

These compact plants have a clove scent as well as colorful flowers. They produce blooms in pink, white, rose, scarlet, and crimson; many are bicolored. The original species comes from Eastern Asia.

Description: China pinks grow 6 to 12 inches high—clumps of blue-gray foliage surmounted continuously with the single, semi-double, or fringed flowers. In Zones 8 to 10, they will live in the garden for 2 or 3 years as short-lived perennials.

How to grow: Dianthus grows and blooms best during cool temperatures of spring and fall and in cool summer locations. In Zones 9 and 10, they're widely used as winter flowering annuals. Plant them in full sun, in well-drained soil on the alkaline side. (Acid soils can be amended by incorporating lime into the soil before planting.) Plant in the garden after danger of frost has passed. Space 6 to 10 inches apart.

Propagation: By seed. Seeds germinate in 8 to 10 days at 70° F. They may be sown outdoors as soon as the soil is workable. Starting indoors 8 to 10 weeks ahead of planting out will bring an earlier display.

Uses: Use China pinks in rock gardens, in rock walls, or planted in cracks in paving stones. Mass them in at the front of beds or borders. Grow them in containers, alone, or combined with other flowers. They're good cut flowers for small arrangements.

Related species: Sweet William (*Dianthus barbatus*) has a cluster of flower tops in pink, white, and red.

Related varieties: The 'Telstar' series has a mixture of scarlet, salmon, rose, pink, and white fringed flowers. Separate colors are available, with 'Telstar Picotee' outstanding. It has crimson flowers edged in white. 'Magic Charms' series is similar, including some speckled flowers. 'Snowfire' has white fringed flowers centered in cherry-red. 'Princess' series is heat-resistant.

Chrysanthemum

Chrysanthemum paludosum, multicaule

Two species of the multitudinous chrysanthemum family are especially popular with gardeners as flowering summer annuals. One bears small, perky, yellow blossoms and the other has white, daisylike flowers.

Description: *C. paludosum* grows about 10 inches in height and has a mounding, trailing habit that spreads to 15 inches. The single, small, white flowers are borne profusely all over the plant. *C. multicaule* is slightly more vigorous, growing to 12 inches with a 20-inch spread. Flowers are single yellow daisies and are visible from a distance. Both will bloom all summer, but if bloom diminishes, shear back by half to encourage new growth and flowering.

How to grow: Grow in rich, well-drained soil in full sun if roots can be kept cool and shaded by other plants; otherwise, in partial sun. An eastern exposure would be ideal for both. Incorporate a slow-release fertilizer in the soil before planting. Plant after the last frost date when the soil has warmed. Space 8 to 12 inches apart for solid coverage.

Propagation: By seed or by cuttings. Germination is 14 to 21 days at 60 to 65° F. Sow 6 to 8 weeks prior to transplanting to the garden. Plants will bloom approximately 10 weeks after sowing. Cuttings root quickly and easily.

Uses: Plant in rock gardens, on slopes, and in the front of beds or borders. Use at gates, along pathways, and at doorsteps where a colorful ground cover is desired. The trailing quality adds grace to hanging baskets, window boxes, and other containers. The white of *C. paludosum* is a good choice in mixed plantings, cooling down hot colors and intensifying dark ones.

Related varieties: 'White Buttons' is the most commonly grown selection of *C. paludosum*. 'Yellow Buttons' is the most popular selection of *C. multicaule*.

Cleome, Spider Flower

Cleome hasslerana

Cleome starts blooming early and flowers continue opening at the top of 6-foot stems. Exceedingly long stamens that extend well beyond the orchidlike flowers—somewhat like a daddy longlegs spider—are what give spider flower its name.

Description: Cleome flowers, with many opening at once, grow in airy racemes 6 to 8 inches in diameter. Flowers are white, pink, or lavender in color. When flowers fade, they are followed by long pods that extend outward from the stem below the terminal raceme. Leaves grow on long stalks from a single stem.

How to grow: Cleome grows well in average soil in full sun or minimal shade. It is very drought-tolerant, although it will look and grow better if it is watered well. Space plants 1 to 3 feet apart.

Propagation: By seed. Sow after the last frost when the ground is warm, later thinning to final spacing. Cleomes may also be started indoors 4 to 6 weeks earlier at a temperature of at least 70° F. Germination time is 10 to 14 days. In the garden, it reseeds prolifically.

Uses: Plant cleome for its height, to back up borders, in the center of island beds, or for statuesque beauty where its dramatic quality stands out. It can also be used as a space-defining hedge, although other plants should hide its bare stems later in the season. Cleome can be used for tall container plantings. It also makes a good cut flower for use in large bouquets.

Related varieties: 'Helen Campbell' is the most popular white variety. 'Rose Queen' is salmon-pink, and 'Ruby Queen' bears rose-colored flowers. Additional color variations including lilac and purple are found in seed mixtures.

Plumed Cockscomb

Celosia cristata v. plumosa

The name *celosia* comes from the Greek word for "burned." These airy, feather duster look-alikes bear the vibrant colors that aptly fit the name. The exotic plumes make superb dried specimens, retaining their color long after harvest.

Description: Shades ranging from electric reds, yellows, pinks, and oranges to more subtle, sand tones are available. Height ranges from 8 to 30 inches. Bloom lasts from June to October.

How to grow: Full sun in average soil is recommended for celosias. Seeds may be sown in the garden after danger of frost has passed and soil has warmed. Initial flowers may last as long as 8 weeks after opening, but removing them will encourage development of side branches and new bloom.

Propagation: By seed. For earlier bloom, celosias may be planted indoors 4 to 5 weeks in advance of planting out. Germination is at 70 to 75° F and takes 10 to 15 days. Plants should not dry out.

Uses: Tall varieties add complementary textures to the center and sides of beds and borders, while the short kinds are good edging plants. They're good container plants, too.

Related species: *Celosia cristata* bears the contorted flowers known as cockscomb. Varieties include: dwarf 'Jewel Box Mixture' and 'Toreador,' a 20-inch variety with large red combs.

Related varieties: The tall 2½-foot celosias include 'Forest Fire,' with orange-scarlet plumes and 'Golden Triumph,' a golden-yellow. Just shorter is the award-winning 'Century Series,' with separate colors of scarlet, red (with bronze foliage), rose, yellow, and cream, as well as a mixture of all colors. Miniatures up to 10 inches are found in the 'Geisha Series' and are especially fluorescent in carmine red, orange, scarlet, and yellow.

Coleus x hybridus

Coleus x hybridus

Coleus is one of the few plants where late blooming is an asset, for the insignificant flowers detract from the beautiful foliage. Tender perennials, they're very frost-sensitive and are used as annuals except in frost-free areas.

Description: Coleus forms a well-branched, spreading plant up to 2 feet tall and as wide. The leaves vary tremendously, from intricately dissected and lobed forms to broad solids. Colors, too, are varied from solid colors of red, bronze, chartreuse, white, pink, yellow, or green, to variations that combine two or more colors.

How to grow: Coleus is ideal in shade and will excel in northern exposures. It will grow in any well-drained, moist soil. As to light, the deeper the shade, the taller the plant. Leaves are less colorful in deep shade.

Propagation: By seed or by cuttings. Sow seeds 6 to 8 weeks before setting outside. Wait until the ground is warm and all danger of frost has passed. Seeds need light to germinate, so do not cover. Seeds germinate in 10 to 15 days at temperatures of above 75° F; lower temperatures inhibit germination. Cuttings root quickly and easily—even in water.

Uses: Coleus are unparalleled shade plants. They are useful as ground covers, massed in the front of borders, or grouped in clusters. Coleus grow well in containers. Indoors, they make good foliage plants.

Related varieties: The 'Wizards' have heart-shaped leaves with contrasting colors. 'Rose Wizard' has patches of rose in leaf centers and is edged with green and white to the margins. 'Saber' varieties have narrow, tapered leaves in many colors. The 'Fiji' series features heavily fringed leaves with contrasting color combinations. Small, deeply lobed leaves distinguish the 'Carefree' series.

Corn Cockle

Agrostemma githago

The name "corn cockle" comes from its appearance in the corn fields of England, where it has been unwelcome for years. However, its 3- to 4-foot height with rosy pink flowers rippling in the wind make it a welcome addition to the garden, where it will bloom from June on.

Description: Plants grow up to 3½ feet tall, with thin, narrow foliage and slender, wiry flower stems. Flower color is a rich, plummy pink. Flowers are often more than 2 inches in diameter, each petal marked with dots or lines to guide insects to the flower center for pollination.

How to grow: Grow in full sun in average soil. Growing in partial shade will cause them to grow taller with weak stems (that may require staking) and reduce flower production. Space plants about 12 inches apart. Deadheading prevents seed formation and encourages bloom throughout the summer.

Uses: Because the foliage is light, it can be planted as a see-through plant surrounded and backed by other flowers. Their delicate grace makes them a good foil for more substantial plants. The flowers can be readily seen if grown at the back of borders or beds. Use them, too, for height in island beds. The informal character lends distinction to cottage gardens with a variety of plantings. They also make good cut flowers.

Propagation: Seeds are large, germination is fast (10 to 12 days outdoors), and growth is rapid. Corn cockle is best direct-seeded into the garden. Plants readily reseed, so they can have their own space in the garden year after year. Currently, seed companies offer many separate selections.

Related varieties: 'Milas' is a somewhat shorter selection, and 'Milas Cerise' is offered for its cherry-red color.

Cosmos

Cosmos bipinnatus

Cosmos is one of the fastest-growing annuals. Some varieties reach up to 6 feet by summer's end. They're natives of Mexico.

Description: Cosmos forms a lacy, open plant with flowers 3 to 4 inches in diameter. These daisies are in pink, red, white, and lavender with a contrasting yellow center. Foliage is feathery.

How to grow: Cosmos grows best in full sun, but it will bloom acceptably in partial shade. Grow in well-drained soil. It does not need fertilizing. Space at least 12 inches apart. Cosmos needs space and is not easily staked. It reseeds vigorously.

Propagation: By seed. Because it grows so fast, sow outdoors after frost danger has passed. Barely cover seeds, since they need light to germinate. For very early bloom, sow indoors 4 weeks prior to planting out. Germination takes 3 to 7 days at 70 to 75° F.

Uses: Because of its height, cosmos should be planted at the back of borders and grouped against fences or other places as a covering. Its informal habit works best in mixed plantings. Cosmos also can provide height for the center of an island bed. The flowers are good for cutting, especially for informal arrangements.

Related species: *Cosmos sulphureus* is the source of the hot red and yellow colors of cosmos. They're also more compact, growing up to 2 feet in the garden. Bloom is heavy from start until frost. A medal winner, 'Sunny Red' has 2½-inch, semi-double flowers of vermilion red. Its companion is 'Sunny Gold.'

Related varieties: Most popular is the 'Sensation' series that comes in mixed colors. Separate colors of this series are also available. 'Candy Stripe' has white petals stippled with crimson. 'Sea Shells' has a unique form with rolled, quilled petals. 'Psyche Mixed' bears semi-double flowers.

Cup and Saucer Vine, Cathedral Bells

Cobaea scandens

The flowers of cup and saucer vine come in white, green, violet, and purple. The name refers to its flowers, which appear to sit within a saucer of foliage. The prominent stamens resemble the clapper of a bell—hence its other common name.

Description: A perennial, cup and saucer vine is grown as an annual in most parts of the country. Rapid-growing, it can reach 25 feet by summer's end. It has leaves composed of 2 to 3 sets of leaflets. The saucer of the flower is a prominent calyx within which the cup, or flower, sits. The hooked tendrils will move within a few minutes after being rubbed on one side—which is why they climb so successfully without support.

How to grow: Cup and saucer vine needs full sun and an average-to-rich soil for best growth. It must have a continuous supply of moisture to grow well. Plant outdoors after all danger of frost has passed, spacing 1 foot apart.

Propagation: By seed. The seeds can be planted in the ground outdoors but, because they germinate somewhat irregularly, earlier and more dependable results can be gained by starting them indoors 8 to 10 weeks prior to outdoor planting. The seeds will germinate in 30 to 60 days at a temperature of 70 to 75° F. They grow rapidly once germinated. Transplant to the garden when all danger of frost has passed and the soil is warm.

Uses: Cup and saucer vine is ideal for screening large areas or covering eyesores. Plant it to cover fences; grow it up and over arches, pergolas, trellises, and porches. It also grows well in a cool greenhouse.

Related varieties: *Cobaea scandens* with flowers that open green and turn deep blue is available; *C. s. alba* is the white form. In addition, a mixture of blue and white forms can be found.

Dahlia

Dahlia hybrids

From huge, dinner plate-sized blooms down to midget pompoms only 2 inches in diameter, dahlias show as much diversity as any summer flowering plant. Once they start blooming in the summer, there is a continuous flood of flowers until frost. They're tender perennials, forming tuberous roots that may be dug and stored in the fall and replanted the following spring. Where the ground does not freeze, they may be left in the ground over winter.

Description: Dahlias grow from 1 to 5 feet tall. Flowers come in every color except blue, and the form is varied: singles; anemone-flowered; peonylike; round, shaggy mops; formal, ball-shaped; and twisted, curled petals. The flowers are carried on long stems above the erect plants. The American Dahlia Society has classified dahlias by both type and size. There are 12 different flower types: single, anemone-flowered, collarette, peony-flowered, formal decorative, informal decorative, ball, pompom, incurved cactus, straight cactus, semi-cactus, and orchid-flowered. Flower size designations are A (large, over 8 inches); B (medium, 6 to 8 inches); BB (4 to 6 inches); M (miniature, not over 4 inches in diameter); Ball (over 3 inches); Miniature Ball (2 to 3½ inches); and Pompom (not over 2 inches in diameter).

How to grow: Dahlias are sun lovers and need air circulation around them. Soil should be fertile, high in organic matter, and moist but well-drained. Incorporate a slow-release fertilizer into the soil before planting. Plant outdoors when the soil is warm and danger of frost has passed. To plant, dig a hole 10 inches deep and as wide. Place the tubers so that the eye is 2 to 3 inches below ground level. Plants growing in pots can be planted at the same level as they were growing in the pot. Space tall varieties 12 to 18 inches apart, reducing the spacing for dwarf plants to as little as 8 inches. Tall varieties, and particularly those with large flowers, must be staked to prevent toppling. Drive the stakes before planting to avoid damaging the plant underground.

Propagation: By seed, division, or cuttings. Most of the large-flowered varieties are grown from tuberous roots available at garden centers or specialist growers. Each fleshy portion must have a piece of old stem with an eye attached in order to grow (unlike potatoes, which can be sliced into pieces so long as there is an eye in the cut piece). At the end of a summer's growing season, a roughly circular mass of tuberous roots will form a clump. These clumps should be stored in a cool but frost-free location until spring. Where the ground does not freeze, tubers can be left to winter in place. In the spring, divide these pieces (an eye attached to a portion of the stem) just before planting. Sow dahlia seeds at 70° F 4 to 6 weeks prior to planting out. Germination will take 5 to 14 days. Cuttings root in 10 to 15 days.

Uses: Taller varieties can be planted as a hedge with shorter flowers growing in front. Groups of three plants can be effective at the back of a border or in the center of large island beds. Compact varieties can be used in the front of beds and borders or planted in containers. For exhibition, disbudding the side buds will result in substantially larger flowers. Dahlias make good cut flowers, especially those with long stems. They may also be floated in a bowl of water.

Related varieties: There are hundreds of varieties; consult your garden center or a specialist grower. A few tuberous, rooted varieties are: 'Los Angeles,' a semi-cactus variety with deep red flowers and petals tipped in white; and 'Canby Charm,' an informal decorative type with pink flowers that can reach a diameter of 12 inches. 'Clown' is golden-yellow with streaks of red in the petals. 'Lavender Chiffon' has lavender-shaded blooms up to 7 inches across. Seed-grown varieties will be available as started plants or can be grown from seeds at home. From seeds, tall varieties include 'Cactus Flowered,' growing to 4 feet with many different flower colors and curved petals. 'Large Flowered, Double, Mixed' will grow to 5 feet and bears large, double and semi-double flowers. Compact varieties include: 'Redskin,' growing up to 15 inches with bronze foliage—a remarkable contrast to the many different flower colors. 'Figaro' grows to 12 inches with semi-double and double flowers.

African Daisy

Arctotis stoechadifolia

In its native South Africa, arctotis bursts into bloom when the spring rains come, although in gardens plants bloom copiously all summer. A tender perennial, it is grown most commonly as an annual. Like many of the plants in the daisy family from South Africa, it's tough enough to live in hot, dry conditions, but a modicum of moisture will bring out stellar blooms. On dull days and at night, arctotis closes its flowers.

Description: The native species has pearly white flowers centered with steel-blue and encircled with a narrow, yellow band. The flowers are held well above the plant, which forms a compact mound. The leaves are handsome grayish-green that combines well with other colors in the garden. Hybrids with flowers up to 4 inches in diameter have brought other colors—yellow, cream, white, purple, orange, and red.

How to grow: Bright sunny days and cool nights are ideal. Arctotis also thrives in mild winter areas with high winter light. The plant needs full sun and will tolerate lots of abuse. With richer soil and moderate moisture, there are larger flowers and lusher foliage. Fertilize only lightly. Where summers are very hot, arctotis may cease flowering but will resume again when cooler weather prevails.

Propagation: By seed primarily, although cuttings of choice kinds will root quickly. Sow indoors 6 to 8 weeks prior to last frost at 65° F. Seeds germinate in 15 to 20 days. Plant 8 to 10 inches apart at the same depth they were growing in the flat or pot. For later flowers, sow outdoors after danger of frost has passed and the soil has warmed somewhat. Thin garden seedlings to 8 to 10 inches apart.

Uses: Plant arctotis in beds or borders where full sun is available. They will tolerate growing in dry rock gardens for early season bloom. They will also bloom indoors in cool sunrooms or greenhouses.

African Daisy, Golden Ageratum

Lonas inodora

The name "African daisy" comes from a portion of its native territory—this plant is found surrounding the Mediterranean Sea, including northern Africa. Because it somewhat resembles the more common ageratum—but with yellow flowers—the name "golden ageratum" is sometimes used. However, the flower clusters are a bit more formal-looking than ageratum.

Description: Although lonas is a member of the daisy family, it does not have the long-ray flowers that give the daisy look. Instead, the small flowers are grouped together in clusters up to 5 inches across. The branched plants grow up to 1 foot tall, and leaves are finely divided into long, narrow segments.

How to grow: Lonas grows best in full sun. It's not particular as to garden soil as long as it is well-drained. It should be planted outside after frost danger has passed. The plant grows best if spaced 6 inches apart; it does not need staking.

Propagation: By seed. Seeds may be sown outdoors in early spring where plants are to grow, thinning to a 6-inch spacing. They may also be started indoors 6 to 8 weeks prior to outdoor planting for earlier bloom. Germination will take 5 to 7 days at 60 to 70° F.

Uses: Plant lonas in flower borders, combined with other flowers in complementary shapes and colors. They blend beautifully in informal mixed plantings and add a bright, golden note to wildflower gardens. For best effect, plant them in groupings, rather than as single plants. They are effective if used to make a bright, golden ribbon through a border. They can also be planted in rows in the cutting garden and used fresh or for dried arrangements. Lonas flowers last a long time on the plant.

Dahlberg Daisy, Golden Fleece

Dyssodia tenuiloba

A charming little plant with sunny flowers, the Dahlberg daisy is now becoming widely available in the spring as a started plant at garden centers. Native to the southern United States down through Central America, it has become naturalized in warmer parts of the world. The plants have pleasantly scented foliage.

Description: The Dahlberg daisy bears many upright, golden-yellow flowers about ½ inch in diameter. The prominent yellow eye is surrounded by ray flowers. The long, narrow leaves are divided, giving a very feathery appearance. Plants grow from 6 to 12 inches high, spreading as much as 18 inches by the end of the growing season.

How to grow: Dahlberg daisies grow well in full sun and well-drained, moderately fertile soil. However, they will also grow and bloom abundantly in poor soil. Unlike many annuals, they thrive in hot weather. For plants started indoors, plant outdoors when the soil is warm and the danger of frost has passed. Space 6 to 12 inches apart. Dahlberg daisies will reseed and appear in the same place the following year. They may winter over in relatively frost-free areas of Zones 9 and 10.

Propagation: By seed. Sow seeds in place when the ground is warm, thinning plants to the proper spacing. For earlier bloom, start seeds indoors 6 to 8 weeks prior to planting out. Germination takes 8 to 12 days at 60 to 80° F.

Uses: Dahlberg daisy can be planted in rock gardens or in pockets among paving stones or patio blocks. It makes a superb edging for beds and borders and can be used as a ground cover plant for sunny areas. Use it also to edge paths and walks. Its habit of reseeding makes it ideal for naturalized gardens. It is also suited for container gardens.

English Daisy

Bellis perennis

In nature, the English daisy, immortalized by poets, bears single flowers. However, breeding and selection have added semi-doubles and doubles to the array of varieties available to gardeners. Particularly in the Northeast, the English daisy has become naturalized. In order to enjoy the improved forms, the gardener must start with named-variety seeds.

Description: Flowers of white, pink, or red rise on 6-inch stems from a rosette of basal leaves. Single and semi-double flowers are centered in yellow, but in fully double varieties this distinguishing feature is covered. Normally, flowers are 1 to 2 inches in diameter; in newer varieties they are larger. Most flowers appear in spring and early summer repeating again in the fall, but in cool and coastal climates they may bloom all year.

How to grow: Grow in full sun or light shade in moist soil, well-enriched with organic matter. When used as an annual, set out as early as the ground can be worked or plant in the fall for earliest bloom when weather warms (except in Zones 3 to 5 where they are not hardy except in well-protected cold frames). Plant 6 to 9 inches apart. Frequently, they are replaced with warm season annuals in late June.

Propagation: By seed or by division. Seeds germinate in 10 to 15 days at 70° F.

Uses: English daisies will liven up small beds and are good for edgings and small containers during the cool spring period.

Related species: *B. rotundifolia* has white flowers; *B. r. caerulescens* bears blue flowers.

Related varieties: The largest-flowered variety is the fully double 'Goliath Mixed,' with flowers up to 3 inches in diameter in shades of white, red, pink, and salmon. Others are 'Pompanette Mixed,' with 1½-inch flowers, and the petite 'Bright Carpet Mixed,' with 1-inch flowers.

Livingstone Daisy

Dorotheanthus bellidiformis (many seed catalogs still list it under *Mesembryanthemum criniflorum*)

Formerly grouped under the name *mesembryanthemum,* Livingstone daisies are now widely dispersed under other names. Frost-tender succulents, they thrive in sunny, dry conditions and locations. Livingstone daisies bloom for weeks in the spring and summer.

Description: Livingstone daisies have flat, succulent leaves up to 3 inches long, with the plants hugging the ground. Flowers have dark centers and are colored pink, white, purple, lavender, crimson, or orange. Plants grow up to 8 inches high and spread to 12 inches wide. The flowers close at night and on cloudy days.

How to grow: Livingstone daisies need full sun and sandy, well-drained soil. They tolerate drought and are resistant to salt spray, making them good for seaside plantings. Livingstone daisies tend to sunburn in hot, humid weather. Space plants 6 inches apart for full coverage.

Propagation: By seed. Sow seeds indoors 10 weeks prior to last frost date. Seeds germinate in 7 to 14 days at 60° F. In frost-free locations, they can be seeded directly into the garden and thinned to the proper spacing. They will reseed, although the colors will not be the same in following years.

Uses: These are ideal plants for mass plantings. They're wonderful sunny ground covers. Plant them in rock gardens; they are especially beautiful on slopes and hillsides. They're among the best plants for seaside locations.

Related species: The primary variety of *Mesembryanthemum occulatum* is 'Lunette,' bearing lemon-yellow flowers with cherry-red centers.

Related varieties: 'Magic Carpet Mixed' combines all colors of Livingstone daisies. 'Livingstone Daisy Mixed' is another blend of all colors. Other available mixes may include a variety of Livingstone daisy varieties as well as similar species.

Swan River Daisy

Brachycome iberidifolia

The Swan River in Western Australia is home to this daisy-flowered charmer. Quite variable in nature, flowers are blue, pink, white, and purple, each one centered with either yellow or black.

Description: The Swan River daisy forms a loose mound up to 18 inches tall with equal spread. Much branched, it holds its many 1½-inch flowers upright on slender stems. The flowers are mostly single with contrasting centers.

How to grow: Brachycome needs full sun and a rich but well-drained soil. Water when soil appears dry, but avoid overwatering. It also grows and blooms better where temperatures of more than 90° F accompanied by high humidity do not continue for long periods of time. To encourage bushiness, young plants can be pinched once. For solid plantings, space plants 9 inches apart in the garden. To reinvigorate bloom if it diminishes, shear plants back to 6 inches.

Propagation: By seed or by cuttings. For early bloom, sow seeds indoors at 70° F 6 weeks prior to planting out after frost danger has passed. Germination will take 10 to 18 days. Seeds may also be sown outdoors after the frost-free date. Thin seedlings to 9 inches. Cuttings will root in 15 days and are very useful for multiplying good forms of brachycome. Adjust humidity to keep leaves firm during rooting, but watch the plants carefully to avoid rot.

Uses: It is the blue brachycome that is so scarce in summer gardens. Because of its mounding habit, brachycome is an ideal hanging basket or container plant. It also accents rock gardens and is useful for edging tall borders. Given bright sunlight, it can be grown in pots indoors.

Related varieties: One selection is 'Blue Splendor.' 'Purple Splendor' will give shades of blue to purple. For a range of all colors, plant 'Mixed Colors.'

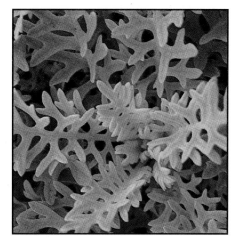

Transvaal Daisy, Barberton Daisy

Gerbera jamesonii

Both common names of this South African native spell out its geographical origin, Transvaal being a province and Barberton a city there. A perennial, it is too tender to live through winter except in parts of Zones 9 and 10, but it will bloom the first year from seed.

Description: Gerbera forms a nice rosette of notched, glossy leaves, from which the flowers grow 12 to 18 inches high, depending on the variety. Flowers are single, semi-double, or double in shades of pink, orange, red, yellow, and white and are up to 4 inches or more in diameter.

How to grow: They grow best in full sun but will tolerate partial shade. They need moist, well-drained soil high in organic matter and high humidity. Use started plants and plant out after last frost and when the ground has warmed. Make sure to plant at ground level. Depending on the variety, space 12 to 15 inches apart.

Propagation: By seed. Be sure to use fresh seeds. Press seeds into the soil but do not cover; they need light to germinate. Sow 14 to 18 weeks before setting out. Seeds will germinate in 10 days at 70 to 75° F.

Uses: Cluster them at the front or side of a bed, or in a border. Mix them with other plants. Individual flowers last a long time on the plant, but when they're done, you need to deadhead to keep new flowers coming. Gerberas are good container plants. As cut flowers, they last up to two weeks.

Related varieties: 'Happipot' is a compact variety with a 10- to 15-inch height. The flowers are single red, rose, pink, salmon, orange, yellow, and cream. 'Parade' is a dwarf series with double flowers in many colors. A taller, cut flower type is 'Gigi,' with 18- to 24-inch stems and 4- to 4½-inch flowers. Many of the flowers are crested.

Dusty Miller

Senecio cineraria, Chrysanthemum cinerariaefolium

The term "dusty miller" originated from the effect of shimmering gray foliage rather than as a name for a particular plant. The name has been commonly applied to a variety of similar plants including *Artemisias, Centaureas,* and *Lychnis.*

Description: *Chrysanthemum cinerariaefolium* grows 1 to 2½ feet tall with finely divided leaflets. It has decorative white daisy flowers about 1½ inches in diameter. *Senecio cineraria* is a bushy subshrub that grows up to 2½ feet tall. The ornamental value is in the finely divided gray foliage.

How to grow: Preference for both plants is full sun and a rather ordinary, well-drained soil, although they will brighten lightly shaded areas, too. Plant in the garden when the soil has warmed and after danger of frost has passed. Space 8 to 10 inches apart. Pinch the tips of plants to induce shapely branching.

Propagation: By seed or by cuttings. Germinate seeds of *Senecio cineraria* at 75 to 80° F and those of *Chrysanthemum cinerariaefolium* at 65 to 75° F. Germination will take 10 to 15 days. Sow seeds 12 to 14 weeks before planting out.

Uses: These are the classic plants to use in urns with bright summer flowers. They are effective in all kinds of planters. However, they also make great ribbons of light in flower beds and borders. They're especially good to use as a bridge between two clashing colors; to intensify cool colors like blue; or to tone down hot colors.

Related varieties: The most commonly available selection of *C. cinerariaefolium* is 'Silver Lace,' with very dissected, feathery leaves. It is not as vigorous a grower as *S. cineraria.* Two varieties of the latter are commonly found: 'Diamond' and 'Silver Dust,' with more silvery and finely divided leaves.

Echium

Echium vulgare

A native of western Europe, including England, echium is really a biennial, producing flowers the year after planting. Its striking flower form of tall racemes is attractive in the garden. The most common form bears blue flowers, but selections are available with rose, pink, mauve, lilac, lavender, and purple flowers.

Description: Long, hairy leaves support a tall spike of flowers. Buds are purple, with flowers opening to a violet-blue. In other forms, the flowers open pink, then fade to blue. Plants are 12 to 24 inches tall and need about 10 to 15 inches of growing space.

How to grow: Echiums thrive in full sun in average soil. Too much fertility causes excess foliage to the detriment of flowering. They will tolerate dry soil, but must have good drainage to grow well. Start plants in July or August in order to develop husky plants for wintering over in locations where they are to flower the following season. Space 8 to 12 inches apart.

Propagation: By seed. Seeds germinate in 14 to 21 days at 60°F. Too high a temperature will inhibit germination.

Uses: Echiums can be used to add a vertical note to beds, borders, walkways, and paths in the garden. The pastel colors combine well with other pastels and white, and strike a happy contrast with sunny, warm colors.

Related species: *Echium fastuosum,* known as "pride of Madeira," is a tender, shrubby perennial for Zones 8 and 9. Great clusters of blue-purple flowers stand well above the foliage in May and June.

Related varieties: 'Blue Bedder' grows to 12 inches high and has cup-shaped flowers. 'Dwarf Mixed' has a mix of colors in purple, lavender, lilac, light blue, mauve, salmon rose, pink, and rose.

Everlastings, Strawflowers

Helichrysum, Everlasting

Helichrysum bracteatum

These double daisy-shaped flowers grow on long stems 18 to 36 inches tall. They come in a wide range of colors: white, yellow, pink, crimson, and bronze. They must have a long season of growth to develop the flowers before fall. Cut for drying before the yellow centers are visible; use wire stems. Air dry upside down in the dark.

Statice

Statice sinuatum

Statice has clusters of small flowers on long stems up to 36 inches in height and bears off-centered flowers in blue, yellow, rose, and white, with other shades less available. Cut the flowers when blooms are at least ¾ open. Air dry them upside down in the dark.

Honesty, Silver Dollar Plant

Lunaria annua

The seedpods of this plant are often used for dried arrangements. The flowers, which bloom on 2- to 3-foot stems, are mauve or white and can be used in fresh arrangements. Cut the stems for drying when the seedpods are beginning to dry, but before the seeds turn yellow. Air dry upside down in a dark place.

Xeranthemum

Xeranthemum annuum

These flowers, also known as "immortelles," grow from 18 to 24 inches tall and have single or double flowers. Flowers are white, pink, rose, violet, and purple. For drying, flowers can be cut at different stages—from half-open buds to fully open flowers. They retain their colors for a long time after drying. Air dry upside down in the dark.

Firecracker Plant

Cuphea ignea

This plant first became popular as an indoor plant, but it's a good tender annual outdoors, too. Its slender, tubular flowers of bright red have a contrasting black band at the tip. It is a native of Mexico.

Description: Firecracker plants form a bushy subshrub up to 1 foot high with an equal or greater spread. Its compact mounding form is heavily covered with tiny, red flowers that appear at all the leaf axils. Leaves are long and narrow.

How to grow: Grow the firecracker plant in full sun in average but well-drained soil. Plant out after all danger of frost is over. Apply an all-purpose, slow-release fertilizer at planting. When planting out, pinch out the tips to increase bushiness. Space them 6 to 12 inches apart, depending on the length of the growing season. They are perennial in frost-free areas and can be sheared back to maintain their shapeliness.

Propagation: By seed or by cuttings. Seeds may be sown in the garden after the soil has warmed. They need light to germinate well—so barely cover them. For earlier bloom, sow seeds indoors 8 to 12 weeks prior to planting out. Seeds germinate in 8 to 10 days at 70 to 85° F. Cuttings root easily in 10 to 14 days.

Uses: Use them as edging plants for borders or in rock gardens. They are also good container plants, with growth flowing over the edges of hanging baskets, window boxes, or other planters. Branches can be cut and used in flower arrangements.

Related species: *Cuphea hyssopifolia*, or "Mexican heather," is a tender perennial used primarily for bedding out, except in frost-free areas. Leaves are tiny, and the plant is nearly obscured by the small white, lavender, or lilac-colored flowers that bloom over a long season. Growing to 1 foot, it spreads wider than its height.

Floss Flower

Ageratum houstonianum

Originally from Mexico and Central America, these fluffy flowers in blue-lavender, white, and pink are favorites for window boxes and edging in summer gardens. One interesting aspect of *ageratum* is that the eye sees the color of so-called blue varieties differently than film, which registers them as pink.

Description: Ageratum is covered with fuzzy flowers about ½ inch in diameter on compact, mounding plants from 6 to 10 inches high. They will spread about 10 inches by season's end. Ageratum blooms continuously from planting out after all chance of frost has passed (it is very frost-sensitive) until fall.

How to grow: Grow in any well-drained soil in full sun or partial shade. Space 6 to 10 inches apart for solid color. Occasional deadheading will improve their performance. They need ample water to make sure that leaves never wilt.

Propagation: By seed. Start seeds indoors 6 to 8 weeks before planting. Cover seeds very lightly, since they need some light to germinate well. Germination time will be 5 to 8 days at 70° F.

Uses: Plant in the front of borders and beds. They also grow well in hanging baskets, window boxes, and other containers. Most of the newer varieties form compact mounds that provide the scarce blue color so seldom found in annuals. Taller, older varieties make good cut flowers.

Related species: Golden ageratum or *Lonas inodora* has the same flower effect in bright yellow.

Related varieties: Several of the popular blue varieties ranging from light tones to deepest violet are 'Adriatic,' 'Blue Danube,' and 'Blue Blazer.' 'Summer Snow' is white, and 'Pink Powderpuffs' is as its name describes. 'Wonder' is a tall variety useful for cutting.

Foliage Plants

Tropical plants are often used for summer planting outdoors in many parts of the country. In frost-free Zones 9 and 10, they may be used as permanent plantings.

Dracaena
Dracaena marginata
This dracaena is used in outdoor container plantings surrounded by geraniums and asparagus fern. It is grown from cuttings.

Polka Dot Plant, Freckle Face
Hypoestes phyllostachya
This plant is used as a ground-covering plant in shade or partial shade during the summer. It is a subshrub that will grow from 1 to 2 feet high. Each leaf has markings in white or pink. It is propagated by seed or by cuttings. The variety 'Pink Splash' has much larger pink markings and is grown from seed.

Moses-in-a-Boat, Moses-in-a-Cradle
Rhoeo spathacea
This semisucculent plant has sword-shaped, metallic-green leaves with purple undersides. The flowers peek out from boat-shaped bracts that appear from leaf axils. This plant is widely used in beds in public plantings in warm parts of the country. They grow in sun or partial shade, resist drought, and flourish in any soil. They are also used as a summer annual in colder climates. A variegated form, *R. spathacea vittata*, has its leaves streaked with pale yellow.

Purple Heart
Setcreasea pallida
This purple-leafed plant is semisucculent and usually a trailer. Native to dry and semidry areas of Mexico, setcreasea is a tough plant. The dramatic, purple foliage contrasts beautifully with chartreuse-colored foliage plants as well as with creamy yellow flowers. Use it in large beds or in front of borders.

Forget-Me-Not

Myosotis sylvatica

A bed of spring bulbs—such as tulips or daffodils—underplanted with forget-me-nots is a sight to behold. Biennials native to cool, moist areas of Europe and northern Asia, they are usually grown as annuals.

Description: Forget-me-nots are small plants seldom reaching more than 12 inches in height and an equal diameter. The tiny flowers are clustered together in racemes at the top of plants.

How to grow: Forget-me-nots relish cool, moist weather with sun or partial shade. In Zones 8, 9, and 10, seeds can be sown in the fall where plants will bloom in the spring. When planting in the spring, plant as soon as the soil can be worked. When plants have finished blooming, replace them with summer annuals. Forget-me-nots will reseed, but seedlings in colder climates will not bloom until late spring or summer.

Propagation: By seed. For early bloom in cold climates, seed indoors in January, planting seedlings outdoors as soon as the soil can be worked. Seeds germinate in 8 to 14 days at 55 to 70° F. Be sure to cover seeds; they need darkness to germinate. When removing plants that have bloomed, shake the ripened seeds onto the ground where you want blooming plants the next spring.

Uses: Plant forget-me-nots in masses for best results. They're suited for rock gardens, as an edging, or in the front of a border. Try them in window boxes and patio planters with spring bulbs. Grow forget-me-nots in meadows, along stream banks, or by ponds.

Related varieties: 'Indigo Compacta' is a darker-colored selection that stays smaller than most varieties. 'Blue Ball' is a compact form with bright blue flowers. 'White Ball' is similar in form but has white blooms. 'Victoria Mixed' combines blue-, white-, rose-, and pink-flowered forms.

Chinese Forget-Me-Not, Hound's Tongue

Cynoglossum amabile

This plant is of special value for the clear, sky-blue color of the flowers. They bloom all summer, and are especially good in cool climates. The Chinese in its common name comes from its origin in Asia, although it also resembles the true forget-me-not (*Myosotis*). "Hound's tongue" refers to its leaves, which have a furry surface and are shaped like a dog's tongue.

Description: Chinese forget-me-not is a biennial most often grown as an annual. The plants grow to 2 feet tall with flowers appearing as sprays above the plant. The foliage is gray-green. There are also pink and white forms that are not widely available.

How to grow: Grow in full sun or partial shade in a rich, well-drained soil, high in organic matter. Except in regions with cool summers, they are more successful in full sun if the soil is kept evenly moist, but not soggy. Feed lightly or mix a slow-release fertilizer into the soil before planting. They may be planted outdoors in spring as soon as the soil is workable. Space 8 to 12 inches apart.

Propagation: By seed. Sow outdoors as early as the ground can be worked. For best color during cool weather, sow seeds indoors 6 to 8 weeks prior to transplanting outside. Germination takes 5 to 14 days at 70° F. Plants will reseed profusely if not kept in check. Seeds stick tightly to clothes and animals that carry them far from the planned location.

Uses: Grow them as a source of sky-blue color in beds or borders. They're also striking in beds all by themselves or mixed with other flowers to tone down hot colors or to complement a range of pastels.

Related variety: 'Firmament,' an award-winner, is widely available.

Summer Forget-Me-Not, Cape Forget-Me-Not

Anchusa capensis

The flowers of this South African native resemble forget-me-nots—resulting in anchusa's common names. Flowers with a bright, true blue color are a rarity for the summer garden. For sheer intensity of color, anchusa matches or exceeds every other blue available. A biennial, it is most often grown as an annual.

Description: Clouds of flowers cover the dwarf plants that grow 12 to 18 inches tall and 10 inches in diameter. Flowers are tiny and held on stems above the plant. Branches are rather top-heavy. A pink and white form is not widely available.

How to grow: Anchusa grows best where summers are cool. In hot areas of the country, they do best in spring or fall bloom, although hot days followed by cool nights suit their needs. They perform best in full sun, but will grow in partial shade on open, well-drained soil. Do not fertilize. Bloom will appear in flushes. When flowering diminishes, shear back to 6 inches to encourage repeat bloom that will take about 3 weeks. Repeat for copious bloom until frost. In mild winter areas, anchusas can be started the summer or fall before and grown outdoors over the winter for early flowering. Elsewhere, sow seeds outdoors several weeks before the last frost, or start in pots indoors and transplant outside after frost danger has passed.

Propagation: By seed. Germinates in 10 days at 60° F.

Uses: A splendid source of blue in the garden, use anchusa wherever you want to soften the strident tones of hot colors such as orange and yellow. It combines well with white. Because summer forget-me-not is compact, use it as an edging for beds and borders.

Varieties: 'Blue Angel' is 10 inches tall, and 'Blue Bird' grows to 18 inches. Both form compact mounds.

Four O'Clock, Marvel of Peru

Mirabilis jalapa

This is a plant whose flowers you wait to see until afternoon—hence, the common name "four o'clock." The name *mirabilis* is from the Latin "wonderful." They open in mid- to late-afternoon and close again the next morning (except on dull days).

Description: Four o'clocks form a well-branched, bushy shrub from 1 to 3 feet tall. Flowering is generous, with plants covered with white, yellow, red, purple, and unusual bicolored flowers. Sometimes different flower patterns appear on the same plant. When closed, the flowers curl up tightly.

How to grow: Full sun in average-to-rich garden soil is ideal for four o'clocks. They will also bloom in partial shade, although plants will become lankier. They are very tolerant of humidity, air pollution, heat, and drought. Plant them outdoors once the danger of frost has passed. Since they are vigorous growers, space them 18 to 24 inches apart. Four o'clocks form tubers which, after frost, can be dug up and stored for replanting the following year. Four o'clocks reseed.

Propagation: By seed or by tubers. In warm climates with a long growing season, you can seed outdoors after the last frost. For shorter season gardens, you'll get earlier bloom by starting them indoors 4 to 6 weeks ahead of planting out. Seeds germinate in 7 to 10 days at 70° F.

Uses: Four o'clocks make a neat, low hedge. They can be used for edging walks and borders or grouped in the center of the border. Because the flowers stay open at night, they're attractive when planted near evening activities—such as lighted pools and patios. Four o'clocks also grow well in large containers.

Related varieties: 'Jingles' bears white, rose, red, yellow, and crimson flowers, many of them splashed with contrasting colors.

Foxglove

Digitalis purpurea

The widely used heart medicine comes from this biennial plant, but its garden value is the bell-shaped flowers in late spring. It's a native of western Europe.

Description: Foxglove grows for months as a rosette of gray-green leaves; then a tall spike surrounded by buds quickly arises, growing from 3 to 7 feet tall. Most flowers, which are white, cream, pink, salmon, lavender, or red, are marked with blotches of contrasting color.

How to grow: Foxglove thrives in light woodlands or at the fringes of tree or shrub plantings. It will grow in average soil if kept moist. When flower spikes appear, fertilize with a general fertilizer. The sturdy spikes normally do not need staking. The seeds are tiny and widely distributed by the wind. To prevent reseeding, cut flower spikes after bloom.

Propagation: By seed. To grow as a biennial, sow seeds outdoors in June or July so husky plants will overwinter. For bloom the first year, sow indoors 8 to 10 weeks prior to planting outdoors. Except for selected varieties, these will bloom in late summer or fall. Seeds germinate at 70° F in 15 to 20 days.

Uses: Foxglove deserves a place in the mixed cottage garden. Plant it in groups at the back of the border, against fences, near tall shrub hedges or woodlands. They're also useful in the perennial border, providing the height that early perennial gardens often lack. They make useful cut flowers.

Related species: *Digitalis lutea* brings yellow flowers to the foxglove clan. It grows to 3 feet.

Related varieties: 'Foxy' has a full range of colors and grows to 3 feet tall. 'Excelsior Mixture' contains many colors of tall-growing foxgloves. 'Apricot' is a buttery, copper color, and 'Alba' is pure white.

Fuchsia, Lady's Ear Drops

Fuchsia hybrida

There are hundreds of named varieties of fuchsias, the beautiful plants with pendulous blossoms that bloom heavily from spring to fall. Most of them have been developed from two species. The name "lady's ear drops" is self-evident, but the name *Fuchsia* is more commonly used. The name honors Fuchs, a German botanist.

Description: Garden fuchsias are all more or less woody plants, some having a more erect, bushy habit; others with long, trailing stems from which blossoms hang. The flowers themselves are composed of a calyx, a brightly colored cylinder or tube that points downward, which is topped by flaring, petal-like lobes called sepals. The calyx can be single or double, and the sepals are either the same color or contrasting. The calyx and sepals may also be wavy and ruffled.

How to grow: Fuchsias bloom more freely when they get some shade. They're at their best in cool coastal or mountain regions with good humidity, but can be grown successfully in most places as long as they are kept moist. Fuchsias are heavy feeders. Apply a slow-release fertilizer at planting or feed biweekly with a water-soluble fertilizer. For large-blooming plants by mid-May, plant 3 to 5 rooted cuttings in a 10- to 12-inch basket. To develop full and shapely plants, pinch out tips as soon as two sets of leaves have formed and continue this process until March 1. Fuchsias are not winter-hardy except in Zones 9 and 10, but they can be stored over winter in temperatures above freezing but below 50° F. Water only enough to keep the root ball from drying out. Light is unnecessary. In January, bring into the light, cut back plants by at least 50 percent, and resume normal watering.

Propagation: By seed or by cuttings. Seeds germinate in 21 to 28 days.

Uses: Fuchsias are at their best in hanging baskets where the pendulous flowers can be viewed from below. They are most often placed where they can be seen frequently—on decks, porches, or beside walkways. Upright varieties are eye-catching in containers raised on railings or porch steps. Fuchsias are also grown as standards or in tree form, with foliage and flowers flaring out from a single stem grown to the desired height.

Related species: *Fuchsia magellanica* is a small-flowered, hardier species.

Related varieties: Selections are so varied that it is best to choose them in bloom at a nursery or garden center. 'Swingtime,' with double, white calyxes and red sepals, is by far the favorite variety. Double 'Indian Maid' has blue-violet calyxes and red sepals. 'Lena' bears double purple and white flowers. 'Jack Shahan' is a single, pink flowered variety with a trailing form. 'Marinka,' with a multitude of small, red, single flowers, has a counterpart, 'Golden Marinka,' with variegated leaves. 'Gartenmeister Bonstedt' is an old upright variety with numerous firecracker-shaped red flowers.

Gazania, Treasure Flower

Gazania ringens

This South African flower likes hot, dry summers and cool winters. Gardeners treasure it for its daisylike flowers.

Description: Gazanias grow in rosette form with attractive notched leaves. In many varieties, these are gray-green on top and silver beneath. Flowers rise 8 to 12 inches on short stems. They're white, pink, bronze, red, yellow, orange, and white, contrasting with bright yellow centers. Some varieties have contrasting stripes in the ray petals.

How to grow: Gazanias prefer full sun and moderately fertile but well-drained soil. The only thing they don't like is heavy soil in hot, humid climates. In Zones 9, 10, and sometimes 8, they'll winter over as perennials. In those areas they'll bloom for 8 or 9 months. Elsewhere, plant out as soon as the danger of frost has passed. Space 8 to 15 inches apart.

Propagation: By seed, cuttings, or division. Sow seeds outdoors after final frost or plant them indoors 4 to 6 weeks earlier. Barely cover seeds, as they need light to germinate. Seeds germinate in 15 to 20 days at 70° F. Cuttings taken in the summer root quickly. In Zones 9 and 10, division can be accomplished by cutting clumps apart and replanting the pieces.

Uses: Plant gazanias in the front of beds and borders. Use them as a ground cover in sunny, dry areas or in rock gardens. They're good cut flowers. Gazanias can be potted for bloom indoors. They are good in containers and window boxes.

Related varieties: The 'Daybreak' series blooms in 'Yellow,' 'Orange,' and 'Garden Sun,' combining yellow and orange. The 'Daybreak Mixture' includes pink and white colors. 'Chansonette' has many contrasting colors between the centers and tips of petals. 'Ministar' has a separate 'Yellow' and 'Tangerine,' as well as a mix.

Ivy-Leaf Geranium

Pelargonium peltatum

Ivy-leaf geraniums have an entirely different character than their zonal geranium cousins. Long, trailing stems make them ideal for containers of all kinds. Their flowers are generally less strident and more toned to the pastel range of their hues. Older varieties are somewhat intolerant of long periods of heat and humidity, but newer varieties are more heat-resistant. The common name springs from the shape of the leaves.

Description: Two distinct groups of ivy-leaf geraniums are available to home gardeners. All of them have the cascading form of ivy geraniums, but a group of single-flowered varieties from Europe are proving more floriferous and heat-tolerant. Semi-double flowered varieties have less bloom, but still make real impact all summer. Many varieties are available—from miniatures with a spread of only 12 inches through vigorous ones that can grow to 5 feet tall.

How to grow: Ivy-leaf geraniums grow best in cool, coastal, or mountain climates with lots of sun. In other locations they may need partial shade. Ivy-leaf geraniums in containers relish full sun if temperatures are not above 85° F for long stretches. Where this occurs, give them northern or eastern exposure where they can be protected from hot midday and afternoon sun. Do not let them dry out. Plant ivy-leaf geraniums outside after danger of frost has passed and the soil is warm.

Propagation: By cuttings or by seed (only one variety so far is seed-grown). Take cuttings from stock plants 10 to 12 weeks prior to planting outside. Pinch tips once or twice to encourage branching.

Uses: Ivy-leaf geraniums are excellent container plants. They develop into shapely hanging baskets clothed with foliage and flowers. As window box plants, they excel and are ideal in patio planters. The single-flowered varieties are also good plants to use as sunny ground covers.

Related varieties: Among the heavy flowering, single-flowered varieties (so-called European types), the 'Cascade' series is representative. 'Sofie Cascade' is a light pink with darker shading toward petal centers. 'Bright Cascade' is a glowing red. 'Lila Compact Cascade' is lavender. Good semi-doubles include 'Yale,' rich crimson; 'Galilee,' a very vigorous hot pink; 'Salmon Queen'; 'Snow Queen'; and 'Beauty of Eastbourne,' cherry red. The seed-grown variety is 'Summer Showers' and includes red, white, pink, lavender, and plum-colored varieties.

Regal, Martha Washington or Lady Washington Geranium or Pelargonium

Pelargonium domesticum

Regal pelargoniums like mild weather and sunny days to perform their best. These plants have large, open-faced flowers above light green, pleated leaves. Exceedingly colorful, they include clear colors of pink, red, white, lavender, and burgundy, with the flowers of many varieties marked with bright patches of contrasting colors. Where nights do not go above 60° F, they will continue blooming all summer. In warmer areas, they will take a midsummer hiatus until cooler nights prevail in the fall. Plant in the garden in the spring when the weather has settled.

Variegated Zonal Geranium

A number of varieties of zonal geraniums are grown for their fancy leaves. Culture is the same as for regular zonals. Probably the most colorful are 'Skies of Italy,' 'Mrs. Cox,' and 'Dolly Varden.' The leaves of 'Ben Franklin,' 'Wilhelm Langguth,' and 'Mrs. Parker' are similar in appearance, rounded with distinct margins of white on the edges.

Scented Geranium

A variety of species pelargoniums have distinctly fragrant leaves when the surface is rubbed. Some have attractive foliage, but in most the bloom is modest. *Pelargonium crispum* has lemon-scented leaves. *P. grossulariodes* is coconut-scented, while *P. nervosum* has the fragrance of lime. *P. fragrans* smells like nutmeg. One of the most popular is *P. tomentosum*, which has a strong peppermint scent. Its foliage is especially attractive, with felted leaves of a rich green. Less common varieties include those with the scent of roses and strawberries.

Zonal Geranium

Pelargonium x *hortorum*

Many gardeners consider zonal geraniums the epitome of summer flowers. Named for the dark, horseshoe-shaped color in the leaves of most varieties, these stalwart garden beauties are tender perennials that must be replanted each year except in the most favored climates. Most *pelargonium* species (true geraniums are hardy perennials) come from South Africa, but through hundreds of years of breeding, the parentage of today's varieties is obscured.

Description: Zonal geraniums are upright bushes covered with red, pink, salmon, white, rose, cherry red, and bicolored flowers on long stems held above the plant. Flower clusters (or umbels) contain many individual flowers and give a burst of color. Plants from 4-inch pots transplanted to the garden in spring will reach up to 18 inches high and wide by the end of summer.

How to grow: Zonal geraniums benefit from sun. They develop into shapely hanging baskets clothed with foliage and flowers. As window box plants, they excel and are ideal in full sun and moderate-to-rich, well-drained, moist soil. Incorporate a slow-release fertilizer into the soil at planting time. Plant after all danger of frost has passed and the soil is warm. Space them 12 inches apart. The only other care requirement is deadheading spent blooms.

Propagation: By seed or by cuttings. So far, the only readily available semi-double, flowered varieties are grown from cuttings. The cuttings root easily. Make cuttings 8 to 10 weeks prior to planting out for husky plants. Seed-grown varieties should be started 10 to 12 weeks prior to garden planting. Seeds germinate in 7 to 10 days at 70 to 75° F.

Uses: Zonal geraniums are among the best plants for formal beds. They can provide pockets of color in any sunny spot. Group 3 or more together for color impact in flower borders or along walks and pathways. They're classics in containers, all by themselves, or mixed with other kinds of plants. Geraniums are also grown as standards—a single stem is trained to the desired height with a bushy canopy of flowers and leaves. Zonal geraniums will bloom through the winter in sunny windows.

Related varieties: There are many varieties available at garden centers in the spring. A few popular semi-doubles are: 'Tango,' a bright orange-red with dark foliage; 'Forever Yours,' a vigorous red; 'Blues,' cherry blossom pink with unique rose and white markings near the center of petals; 'Schone Helene,' a 2-toned salmon; and 'Snowmass,' pure white. Seed-grown singles are generally found in series of many colors. Widely planted are 'Orbit,' 'Elite,' 'Ringo,' 'Bandit,' and 'Hollywood' varieties.

Gladiolus, Glad

Gladiolus hybridus

The name *gladiolus* means "little sword" in reference to the sword-shaped leaves of the plant. Every flower color but blue is represented in modern hybrids, and the flowers themselves vary immensely. They are members of the iris family.

Description: The erect spikes of flowers, from 1 to 4 feet tall, grow through the swordlike leaves from the corm, a modified stem planted underground. The individual flowers are classified by size by the North American Gladiolus Council, from miniatures with flowers under 2½ inches in diameter to giants over 5½ inches in diameter.

How to grow: Gladiolus grows best in well-drained soil high in organic matter, in full sun. Shelter from heavy winds. Where the ground does not freeze, corms may be left in the ground from year to year. Elsewhere, plant each spring in succession to assure continuous bloom. Plant the first about the time deciduous trees are sprouting new foliage, continuing about every 2 weeks until the first of July. Bloom occurs 60 to 70 days after planting. Fertilize a month after planting and again just before the first flowers open. Water regularly if dry.

Propagation: By corms. The tiny corms that form around each corm can be saved at digging (keep separate and label by variety), then planted in the spring for size increase.

Uses: Glads can be used to provide a succession of color, especially in perennial borders when early blooming perennials have finished. Plant them in clusters or groups. They make superb cut flowers, and if wanted primarily for cutting, can be planted in rows in the cutting garden.

Related varieties: There are named varieties by the hundreds.

Godetia, Farewell-To-Spring, Clarkia

Clarkia amoena

The name of this genus honors Captain Clark of the Lewis and Clark expeditions. The species (formerly called *Godetia* botanically) has been improved to produce varieties for spring gardens as well as for cool coastal and mountain locations in the summer.

Description: Godetias produce cup-shaped blossoms in clusters at the tips of strong stems. Flowers are white, pink, red, or lilac with contrasting colors in most. There are also double varieties. Foliage is gray-green. Height ranges from 10 inches up to 2½ feet, and they grow about 10 inches wide. Shorter varieties have a mounding habit.

How to grow: Godetias grow best during the cool weather. In Zones 9 and 10, sow outdoors in the fall for earliest bloom in the spring. In other zones, seed in the garden as early as a seedbed can be prepared. Grow in light, sandy loam in full sun or partial shade. Space plants 12 inches apart. Taller varieties may need staking.

Propagation: By seed. Because they do not transplant well, sow seeds directly in the soil outdoors. Barely cover; they need light to germinate.

Uses: Plant in beds and borders, grow in rock gardens, and naturalize in open meadows. Tall varieties make good cut flowers.

Related species: Many of the flowers usually referred to as clarkias are hybrids of *C. unguiculata* and *C. pulchella* (*Clarkia elegans*). Each species has a variety of garden forms, including double-flowered varieties. Generally, the flowers of clarkias grow along the stem, facing outward, and are about 1 inch in diameter. Colors include white, pink, salmon, and purple.

Related variety: F₁ hybrid 'Grace' is available in red, shell pink, rose-pink, and a mixture of colors.

Ornamental Gourds

Yellow-Flowered Gourd
Cucumis pepo olifera

These are closely related to squash. Hard-shelled fruits of many shapes and colors (both solid and striped) grow on long-stemmed vines.

White-Flowered Gourd
Lagenaria siceraris

This is a rapidly growing vine with large fruits of many sizes and shapes. Depending on the shape, they are often known as bottle gourd, calabash, dipper gourd, siphon gourd, snake gourd, and sugar-trough gourd. Besides being used as ornaments and as containers, they are also used as musical instruments.

Dishrag Gourd, Vegetable Sponge
Luffa aegyptiaca

The long, gourdlike fruits have a fibrous skeleton, which, once the skin is removed, can be used for scrubbing purposes. They grow on a vigorous vine.

How to grow: Full sun, a rich soil high in organic matter, and plentiful moisture are important for good growth by gourds. Sow outdoors when the ground is well-warmed and all danger of frost has passed. Plant seeds in hills of 6 to 8 seeds to a group. Thin seedlings to 4 per hill, selecting the strongest ones. Space hills 8 feet apart.

Propagation: By seed. Roots of gourds resent disturbance, so sow in place outdoors. If started earlier indoors, plant in peat pots that can be transplanted into the ground, pot and all. Seeds germinate in 4 to 8 days at 70° F.

Uses: The vines of gourds can be used to grow over arbors, trellises, pergolas, fences, and arches, or may be left to grow on the ground. Their rapid growth will allow them to reach 15 to 30 feet. After harvesting mature fruit, wash well, dry, then coat with floor wax or varnish before using in ornamental arrangements.

Cloud Grass, Wild Oats, Quaking Grass, Job's Tears, Golden Top, Wheat Grass

Agrostis nebulosa, Avena sterilis, Briza maxima, Coix Lacryma-Jobi, Lamarkia aurea, Triticum aestivum

Ornamental grasses have long been a primary ingredient in dried flower arrangements and winter bouquets. Recently, their use as ornamentals in the landscape has grown dramatically. There are about 10,000 species of grasses, and most of them are perennial, including the bamboos. The following is just a small sampling of the annual varieties that are widely grown both for adornment of the garden and for enduring pleasure in the home. Perhaps 150 different ornamental grasses are used in gardens, with more being tamed for this use all the time.

Description: Cloud grass (*Agrostis nebulosa*) from Spain, growing to 15 inches tall, is grown primarily for its airy flower heads, which are much larger than the sparse foliage. The flower heads dry well but aren't suitable for dyeing.

Wild oats (*Avena sterilis*) from the Mediterranean are now naturalized in the United States. Favored by flower arrangers, they're also a lovely feature in the garden, especially when light strikes from behind so that the hanging spikelets are highlighted. They grow up to 18 inches tall.

Quaking grass (*Briza maxima*) from the Mediterranean was one of the first grasses grown for its ornamental value. The loose flower heads shake at the slightest breeze. They grow to less than 1 foot tall.

Job's tears (*Coix Lacryma-Jobi*) from the tropics have large, tear-shaped grains that are used for making bead necklaces and other ornaments and crafts. As garden plants, they are grown for their seeds. They grow up to 3 feet tall.

Golden top (*Lamarkia aurea*), another Mediterranean import, has erect, silky plumes on

Héliotrope, Cherry Pie

Heliotropium arborescens

Chinese Hibiscus, Hawaiian Hibiscus, Rose of China

Hibiscus rosa-sinensis

one side of the stalk like a toothbrush. The flower heads range from whitish to yellow and tones of purple. It grows up to 1 foot high; clumps are effective in the front of a border. It is very good for drying.

Wheat grass (*Triticum aestivum*) grows to 3 feet tall and is topped with grains evenly spiraled around the stem. A cereal grain in real life (but not the common one we know), wheat grass is prized by floral arrangers.

How to grow: All the annual grasses thrive in full sun on well-drained soil. They'll survive and seed in poor soil even under dry conditions, but growth will be richer and flowering more luxuriant in fertile soil with adequate moisture. In order to prevent reseeding, harvest the flower heads before they're fully dry.

Propagation: By seed. Sow in place in the spring when soil becomes friable. Plant 12 to 15 seeds in an area 1 foot square in well-worked soil and cover ½ to 1 inch deep. Most varieties will tolerate frost, but wait to plant tropical kinds until the soil is warm and frost danger has passed. Save some of the harvested seed stalks for replanting the following year.

Uses: Ornamental grasses are indispensable to many harvest arrangements, door hangings, and other crafts. The tall spiky kinds add line, and the feathery, soft heads of others provide a graceful note to arrangements. In the garden, plant grasses in clumps so their impact is heightened. Short varieties gracefully tie down the front of the border. Taller ones, unless their foliage is especially attractive, deserve middle of the border position where flower heads can be treasured beginning in July. Varieties grown only for flower arrangements can be planted in the cutting garden. Ornamental grasses are also showing up in container gardens, by themselves, or combined with flowers. In northern climates, many varieties of annual grasses remain attractive in the garden until heavy snows cover them.

Fragrance is one of the most alluring attributes of heliotrope. Flowers are deep blue, violet, lavender, or white in copious quantities during the summer. A perennial shrub in South America, we use it in the United States, except in frost-free areas, as an annual.

Description: Heliotrope is a branched shrub with long, gray-green leaves with deep veins. In nature it grows to 4 feet, but as a summer plant a height of 1 foot and equal spread is reasonable. Many tiny flowers are clustered in the large heads carried well above the foliage. The most commonly available varieties are deep blue and white.

How to grow: Any good garden soil with medium fertility in full sun will grow good heliotropes. Normally, plants are started early indoors (from seed or cuttings) and transplanted outdoors when danger of frost has passed and the ground is warm. Depending on the size of transplants, space from 8 to 15 inches apart.

Propagation: By seed or cuttings. Sow seeds 10 to 12 weeks before planting out. Seeds germinate in 7 to 21 days at 70 to 85° F. Root cuttings in 4-inch pots in February in order to have husky plants for planting outdoors in May. Pinch the tips of both seedlings and cutting varieties to create bushy plants.

Uses: Tuck heliotropes into rock gardens, or grow them in the front of borders. Plant them by doorsteps where the fragrance will be appreciated. They are superb as container plants. Grow them indoors if you can provide enough sunlight. To use as cut flowers, plunge the stems and necks deep in water and hold in a cool, dark place for several hours before arranging.

Related varieties: 'Marine,' grown from seed, has dark violet-blue flowers.

Hardy only in frost-free parts of Zones 9 and 10, hibiscus is widely used as an annual elsewhere. It is a member of the mallow family and is found throughout the year in garden centers as a blooming pot plant for indoor enjoyment, but it can be used outdoors as well.

Description: In nature, they're shrubs up to 15 feet tall, but for summering outdoors they will probably reach a maximum of 3 feet tall and wide. The glossy, evergreen foliage is a handsome background for the large—up to 6-inch—flowers. These flaring bells with a distinctive column of yellow stamens in the center are red, yellow, pink, salmon, orange, or white.

How to grow: Hibiscus needs full sun for best bloom production, but it can tolerate partial shade. Soil should be rich, high in organic matter, and be well-moistened. Hibiscus also grows best in high humidity. Primary use in all but frost-free areas is as a container plant. Apply slow-release fertilizer to the soil before planting in the container. Hibiscus can be pruned to make it more shapely by pinching out the tips of young growth to induce branching.

Propagation: By cuttings. Semi-hardwood cuttings root quickly in summer under mist.

Uses: Hibiscus is best used in containers. It can be cut back severely in the spring to maintain its size.

Related species: *Hibiscus rosa-sinensis cooperi* has brightly variegated leaves in pink and white; blooms are red. *Hibiscus schizopelalus* has finely divided, pink blooms. *Hibiscus moscheutos*, or rose mallow, is a perennial with large flowers. 'Disco Belle Mixed,' grown from seed, has large flowers in red, pink, and white.

Related varieties: There are hundreds of named varieties of *Hibiscus rosa-sinensis*.

Hollyhock

Alcea rosea

These tall, stately plants have long been favored by artists when painting scenes of romantic cottage gardens. Hollyhocks have also been a favorite children's plaything—the flowers can be turned into "Southern Belles" complete with long, ruffled skirts.

Description: Most varieties will grow to 6 feet or taller, the stems surrounded by hibiscuslike flowers in every color except blue. Flowers can be single, semi-double, or double, and are waved or fringed. Leaves are large, round, and coarse.

How to grow: Plant in full sun where there's good air movement to avoid rust. Water and feed heavily and spray with a fungicide if rust develops. Staking may be necessary with very tall varieties or if the site is very windy. Plant 12 to 15 inches apart in clumps. Hollyhocks are prolific reseeders, although they will not come true to type this way. To prevent undesirable colors, deadhead the spent flowers.

Propagation: By seed. Most varieties are biennial but, if seeded early enough indoors, can be treated as annuals for the garden. Sow seeds indoors in February or March for flowers the first year. Barely cover seeds (they need light to germinate) and expect germination in 10 to 24 days at 70° F. Plant outdoors after final frost where they'll bloom from July until frost.

Uses: Since hollyhocks are bold in scale, they add height to the rear of a border. They can also be used as a bright clump beside garden paths or at doorsteps.

Related varieties: 'Powderpuff Mixed' provides a wide range of colors with very double flowers. 'Majorette' produces semi-double and laced flowers on 3-foot stems. 'Summer Carnival' with double blooms will flower as an annual if sown early indoors.

Impatiens, Busy Lizzie, Patience

Impatiens wallerana

Impatiens flower in all colors (except true blue and yellow). Their tidy and mounding habit makes them ideal low-maintenance plants. Impatiens were stowaways on trading ships from Africa and naturalized in Central and South America.

Description: Breeders have developed compact, self-branching plants whose flowers are borne above the foliage. Flowers are white, pink, rose, orange, scarlet, burgundy, violet, and many variants. Other varieties have star-shaped patterns of white against colored backgrounds. Double varieties are also grown. Foliage is deep, glossy green or bronze in color. Most varieties grow 12 to 15 inches high in dappled shade. Heavy watering encourages vigorous growth; higher light dwarfs them.

How to grow: Impatiens will grow in any average soil. In cool or coastal areas, impatiens will grow and bloom well if their roots are kept well-watered. In deep shade, bloom diminishes.

Propagation: By seed or by cuttings. Sow seeds 10 to 12 weeks before the last frost date. Impatiens need light to germinate; do not cover seeds, but keep moist. Germination takes 10 to 20 days at 75° F. Use a sterile soil mix, because young impatiens seedlings are subject to damping off disease. A fungicide is recommended. Cuttings root in 10 to 14 days.

Uses: Impatiens can be used in beds, borders, planting strips, and containers. Their mounding habit is beautiful in hanging baskets and planters. Impatiens can be grown indoors in bright, filtered light.

Related varieties: There are many varieties: 'Accent,' 'Dazzler,' 'Impulse,' 'Super Elfin,' and 'Tempo,' to mention a few. Vigorous series such as 'Blitz' or 'Showstopper' are ideal for containers. Double varieties include 'Rosette,' 'Duet,' and 'Confection.'

New Guinea Impatiens

Impatiens species

When a plant hunting expedition went to Southeast Asia, they made significant discoveries. Species impatiens found there are now being developed into varieties quite different from traditional impatiens.

Description: New Guinea impatiens form compact, succulent subshrubs with branches growing 1 to 2 feet tall by summer's end. Leaves are long and narrow, green, bronze, or purple. Flowers, growing up to 2 inches in diameter, are white, pink, lavender, purple, orange, and red.

How to grow: Fertile, moist soil high in organic matter is preferred by New Guinea impatiens. They are more sun-loving than the other impatiens. They will tolerate more sun if their roots are kept moist. Incorporate a slow-release fertilizer into the soil before planting. They should only be planted after the danger of frost has passed and the ground has warmed. Space 9 to 15 inches apart.

Propagation: By seed or by cuttings. Only two varieties of New Guinea impatiens are available from seed so far. Sow 10 to 12 weeks before planting outside. Germinate at 75 to 80° F. Do not cover, since seeds need light to germinate, but mist to keep moist. Cuttings root quickly and easily in 2 to 3 weeks.

Uses: Impatiens should be used in masses of color in beds and borders. Cluster three or more in groups beside garden features. Plant them in containers and in hanging baskets.

Related varieties: 'Tango,' grown from seed, has fluorescent-orange flowers. 'Sunshine' hybrids, grown from cuttings, are a series that include many with variegated foliage and flowers in all colors—white, pink, red, orange, lavender, and purple. They also have bicolors. Look for constellation and meteorological names: 'Cirrus,' 'Gemini,' etc.

Joseph's Coat, Love Lies Bleeding, Prince's Feather

Amaranthus tricolor, A. caudatus

Brightly colored foliage in yellow, red, and orange is the appeal of various ornamental varieties of *A. tricolor*, hence the common name of "Joseph's coat." *A. caudatus* is known as "love lies bleeding" for its brightly colored ropes of flowers in red, white, or bright green.

Description: These tropical foliage and flowering plants with their bright plumage vary in different, visually stimulating ways. Because they grow rapidly in hot weather, choose different amaranthus for specific needs of color and texture.

How to grow: Plant in warm soil after all chance of frost has passed and in full sun to develop the most vibrant color. Amaranthus tolerates poor soil, heat, and drought. Poor drainage or excessively wet soil may cause root rot.

Propagation: By seed. Start indoors at 70° F 6 weeks prior to planting out or sow directly in place.

Uses: Because of its height, *A. tricolor* makes a good background plant. The shorter *A. caudatus* is useful grouped in mid-border. Several plants together will effectively highlight their tassels. They make striking container plants. The flowers may also be cut and dried.

Related species: Prince's feather (*A. cruentus*) has purple or red spikes that will reach 5 feet by season's end.

Related varieties: Plants of *A. tricolor* can grow to 4 feet high and spread 2 feet wide. Varieties include 'Flaming Fountains,' with long, willowy, crimson leaves; 'Joseph's Coat,' with yellow, scarlet, and green foliage; and 'Illumination,' which adds bronze to the previous colors. Varieties of *A. caudatus* are shorter, up to 2 feet high with a 2-foot spread and include 'Green Thumb,' with upright, green spikes; 'Pigmy Torch,' with erect, maroon spikes; and 'Love Lies Bleeding,' with blood-red flowers.

Lantana

Lantana hybrida

These shrubby plants are abundantly covered through the summer with brightly colored blossoms. The garden varieties bear white, yellow, gold, orange, and red flowers; usually the older flowers in each cluster are a different color than the younger ones.

Description: Lantanas are woody shrubs with large, rough leaves. They grow about 3 feet tall and as wide over a summer's growth. When protected against frost, they can grow to 15 feet or more in height over a period of years.

How to grow: Lantana needs full sun and hot weather to perform best. It is actually best in poor soil. It is very frost-sensitive, so plant outdoors after the ground has warmed thoroughly. Space the plants about 18 inches apart. Pinch the tips of plants as soon as they have made 2 sets of leaves and repeat 3 or 4 times. This will promote bushiness. Plants may be dug 6 weeks before frost, cut back, and potted for indoor bloom in sunny locations.

Propagation: By cuttings. For May or June planting outdoors of 4-inch pots, take cuttings in February or early March. For larger hanging baskets, take cuttings in January. Dipping in a rooting hormone speeds rooting. Root under mist or keep from wilting during rooting.

Uses: Lantanas are most often used in containers. They grow well in sunny window boxes, hanging baskets, or patio planters. They can be used in ground beds if soil is not too rich.

Related species: *Lantana montevidensis* is a widely grown, pink-lavender flowering variety. Its growth is more trailing.

Related varieties: 'Confetti' has flowers with pink, white, and red colors intermixed. 'Radiation' has tones of orange and red, while 'Pink Caprice' combines pink and yellow in the same flower clusters. There are many other varieties.

Larkspur, Annual Delphinium

Consolida ambigua

Larkspur resembles the delphinium, with its stately spikes of flowers in cool pastel colors. Formerly lumped with delphiniums, botanists split them off and named them *Consolida*, an old Latin term for "an undetermined plant."

Description: Larkspur grows up to 4 feet tall with delphiniumlike flowers, single or double, evenly spaced around the long stem above lacy, gray-green foliage. Although blue is favored, larkspur also flowers in pink, salmon, rose, lavender, purple, and white.

How to grow: Grow in moist but well-drained soil in full sun. If exposed to high winds, larkspur may need staking. It performs best in cool weather. In Zones 7 to 10, seeds may be sown early enough in the fall so that young plants would bloom early in the spring. In other zones, seeds can be sown late in the fall so that they would germinate in the spring. Remove spent blossoms to encourage bloom.

Propagation: By seed. Sow in place because larkspur does not transplant well. Sow in the fall or as soon as the ground can be worked in the spring. For summer and fall blooms in cool climates, successively sow 2 to 3 weeks apart until mid-May.

Uses: Groups of delphinium backing informal annuals can give a cottage garden look. Group them at the side or at the back of the flower border or center them in island beds to lend height. They're good cut flowers and may be dried for winter bouquets.

Related species: Many of the true perennial delphiniums may be grown as summer annuals. 'Pacific' hybrids are widely grown and hybrids of *Delphinium belladonna* are also planted. Compact hybrids (2 to 3 feet high) grown from seed are 'Blue Springs' and 'Blue Fountains.'

Related varieties: A favorite is the 'Imperial' series that branches freely from the base.

Lisianthus, Prairie Gentian

Eustoma grandiflorum

This native plant of the Midwest to Mexico has come into vogue recently because of widespread breeding efforts. New hybrids have been developed for flowering pot plants, cut flowers, and garden use. The primary color is a bluish-purple, but it also blooms in pink or white.

Description: Prairie gentians grow up to 3 feet tall, are branched, and are surmounted with cup-shaped, poppylike blooms that open wide in full sunlight. Flowers are about 3 inches in diameter. Although most are single-flowered, semi-doubles are also available.

How to grow: Prairie gentians can be grown as annuals by starting them early; otherwise, they are biennials, grown by seeding them the summer before, then wintering them over as small plants in cold frames or heated greenhouses. Grow them in full sun in moist soil. Space 8 to 12 inches apart. Pinch out the growing tips to induce branching and more flowers.

Propagation: By seed. Sow seeds 3 months before planting out when danger of frost has passed. Germination takes 10 to 12 days at 75° F. Because they form a taproot that makes transplanting difficult, prairie gentians should be transplanted to individual pots when they reach the 3-leaf stage. Early growth is slow, picking up when weather warms.

Uses: Grow prairie gentian where you want a strong show of color in moist soils. Because the flower form is so attractive, plant them where they can be viewed close up. They grow well in containers. They are superb as cut flowers.

Related varieties: Varieties include: the 'Yodel' series, with blue, deep blue, mid-blue, lilac, pink, rose, and white flowers. It is also available as a mixture of all colors. The 'Lion' series is semi-double, offered in white, pink, and blue.

Lobelia

Lobelia erinus

Few flowers have the intense blue provided by some varieties of lobelia. They are perennials, but too tender to live over the winter in most parts of the country and are grown as annuals.

Description: These lobelias have small, round leaves and flowers up to ½ inch in diameter. Some varieties are compact and mounding; others are definite trailers. The most prominent flower color is blue, but there are also crimson, pink, and white varieties. The trailing ones will reach 12 to 18 inches by summer's end; the mounding ones grow 6 to 8 inches high.

How to grow: Lobelia grows best in cool areas or where cool nighttime temperatures moderate the weather. They will bloom well in partial shade if their root areas are mulched and kept moist. Space 4 to 6 inches apart in the garden or in containers.

Propagation: By seed. Seeds are tiny and need light to germinate, so they should not be covered. Start plants indoors 10 to 12 weeks before planting outdoors. Seeds germinate in 20 days at 70 to 80° F. Seedling growth is slow, and the early stages should be watched carefully to prevent damping off. A fungicide is recommended. Don't try to separate individual seedlings at transplanting; instead, plant clumps of several seedlings.

Uses: Use the mounding forms for edgings, as pockets in rock gardens, between patio stones, or in the front of taller plantings beside walks and pathways. The trailing varieties can cascade over rock walls and are among the best for containers of all kinds.

Related varieties: Mounding forms include: 'Crystal Palace,' deep blue flowers and bronze foliage; 'Cambridge Blue,' sky-blue flowers; 'Mrs. Clibran,' dark blue with white eyes; and 'Rosamund,' cherry-red. Some trailers are: 'Sapphire,' deep blue with white eyes; 'Blue Cascade,' light blue; and 'White Cascade.'

Lotus Vine, Parrot's Beak

Lotus berthelotti

The scarlet flowers from which the name "parrot's beak" is derived are a short-term bonus from this lovely plant. It's the smoky gray, feathery foliage that makes this plant such a beautiful addition to summer container plantings. A native of the Canary Islands, it's a member of the legume or pea family. It is only hardy in frost-free parts of the United States.

Description: Lotus vine (which is really a trailer) can grow up to 3 feet in length by the end of the season. It has many-branched segments covered with very fine, gray-green leaves. In sun, they're almost iridescent. The blossoms that appear in June or early July are up to 1 inch long with curved petals. They're scarlet to crimson, lightening to an orange-red as they fade.

How to grow: Grow lotus vine in full sun. Normally, it is used in containers and will be satisfied with any commercial potting soil mix. In the wild, it will tolerate summer drought and periods of moisture shortage, but will grow more lushly if given adequate water. Add a slow-release fertilizer to the soil at planting time for continuous feeding during the summer. Space 8 to 12 inches apart in containers.

Propagation: By cuttings. Take cuttings 8 to 10 weeks prior to planting out (after all danger of frost has passed). Strip the foliage off the bottom 1 inch of cuttings and insert in a soil mix. Keep humidity high during rooting. Pinch tips to induce branching.

Uses: Lotus vine is one of the best plants for dressing up mixed container plantings. The trailing habit covers containers, adding color to window boxes, hanging baskets, and planter boxes. Lotus is especially good with white or pastel colors and combined with geraniums of all kinds in planters.

Love-in-a-Mist, Devil in a Bush

Nigella damascena

These frothy, quick-to-bloom annuals add an airy note to garden plantings with their soft colors combining well with other flowers. Nigellas are native to Mediterranean areas.

Description: Love-in-a-mist grows up to 2 feet tall and has many branches. The finely cut foliage is lacy, and the flowers float above the foliage, which is highlighted by large bracts on which the flowers sit. Flowers are most often powder-blue, but there are also pink, rose, and white varieties.

How to grow: Nigella thrives in any sunny location in soil of average fertility or better. Sow the seeds outdoors in the spring as early as the ground can be worked. Thin to a spacing of 5 to 15 inches. For continuous bloom all summer, make successive sowings until early July. Protect them from high winds and stake the plants if necessary.

Propagation: By seed. For earlier bloom, start them indoors 4 to 6 weeks before outdoor planting. Because they are difficult to transplant, start them in peat pots that can be transplanted into the garden, pot and all. Seeds germinate in 10 to 15 days at 65 to 70° F.

Uses: Nigella is a good see-through plant, allowing the plants behind to peek through. Consider using it with other pastels and creamy whites. It's best in informal situations. The seedpods are widely used for winter arrangements. Cut them off after they have ripened and dry them upside down in a dark place.

Related species: *Nigella hispanica* has mid-blue flowers with black centers and red stamens.

Related varieties: 'Persian Jewels' combines the most popular blue with white, pink, rose, mauve, lavender, and purple. 'Miss Jekyll' has semi-double flowers in sky-blue. 'Miss Jekyll Alba' is similar, but with white flowers.

Lupine

Lupinus species

There are many kinds of lupines, both annuals and perennials (some are grown as annuals because they are short-lived in many regions). The most widely planted are hybrids grown under the name of *Lupinus regalis*, which have stout spires of many colors. Lupines are members of the legume or pea family and bear the typical pea-shaped flower.

Description: The best known are Russell hybrids, which, under favorable conditions, can grow up to 5 feet tall. Compact varieties topping out at 18 inches are also available. A rosette of foliage is composed of many leaves resembling bird's feet. The flower stalk appears in late May or early June surrounded with many flowers of varied colors—white, pink, red, blues of many hues, yellow, and apricot. Many have bicolored flowers, usually including white contrasting with another color.

How to grow: The so-called perennial lupines grow best in areas with cool summers and mild winters. Elsewhere, they are best treated as annuals, planted into the ground in spring as soon as the soil can be worked. They resent root disturbance and should be planted out from 4-inch or larger pots in order to bloom the first season. Lupines want full sun; moderately rich, well-drained soil; and continuous moisture. They grow best in acid or neutral soil. The tallest varieties should be planted in areas protected from high winds, or staked to prevent toppling. Plant largest varieties 12 to 15 inches apart; shorter ones in a 3- to 5-inch spacing.

Propagation: By seed. For husky plants, start seeds in January to transplant outdoors as soon as the ground is workable. Since seeds are very hard, soak them overnight or cut a small nick in the seed coat prior to planting. Germination takes 15 to 25 days at 55 to 70° F.

Uses: The tall lupines are unparalleled for bright color in late May and June. They add a vertical note to the mixed border, as well as in planting beds. Plant them in groups of at least three. Use them at the ends or centers of plantings, fronted by lower-growing varieties.

Related species: The Texas bluebonnet (*L. carnosus* or *L. texensis*) is an annual that covers thousands of square miles of southwestern countryside in the spring. Flower color is mostly blue with some whites. Seeds are available. *L. luteus* is a yellow-flowered, fragrant, annual species. The blue lupine (*L. hirsutus*) is an annual variety native to Europe that is sometimes grown in gardens.

Related varieties: The tall Russell varieties are available as separate colors: 'Yellow,' 'White,' 'Red,' 'Pink,' 'Carmine,' as well as bicolors of blue and white, cream and white, and pink and white. Mixtures of all colors are also available. 'Minarette' is a dwarf mixture of colors.

Magic Carpet Plant

Polygonum capitatum

This nonhardy creeping plant makes a lovely ground cover for sun or shade. It deserves to be more widely grown for the carpet it creates over rolling terrain. A member of the buckwheat family, it comes from the Himalaya mountains of Asia.

Description: This charmer creeps across the ground and seldom reaches more than 3 inches in height, but each plant can reach up to 2 feet in diameter from its long trailing stems. Each bright green leaf is marked with a V-shaped purple band. The flowers, lifted above the foliage on short stems, are round, fluffy balls of pink, up to ½ inch in diameter.

How to grow: In frost-free areas, magic carpet plant can make a permanent ground cover. Elsewhere, it is good for covering large amounts of ground quickly. Grow it in either sun or partial shade in average or richer soil that is well drained. Space plants 8 to 10 inches apart for summer coverage. Plant outdoors as soon as all danger of frost has passed. Pinch the tips of small plants to induce branching.

Propagation: For good-sized plants that will grow quickly to cover the ground, start indoors 8 to 10 weeks prior to planting in the garden. Seed germination takes 15 to 25 days at 65 to 75° F.

Uses: Plant it in small pockets for its small, cloverlike blossoms. Use it like any ground cover—underplanted near bushes and shrubs—for providing a carpet of green. Plant it beside walks and pathways or next to ponds or streams. Its trailing stems are especially attractive creeping over rocks or walls. It's also a good trailing plant to use in flowering containers. Plant near the edges so the small stems will cover the maximum outside surface of the container. It's a charming indoor plant in hanging baskets. Give it medium-to-high light and pinch the tips to make it bushy.

Mallow, Cheese

Malva sylvestris

Although in nature it's a biennial and occasionally a perennial, malva is usually grown as an annual in gardens. Related to hollyhocks, this native of Europe is now naturalized in parts of the United States. The purple-pink-lavender flowers are often veined with a darker color.

Description: This mallow grows up to 4 feet tall and has round or kidney-shaped, lobed leaves. The flowers on 2-inch stalks come from the leaf axils of the upper stalk. The flowers are up to 2 inches in diameter.

How to grow: Grow this mallow in full sun. It's indifferent to soil, growing equally well in average and rich fertility. Keep well watered to ensure lush growth. Protect from high winds to prevent toppling. Space plants 10 to 15 inches apart.

Propagation: By seed. Sow seeds in place where plants are to grow. Thin to 10 to 15 inches apart. For earlier growth and bloom, start indoors 6 to 8 weeks prior to planting out after frost danger has passed. Seeds germinate in 10 to 15 days at 70° F. Barely cover seeds; they need light to germinate.

Uses: This mallow can be used in beds and borders. Plant mid-border or at the ends. Use it at the edge of woodlands in full sun. It can be cut and used for arrangements, especially if the entire bloom spike is used in bouquets.

Related species: *Malva nicaeensis* is similar but shorter, growing up to 2½ feet tall, with slightly smaller blooms. *M. verticillata crispa* is a tall species with curled and crisped, round leaves. It grows up to 6 feet tall.

Related varieties: *M. sylvestris* ssp. *mauritiana* has rich purple-pink flowers with dark purple veins. Some of the flowers are loosely doubled.

Flowering Maple

Abutilon hybridum, A. megapoticum variegatum, A. striatum thompsonii

Once considered houseplants, flowering maples are being used increasingly for summer color in the garden. Their common name comes from their leaf shape—roughly maple-shaped. Flowering maples are semiwoody shrubs, hardy only to Zone 9. They'll grow about 2 feet high by summer's end.

Description: *A. megapoticum variegatum* has leaves marked with light and dark green patches, bearing yellow and red flowers with large, dark purple, pollen-bearing anthers. Older plants trail. *A. striatum thompsonii* is upright with orange-salmon flowers. Varieties of *A. hybridum* bear white, yellow, salmon, or purple flowers.

How to grow: Plant in well-drained soil and water only if dry. Incorporate a slow-release fertilizer into the soil before planting. Plant 12 to 15 inches apart. In Zones 9 and 10, flowering maples will benefit from partial shade, otherwise full sun and eastern exposure are preferred. During vigorous growth, pinching tips will encourage branching. Dig and bring indoors before frost.

Propagation: By cuttings or by seed. Start seeds indoors in winter (germination time is 3 to 4 weeks) with bottom heat at 70° F for outdoor bloom. They are also easily propagated from semi-mature cuttings.

Uses: Use in small spaces where the attractive foliage and dainty bells can be viewed close up. They also make ideal container plants especially in raised situations where their flowers can be seen more easily. For indoor use, repot before frost and cut back by half before bringing indoors. Provide at least 4 hours of direct sunlight indoors for good blooming. Pinch tips to induce bushiness.

Related varieties: Varieties from seed include 'Benary's Giant,' with drooping, crimson-rose bells.

Cape Marigold, African Daisy, Star-of-the-Veldt

Dimorphotheca **hybrids**

A member of the composite or daisy family, these are sometimes called *Osteospermum*, depending on which botanist classified closely related plants. They are not closely related to true marigolds.

Description: Cape marigolds grow up to 1 foot tall, in a loose mound heavily covered with flowers during cool seasons or in cool climates. Flowers are 3 to 4 inches in size in yellow, white, salmon, or rose. The reverse sides of the petals are colored in shades of blue or lavender.

How to grow: African daisies thrive in light, sandy soil and will tolerate drought. They prefer cool, dry weather in full sun in coastal or mountain climates. They turn scraggly in hot, humid parts of the country during summer. In such locations, plant them as soon as the ground can be worked for cool season beauty, replacing them later with heat-tolerant plants. They flower best when temperatures are 45 to 50° F. They are good winter annuals (actually semi-hardy perennials) in areas with only a few degrees of frost (Zones 8 to 10). Space 8 to 12 inches apart. Do not fertilize.

Propagation: By seed or by cuttings. Sow outdoors in spring after the last frost or start indoors 6 to 8 weeks in advance of planting out. Seeds germinate in 10 to 15 days at 60 to 70° F.

Uses: Tuck cape marigolds into chinks of rock walls or plant them in sunny rock gardens. Use them for large drifts of color through borders and beds. Plant them at the edges of containers. Cape marigolds combine well with other container plants. They're good cut flowers, too.

Related varieties: 'Starshine' bears flowers of pink, rose, carmine, and white. 'Tetra Pole Star' is a white variety with violet centers. 'Tetra Goliath' is an orange-flowered variety with unusually large blooms.

French Marigold, American Marigold

Tagetes patula, Tagetes erecta

These all-American plants come in such an array of bright colors over a long season that they're a mainstay of gardeners everywhere.

Description: American marigolds can be tall plants, growing up to 36 inches high, although breeding has produced shorter heights. They have large, fully double flowers in yellow, gold, and orange. French marigolds are bushier and more compact with smaller flowers. Their flowers come in many colors and forms. They usually grow no more than 12 inches. Triploids, a cross between French and American marigolds, resemble French marigolds, but have larger flowers.

How to grow: Marigolds grow best in full sun with moist, well-drained soil, although they will tolerate drier conditions. Plant them outdoors as soon as all danger of frost has passed. Space French marigolds 6 to 10 inches apart, Americans 10 to 18 inches apart. They require no deadheading.

Propagation: Seeds may be sown in place. For earlier bloom, start indoors 4 to 6 weeks prior to outdoor planting. Seeds germinate in 5 to 7 days at 65 to 75° F.

Uses: Grow taller ones to the center or rear of beds and borders, or as planting pockets in full sun. Plant them in containers.

Related species: *Tagetes tenuifolia*, or signet marigolds, bear many small, yellow or orange flowers. 'Lemon Gem' and 'Tangerine Gem' are two examples.

Related varieties: The flat-petaled, double, French marigolds include many series: 'Aurora,' 'Sophia,' and 'Early Spice.' Fully double, crested series include 'Boy,' 'Bonanza,' 'Hero,' 'Little Devil,' and 'Janie.' Single-flowered series are 'Disco' and 'Espana.' American marigold series include: 'Inca,' 'Perfection,' 'Voyager,' and 'Discovery.'

Pot Marigold, Field Marigold

Calendula officinalis

These beauties bloom in all shades of white, gold, yellow, and orange. Some varieties have flower petals tipped in contrasting colors. They're known as stalwarts of the cool season garden, growing all winter in Zones 8 to 10.

Description: Cultivated calendulas grow 12 to 24 inches tall with rich green leaves. Plants will spread 12 to 18 inches. Flowers can be single daisies, semi-double, or fully double. Flower size ranges up to 4 inches in newer varieties.

How to grow: Calendulas thrive on poor to medium soil in full sun with moderate moisture. They will survive several degrees of frost, and if properly hardened off, can be planted in the spring as soon as soil is workable. Plant 10 to 15 inches apart. Pick off the spent blooms for continued bloom. For fall bloom, sow seeds in July. In cool damp weather, mildew is occasionally a problem.

Propagation: By seed. For earliest bloom, sow seeds indoors 4 to 6 weeks early at a temperature of 65 to 70° F. Germination takes 10 to 14 days. After transplanting, the seedlings grow in cooler temperatures (50 to 55° F) until planting outside. Seeds can also be sown outdoors when the soil is workable, then thinned to a 10- to 15-inch spacing. For winter bloom in Zones 8 to 10, seeds should be sown in late fall.

Uses: Plant in beds, borders, planting pockets, and containers in full sun. Calendulas also make good long-lasting cut flowers.

Related varieties: The 'Bon Bon Series' has separate shades of yellow and orange, and a mixture that also includes apricot and soft yellow. The 'Fiesta Gitana Series' bears semi-double flowers in yellow, orange, and a mixture, with most of the flowers having dark centers. Taller 'Pacific Beauty' have large flowers on strong stems and are good for cutting.

Meadow Foam, Fried Eggs

Limnanthes douglasii

Here's a West Coast native with many of the attributes of flowers from Mediterranean climates. As the weather warms, rain triggers germination, and the flowers quickly come into bloom. It's at its best for spring bloom. *Limnanthes* comes for the Greek word for "marsh." "Fried eggs" (sunny side up) typifies its look of a great yellow center surrounded by white.

Description: Meadow foam grows up to 1 foot tall with many branches, giving it the appearance of a low mound or bush. It has finely divided, green leaves. The flowers are up to 1 inch in diameter. Typically, they are golden-yellow surrounded by white, but in some forms the petals are all yellow—still others are all white or white with pink veins.

How to grow: Meadow foam prefers full sun and moist, medium-rich soil. In coastal or mountain areas where the summers remain cool, it will continue blooming all summer. In other climates, enjoy it for spring bloom before weather gets torrid. In nearly frost-free areas of Zones 8, 9, and 10, seeds may be sown in the fall and allowed to overwinter for earliest spring bloom. Space plants 4 to 6 inches apart. Plants will reseed for next year.

Propagation: By seed. Sow seeds in fall in mild climates or as soon as ground can be worked elsewhere. For earlier bloom, start seeds indoors 6 to 8 weeks prior to planting out. Seeds germinate in 14 to 21 days at 65 to 70° F.

Uses: Grow it in rock gardens, near pools or ponds, and along walks and pathways. Use it as an edging for beds or in front of borders.

Related varieties: Named varieties of the typical form are not available. Special forms include: *Limnanthes douglasii sulphurea*, with all-yellow flowers; *L. d. nivea*, all white; and *L. d. rosea*, white flowers veined with rose.

Melampodium

Melampodium paludosum

Large, bright green leaves have many perky, little yellow, daisylike flowers peering forth all summer long. A member of the daisy family, it hails originally from Mexico and Central America. *Melampodium paludosum* is one of 36 species in the genus. The name *melampodium* comes from the Greek and literally translated means "black foot," referring to the color of the stalks.

Description: Melampodium forms a vigorous, bushy plant 10 to 15 inches high in the garden. It will be 15 to 20 inches in diameter by the end of summer. The leaves are large and rough. They are paired, and each pair is at right angles to the next. The flowers are small, up to 1 inch in diameter.

How to grow: Melampodium needs full sun. An average-to-rich, moist but well-drained soil is satisfactory. Plants should not be allowed to dry out. Plant outdoors as soon as all danger of frost has passed and the ground is warm. Space 10 to 15 inches apart.

Propagation: By seed. Sow seeds indoors 7 to 10 weeks prior to planting outdoors. Seeds germinate in 7 to 10 days at 65° F. For easier transplanting, grow in peat pots that can be transplanted into the garden, pot and all.

Uses: Plant melampodium where you want some contrast between flowers and foliage. Melampodium can be used as a sunny ground cover or be planted in rock gardens in the front of flower borders. Grow in window boxes, patio or deck planters, and in hanging baskets.

Related varieties: 'Medaillon' is the most planted variety. It grows up to 20 inches tall and as wide, covered all summer with small, golden-yellow flowers.

Mignonette

Reseda odorata

Here's a plant of little apparent virtue until a bit of its sweet aroma wafts your way. Its wonderful aroma has brought it a long way from its native home in North Africa to its place in the gardens of kings, presidents, and common folks.

Description: Mignonette is a spreading plant that grows up to 2 feet high and is covered with spikes of many small flowers—greenish-white or yellowish-green in color. The flowers are very fragrant and are able to perfume large areas.

How to grow: Mignonette grows best in well-drained, moderately rich, slightly alkaline soil. It does best in partial shade in the hottest parts of the country. Transplant it into the garden as soon as the soil can be worked. Space 10 inches apart. Pinch the tips of young plants to encourage branching. Mignonette reseeds itself in the garden.

Propagation: By seed. In mild climates, seeds can be sown in place the previous fall. Otherwise, sow in the spring and thin to the proper spacing. In other areas of the country, an early bloom can be developed by sowing seeds indoors 5 to 6 weeks prior to planting out. Do not cover seeds; they need light to germinate. Seed germination takes 5 to 10 days at 70° F. Seedlings do not like transplanting; grow them in peat pots that can be planted in the garden, pot and all. Because there is a short season of bloom, repeat sowings for several weeks for continuous flowering.

Uses: Plant mignonette where the spicy scent will be noticed—tucked into a corner of the flower bed, near paths and walks, and under windows. Do the same with containers on decks, porches, and patios. Cut flowers maintain the same fragrance.

Related varieties: 'Fragrant Beauty' has red-tipped, lime-green flowers. 'Red Monarch' has more red in the flowers. Both are very fragrant.

Monkey Flower

Mimulus hybridus

The name "monkey flower" comes from the physical appearance of the flowers or from the name *mimulus*, stemming from a root word meaning "mimic." In either case, the low-growing flowers are a good way to brighten up the shade.

Description: Mimulus forms neat, compact mounds seldom reaching over 10 inches in height, but spreading wider. The open-faced flowers are frequently painted with contrasting color markings on the background of yellow, pink, red, burgundy, and other warm-hued tones.

How to grow: Mimulus is not frost-tolerant, but prefers cool weather. It will thrive in moist soil, even in boggy conditions with occasional flooding; it will also bloom beautifully in dappled shade. Plant out after all danger of frost has passed, spacing plants 6 inches apart. Work a slow-release fertilizer into the soil at planting for feeding all summer. Where keeping an even soil moisture level is a problem, a mulch is suggested. Deadheading spent flowers occasionally will improve their appearance.

Propagation: By seed. Sow seeds indoors 10 to 12 days prior to planting outdoors. Do not cover the fine seeds. Germination takes 7 to 14 days at 70 to 75° F.

Uses: Mimulus thrives nears ponds, pools, and streams. Grow it in shady borders and, because of its small stature, in front of a border or as an edging. Mimulus is also a perfect container plant. It will bloom indoors under cool conditions (and high indoor light).

Related varieties: 'Calypso' is a mixture of many colors of 2-inch flowers, both solids and marked bicolors. 'Malibu' is another mixture in shades of red, yellow, and orange. 'Viva' is a single variety with yellow flowers marked with bright red.

Morning Glory Vine

Ipomoea nil, purpurea, tricolor

A group of twining vines with bell-shaped flowers, they have also become intertwined botanically under the name "morning glory." The name comes from the flowers, which last a single day. These rapidly growing vines are closely related to the sweet potato. Flowers are white, blue, pink, purple, red, and multicolored. There are even double forms. Because they're quick, easy, and dependably colorful, they're the most popular annual vine.

Description: The vines grow quickly to 10 feet or more only two months after seeds sprout. The leaves are heart-shaped, and the flowers are normally open from dawn to midmorning, but new varieties will stay open longer, especially on overcast days.

How to grow: Requirements are undemanding. Morning glories will thrive in full sun in any soil, especially if it is not too fertile or too moist. Sow the seeds outdoors when all danger of frost has passed. Provide support. Because they grow by twining, they need extra help if planted around large posts. Plant 8 to 12 inches apart.

Propagation: By seed. Soak the seeds in water for 24 hours before planting to speed germination. In the North, earlier bloom can be achieved by starting indoors in peat pots 4 to 6 weeks before planting out. Germination takes 5 to 7 days at 70 to 80° F. Transplant the peat pots to the garden—pot and all—without disturbing the roots.

Uses: Morning glories are splendid for enhancing fences or for covering up eyesores. They will rapidly cover fences, arches, pergolas, and trellises or can be made into their own garden feature with stakes and twine. They don't have to grow up. They're just as effective as trailers from hanging baskets and window boxes.

Related species: Moon flower (*Ipomoea alba*) has large, fragrant, white flowers that open in the evening and close before midday. *Convovulus tricolor,* known as "dwarf morning glory," forms bushy plants with pink, blue, purple, and rose flowers. 'Blue Ensign' is a selection with blue flowers and contrasting yellow and white centers. *Evolvulus glomeratus* is a prostrate plant, 10 to 15 inches in diameter, with many small, morning glorylike flowers in bright blue. 'Blue Bird' is one selection.

Related varieties: Most famous is 'Heavenly Blue' for refreshing azure color. 'Scarlet Star' has a strong pattern of red and white. 'Pearly Gates' has large, white flowers. 'Early Call Mixture' has white, pink, crimson, lavender, blue, and violet flowers.

Nasturtium

Tropaeolum majus

Nearly every kid who's been near a garden has grown a nasturtium. And today's salad-conscious adult has certainly enjoyed the peppery tang of nasturtium leaves and flowers among the greens. A native of Mexico, they're among our garden favorites.

Description: Nasturtiums started out as vigorous, vinelike plants, and many of them still are. Breeders have altered them so that some are now bushy, compact plants only 12 inches tall. The leaves are nearly round. Flowers with bright, open faces have long spurs behind them.

How to grow: Don't overdo the care with nasturtiums. They need full sun in a dry, sandy, well-drained soil. They're at their best in regions with cool, dry summers, although they will grow elsewhere, too. Sow seeds outdoors in the ground after the last frost. Depending on variety, space them 8 to 12 inches apart. The vigorous varieties can only be trained upward by tying them to supports; they have no means of attachment. Nasturtiums will reseed vigorously but will not be the same colors you planted.

Propagation: By seed. Seed germination takes 7 to 12 days at 65° F. Do not cover the seeds; they need light to germinate.

Uses: Dwarf varieties are good for flower borders, beds, edging paths, and walks. Vining varieties can be tied to fences or posts and trailed from window boxes, hanging baskets, or other containers. Nasturtiums are good cut flowers, too.

Related species: *Tropaeolum peregrinum,* or canary creeper, is a vigorous vine with bright yellow flowers.

Related varieties: 'Dwarf Double Jewel,' in separate colors and a mix, has light yellow, gold, orange, rose, crimson, and brownish-red flowers. It grows 1 foot high. 'Double Gleam' grows to 3 feet with similar flower colors. 'Climbing Mixed' will grow to 6 feet.

Nemesia

Nemesia strumosa

Nemesias are spectacular in cool, maritime areas or mountain gardens where nights remain cool throughout summer. In other places, enjoy them early since they fade in the hot, humid days of summer. They are originally from South Africa. They resemble snapdragons and linaria, to which they're related.

Description: Nemesias grow from 1 to 2 feet tall, with sparsely branched plants. They grow erect, with the flowers carried in large clusters at the top. There's a wide color range, including yellow, orange, brown, pink, red, and lavender-blue.

How to grow: Nemesias like fertile, well-drained soil and prefer full sun, although they will tolerate partial shade. Transplant started plants after the last frost date. Space them 6 inches apart. Pinch the tips of seedlings to increase branching.

Propagation: By seed. Sow seeds indoors 4 to 6 weeks before the last frost date. Seeds germinate in 7 to 14 days at 55 to 70° F. In areas with cool, dry summers, seeds can be sown outdoors as soon as the ground can be worked for later bloom that will continue until fall.

Uses: Use them for edgings, in rock gardens and walls, and for borders. They're splendid container plants and make good cut flowers, too.

Related species: *Nemesia versicolor* is a similar, more compact species. It has a variety of colors including truer blues. 'Blue Gem' is a very compact variety growing to 10 inches high with blue flowers.

Related varieties: 'Carnival' is a mixture of colors on plants that grow up to 2 feet tall. 'Tapestry,' in addition to a wide range of colors, has a good balance of blue and white. 'Fire King' is a scarlet-flowered variety.

Nicotiana, Flowering Tobacco

Nicotiana alata grandiflora

Related to the tobacco plants of commerce, flowering tobacco has been bred for its ornamental value. The flowers are in a variety of colors, including an intriguing lime-green. In addition, flowers have a rich, pervasive scent.

Description: A low rosette of large, flat leaves supports the tall flowering stems covered with star-shaped flowers. Flower colors include white, pink, maroon, lavender, green, red, and yellow. The plants grow up to 3 feet tall.

How to grow: Nicotiana grows best in fertile, humus-rich, moist, well-drained soil in partial shade, or full sun in cooler areas. They are tough plants that will tolerate high temperatures. Before planting out, incorporate a slow-release fertilizer in the soil. Transplant to the garden when all danger of frost has passed, spacing 8 to 12 inches apart.

Propagation: By seed. In areas with a long growing season, seeds may be sown in place, thinning the seedlings to the right spacing. Elsewhere, start the plants indoors 6 to 8 weeks prior to planting out. Seeds germinate in 10 to 20 days at 70° F. Don't cover seeds; they need light to germinate.

Uses: Nicotiana is a plant that can give much-needed height to beds and borders. Group them in clusters for more impact. They're also good for containers.

Related species: *Nicotiana sylvestris* is a very fragrant species with white flowers. It grows up to 4 feet tall.

Related varieties: The most popular series is 'Nicki' hybrids with separate colors of 'White,' 'Rose,' and 'Pink,' as well as a mixture. 'Limelight' is a lime-green variety. More compact varieties growing up to 18 inches are the 'Domino' series. Included: 'White,' 'Purple,' 'Red,' 'Lime-Green,' and 'Pink with White Eye,' as well as a mixture.

Nierembergia, Cup Flower

Nierembergia hippomanica violacae

The name "Cup Flower," although not much used, refers to the shape of the flower, which is somewhat like an open-faced bowl. Native to Central and South America, they are tender perennials grown like annuals in most of the country. In frost-free areas, they will winter over with good drainage.

Description: Nierembergia has attractive thin, narrow leaves topped at the ends with bluish or purple flowers. A small yellow spot in the center of each flower highlights the display. The plants grow outward rather than up, to 6 inches high, and will spread a foot.

How to grow: Grow nierembergia in full sun in well-drained soil with adequate moisture. Medium fertility is adequate to grow them well. Flowers hold their color without fading in full sun. Transplant to the garden when all danger of frost has passed. Pinch them to encourage more branching and a higher production of flowers. For full coverage, plant them 5 to 6 inches apart.

Propagation: By seed. Sow seeds indoors 10 to 12 weeks prior to planting in the garden after the last frost. Seeds germinate in 14 to 21 days at 70 to 75° F. Plants will not grow rapidly until the soil is warm.

Uses: Grow nierembergia as a flowering ground cover in full sun, massed in large patches or beds. It's an ideal edging plant for beds and borders, traveling along paths and walkways with ease. It's also a good plant for rock gardens. Use it in window boxes, hanging baskets, and patio planters, usually with other plants for height and mass.

Related species: *Nierembergia repens* is a creeping species with creamy white flowers.

Related varieties: 'Purple Robe' is the only variety widely available. It has been selected for uniformity and has glowing violet-blue flowers.

None So Pretty

Silene armeria

Small patches of sticky fluid on the stems of these flowers entangle flies and are the reason for the common name. A native of southern Europe, it's now naturalized in parts of North America. The most prevalent color of these annual plants is pink, but there is a white-flowered one, too.

Description: The plants grow a clumplike rosette with narrow leaves and flowering stems rising 1 to 2 feet tall. The many flowers are in branched clusters, with each flower about ¾ inch in diameter. The 5-petaled flowers faintly resemble a star.

How to grow: Grow silene in full sun in ordinary garden soil with good drainage. Transplant well-hardened plants to the garden as soon as the ground is workable in the spring. Space plants 6 to 9 inches apart.

Propagation: By seed. Sow seeds indoors 8 to 10 weeks before transplanting to the garden. Seed germination takes 15 to 20 days at 70° F.

Uses: Their modest size adapts well to rock gardens and in planting pockets. Use them in beds and borders, planting them near the front for the best show. Silenes bloom over a long season and look good in mixed plantings and old-fashioned cottage gardens. They'll also grow well in containers, preferably combined with other flowers with more substance. However, the airy stems with small clusters of flowers will give an open look to the container garden. They are not long-lasting as cut flowers.

Related species: *Silene gallica* ssp. *quinque-vulnera* has white flowers with ruby-red centers. This plant grows 12 to 18 inches high. *Silene pendula* has drooping sprays of flowers in pink, shell pink, rose, and white. It grows up to 12 inches high.

Ornamental Corn

Zea mays

The same corn species that brings the world field corn, popcorn, and sweet corn has turned up some ornamental varieties that are worth growing in the garden for their statuesque beauty. Corn belongs to the grass family, a widely diversified group that includes bluegrass and bamboo.

Description: A single seed of corn grows a tall stalk with long, broad leaves topped by a tassel. Pollen from the tassel fertilizes the ears of corn growing from the stalk below. It can grow up to 10 feet tall.

How to grow: Corn needs rich, fertile soil and full sun. The soil must be well drained and moist. Wait to plant corn until after the last frost-free date and the soil is warm. Plant seeds 1 inch deep. Space plants 6 to 15 inches apart. Corn forms a series of brace roots to support it, so it will not need staking.

Propagation: By seed.

Uses: Corn is tall and requires space to accommodate it. It's useful as a fast-growing screen and as a plant for the back of the border. Ears of ornamental corn are used in many kinds of dried arrangements—from door hangings to centerpieces.

Related varieties: Some corn are grown for their ornamental leaves. *Zea mays gracillima variegata* is a dwarf (3 to 4 feet high) with leaves having long stripes of white. *Z. m. japonica variegata* and *Z. m. j. quadricolor* are tall, with long stripes of yellow, white, or pink running lengthwise on the leaves. Corn grown for its unusual ears include: 'Rainbow,' whose ears have kernels of deep red, yellow, orange, and blue and 'Strawberry Ornamental Popcorn,' bearing small ears with cranberry-colored kernels. It pops like conventional corn but has flecks of ruby-red throughout.

Ornamental Cabbage, Ornamental Kale

Brassica oleracea

The fancy-leaved cousins of our familiar vegetables make a bold statement in the cool season garden. In fact, the ornamental forms are edible, too, but the cabbage is bitter, and when the white, pink, red, and purple leaves are cooked, they turn an unappetizing gray. Tolerant of mild frosts, they're colorful all winter in mild climates.

Description: Bold, round plants whose center leaves (not flowers) color up in cool or cold weather, ornamental cabbage and kale grow 18 to 24 inches in diameter and can grow 18 to 24 inches tall.

How to grow: Their primary use is in the fall because the period of cool weather in spring after hard freezes cease is too short. Grow in large pots in a soil mix and feed weekly with a water-soluble fertilizer as recommended on the package. Transplant to the garden or display container in September. Before transplanting, remove tatty bottom leaves. Plant into the ground so that the crown of leaves is flush with the soil surface (roots will grow along the buried stem).

Propagation: By seed. Sow 6 weeks in advance of outdoor planting at 65° F. Do not cover the cabbage seeds since light aids germination. Conversely, cover kale seeds with ¼ inch of soil.

Uses: Kale or cabbage are best planted in areas where you can peer into the center—on slopes, doorsteps, decks, and patios. They're also successful in ground beds and in large plantings.

Related varieties: 'Dynasty Series' cabbage in pink, red, or white have semi-waved leaves. Ornamental kale in red or white include: 'Chidori Series,' heavily fringed and especially uniform, and the 'Peacock Series,' which is more compact than others.

Ornamental Peppers

Capsicum species

Ornamental peppers are the only summer annuals grown primarily for the attractiveness of their fruit. That, combined with their contrast of foliage and form, is what makes them popular in the summer garden.

Description: Ornamental peppers grow into small bushes 12 to 18 inches high and as wide. Their dark green leaves are topped by bright-colored fruits that form in July and hold on the plant until frost. Depending on variety, fruits may be red, purple, yellow, or orange; the shapes range from conical to slim and tapered. There are even twisted forms. The small, white flowers that appear prior to the fruit are pretty but inconspicuous.

How to grow: Ornamental peppers prefer full sun in rich, well-drained soil and perform best in hot weather. They're remarkably drought-tolerant, but will grow better if watered when soil becomes dry. A slow-release fertilizer should be incorporated before planting. Plant when the soil is warm and the weather has settled down.

Propagation: By seed. Sow seeds 8 weeks prior to planting out after last frost date. Cover seeds, germinating at temperatures above 70° F. Germination time is approximately 12 days. Sow in June or July for potted plants in late fall.

Uses: Bright-colored fruits on glossy, green plants decorate borders or bed edges. Ornamental peppers have been used traditionally as an indoor pot plant for holiday enjoyment.

Related varieties: 'Fireworks' is a variety whose cream-colored, cone-shaped fruits turn a brilliant red. 'Holiday Cheer's' fruits start out cream-colored, then turn orange and bright red with all colors mixed on the plant. 'Holiday Flame,' an F_1 hybrid, has tapered, yellow fruit that turns red. Fruits of F_1 hybrid 'Masquerade' start out purple, then turn consecutively yellow, orange, and red.

Pansy

Viola x *wittrockiana*

Pansies are the ultimate in cool season color, blooming until weather turns torrid. They are related to violets.

Description: Pansies grow on sprawling plants that produce flowers continuously as they grow. Flowers range from 2 inches in diameter up to giants of 5 inches or more. Some have clear colors, but many have the unique faces that are so appealing to kids of all ages. The color range is complete.

How to grow: In mild winter areas, plant as soon as the weather cools in late summer. Even areas with short freezes can enjoy winter pansies; once the weather warms, they'll start opening blossoms. Elsewhere, enjoy them for a short season in the spring. Plant in the garden as soon as the ground can be worked. Space 6 to 9 inches apart. If plants become lank and leggy, shear back halfway to force new growth and bloom. Pansies prefer full sun and cool, moist soil. A bit of shade will help them extend the season in hot climates.

Propagation: By seed. Start seeds 6 to 8 weeks prior to planting out. They will germinate in 10 to 15 days at 68° F. Do not cover seeds; they need light to germinate.

Uses: Plant them anywhere you want spots of color. They are suitable for the front of borders and beds, in small groups among other flowers, in cottage garden plantings, and in containers.

Related species: Several varieties of violas, which are derived from *Viola cornuta* and *V. tricolor* include 'King Henry,' deep violet with a yellow eye; 'Helen Mount,' often called 'Johnny Jump Up' for its yellow and violet-faced flower; and 'Prince John,' a clear yellow.

Related varieties: The largest flowers of all are in the 'Super Majestic Giant' series. 'Majestic Giants' are somewhat smaller. The most widely planted include these series: 'Crown,' 'Crystal Bowl,' 'Imperial,' 'Maxim,' and 'Universal.'

Perilla, Beefsteak Plant

Perilla frutescens

A member of the mint family, its foliage and stems have a pungent fragrance when the leaves or stems are crushed. It is widely used as a flavoring in Oriental cuisines and can be used to dye rice pink.

Description: Perilla has the square stems typical of mint family members. The oval leaves can be green, purple, or bronzy, although the most common are a deep purple. They also have a most attractive, metallic sheen. The leaves are deeply veined and crinkled, adding to its attractiveness. Plants can grow as tall as 3 to 4 feet. Flowers are not noteworthy and appear at the end of summer.

How to grow: Perilla will grow equally well in sun or in shade, but low light will create a lankier plant. Average garden soil is satisfactory. Since they are tender annuals, plant them in the garden after all danger of frost has passed, spacing them 12 to 15 inches apart. Pinch the tips once or twice to form a bushier plant.

Propagation: By seed or cuttings. Sow seeds outdoors after the last frost date. Thin to the desired spacing when the seedlings are 3 or 4 inches tall. For larger plants earlier, sow seeds indoors 4 to 6 weeks prior to transplanting into the garden. Because perillas are difficult to transplant, grow them in peat pots to prevent root disturbance when transplanting. Seeds germinate in 15 to 20 days at 65 to 75° F. Cuttings root quickly and easily, even in water. Plants in the garden will self-sow readily.

Uses: Plant it in beds or borders. Use it as a ribbon to contrast with other foliage and flower colors. Its bushy habit makes a good edging for pathways and along walks. Try it as a low hedge.

Related variety: 'Crispa' has attractively curled leaves and grows 2 to 3 feet tall.

Petunia

Petunia x hybrida

Anyone who's been close to a garden is familiar with petunias, a longtime favorite for undiminished color through a long season. Actually tender perennials, they will flower through the winter in nearly frost-free climates. The name "petunia" comes from a South American word for "tobacco," to which they're related along with tomatoes and potatoes. A plant that has long had the eye of breeders, petunias have flowers with charming variations—open bells, crisped, curled, waved, and doubled up into fluffy balls. The enormous color range even includes a yellow.

Description: Garden petunias are divided into two types: multifloras and grandifloras. Each has single and double forms, with grandiflora petunias being larger in each case. Recently, the distinction has become blurred as seed companies have introduced larger-flowered multiflora petunias named 'floribundas.' Always more flowerful and weather-tolerant in the garden than their larger cousins, they were never as popular as the bigger-flowered kinds. Now these new hybrid 'floribundas' are capturing the hearts of gardeners everywhere.

How to grow: Well-drained soil in full sun suits petunias best. They grow well in cool temperatures and will stand a few degrees of frost if plants have been well-hardened before planting. Incorporate a slow-release fertilizer into the soil before planting. Space petunias 12 inches apart. To promote more branching and increased bloom, shear plants back halfway in midsummer. Deadheading is extremely important—as the plants set seed, flowering is greatly reduced.

Propagation: By seed. Start seeds indoors 10 to 12 weeks prior to planting outdoors. Seeds are very fine and can be more evenly sown by mixing thoroughly with a pinch of sugar. Do not cover the seeds as they need light to germinate. Seeds germinate in 10 to 12 days at 70 to 75° F.

Uses: Beds, borders, walkways, paths, containers—all will accommodate an abundance of petunias. Some varieties are especially recommended for containers, since they mound up and billow over the edges. The multifloras (and 'floribundas') are especially recommended for mass plantings because they give the most flowers per plant, nearly undaunted by drenching rains and high winds. The intricate, double varieties are probably best in containers for greatest enjoyment of their complex flowers. Petunias also make good, informal cut flowers.

Related varieties: Grandifloras: 'Super Cascades,' 'Super Magics,' 'Falcons,' 'Ultras,' and 'Flashes.' All of these are series petunias and are available in many colors—some are veined. Multifloras: 'Madness,' 'Carpet,' and 'Celebrity' are three of the newer series with larger flowers and good garden habits.

Annual Phlox, Texas Pride

Phlox drummondii

These bright-colored plants originally hail from Texas, but breeders have civilized them to be some of the most dependable garden performers. The name *Phlox* comes from the Greek word meaning "flame," identifying its bright colors.

Description: Annual phloxes grow from 6 inches to 1½ feet tall. The flowers are in large clusters of many colors and many shapes. Colors include pink, red, rose, white, lavender, scarlet, crimson, and yellow.

How to grow: Annual phloxes grow best in well-drained, sandy soil, high in organic matter. They require full sun and must receive continuous moisture during the growing season. Good air movement around the plants will prevent mildew. Plant in the garden as soon as the danger of frost has passed. Space 6 inches apart. Pinch the tips to encourage branching. At midsummer, shear the plants back halfway to reinvigorate flowering.

Propagation: By seed. Sow plants outdoors where they are to grow after the last frost is due. Thin to the desired spacing. For earlier bloom, start plants indoors 4 to 6 weeks before setting out. Seeds germinate in 15 to 20 days at 55 to 65° F. Transplant in clumps of several plants to get a full color range.

Uses: Grow phlox in beds or at the front of borders. Use them as edgings. Intermix them with other flowers in informal plantings and cottage gardens. Phlox are good container plants and hold well in water when cut.

Related varieties: 'Petticoat Mix' are very dwarf with a mix of all colors. 'Cecily' is a mixture with a high number of bicolors with contrasting eyes. It is also a dwarf variety. 'Tall Finest Mixed' has large flower heads on plants up to 20 inches tall. 'Twinkle,' an award winner, is a mix of ringed, pointed, starlike flowers.

Pocketbook Plant

Calceolaria herbeofruticosa

The shape of the flower, resembling a little pouch, is the origin of both the common name and the botanical name of this plant. It comes from the Latin *calceolus* or "slipper."

Description: Flowers appear like clusters of small grapes, although they're held upright rather than trailing and cover the foliage when in full bloom. In their preferred cool climates, they bloom all summer but can be used for fall, winter, and spring bloom in frost-free areas. Their ultimate height is 8 to 12 inches by 10 inches wide.

How to grow: Pocketbook plant grows best in moist soil with partial protection from intense summer sun. For spring and fall use, full sun will increase flowering. To induce repeat flowering, cut back plants when blossoms fade.

Propagation: By seed or by cuttings. Sow seeds 6 to 8 weeks prior to last frost without covering. They germinate in 8 to 18 days at 60° F. They may also be sown outdoors. Seedlings must be thinned to 6 inches apart.

Uses: Plant them near water—by stream banks, at pool edges, or near bogs and moist woodlands in partial shade. So long as their roots are kept moist, they will also make good container plants.

Related species: Good for the partially shaded rock garden is *Calceolaria falklandia,* a dwarf, tufted native of the Falkland Islands with purple spotted, primrose-yellow flowers. It survives winter only in frost-free gardens. *Calceolaria mexicana* is an annual with typical yellow flowers that bloom all summer.

Related varieties: 'Goldcrest,' 'Golden Bunch,' and 'Midas' are all sunshine-yellow in color. 'Goldcrest' has larger flowers than the others.

California Poppy

Escholtzia californica

California hillsides are covered in spring with the golden-orange of California poppies. Gardeners now have a choice of color—white, rose, scarlet, crimson, or salmon.

Description: Perennials in mild winter areas, California poppies have finely cut, blue-green foliage in contrast to silky flower cups on slender, wiry stems 12 to 15 inches tall.

How to grow: The best planting location for California poppies is sandy, slightly alkaline soil in full sun. They tolerate poor and dry soils as well. In all but Zones 8, 9, and 10, treat them as annuals that bloom best during the cool weather. In cool seasons and maritime climates, they will continue blooming all summer if dead flowers are picked off.

Propagation: California poppies are tap-rooted plants that don't transplant well, so they should be sown in place. In mild winter areas, this is best done in the fall, as small plants will winter over for earliest spring bloom. Elsewhere, sow as early in the spring as the ground can be worked. (If you want to start them indoors, transplant before the taproot is established.) Seeds will germinate in 4 to 10 days when the soil temperature is at 60° F. Water well.

Uses: Grow them in rock walls or rock gardens or as part of naturalized meadow plantings. Reseeding will occur and the offspring of hybrids will revert to the golden-orange colors of their ancestors.

Related varieties: 'Aurantica Orange' is the golden-orange color of the original, although the flowers are larger. 'Ballerina' is composed of semi-double and double flowers in yellow, rose, pink, scarlet, and orange. 'Milky White' is a creamy white selection. 'Thai Silk Pink Shades' has flowers with petals enhanced by wavy edges and fluted form.

Horned Poppy, Sea Poppy

Glaucium flavum

This flower is a native of maritime Europe, North Africa, and eastern Asia. It is also naturalized in parts of North America. Although each flower only lasts a day, the succession of bloom lasts for several weeks.

Description: Several branched stems grow from a rosette of leaves. The crinkly, gray-green leaves also appear on the stems and below each flower. The golden-yellow flowers are open and about 2 inches in diameter. Occasionally, there are orange or red flowers. The roots of the horned poppy are poisonous.

How to grow: Horned poppies need to be grown in full sun in well-drained soil. Space 12 to 18 inches apart. The easiest way to grow them is seeding where they are to bloom and thinning them to the desired spacing.

Propagation: By seed. Glaucium can be grown as a biennial by sowing seeds in the ground the previous fall. For earlier bloom, sow indoors 8 to 10 weeks prior to planting in the garden, after danger of frost has passed. Germination takes 8 to 15 days at 60 to 65° F. Transplant the seedlings to individual pots when three leaves have formed, but before the taproot has developed. Then transplant to the garden without disturbing the root system.

Uses: Plant in clusters in mid-border or grow them at the sides. Use them at the end of a path, or at the corners of beds. The contrast of the gray-green foliage should be mixed with other greens, including chartreuse. The dramatic seedpods can be used in dried arrangements.

Related species: A showy, red-flowered species is *Glaucium grandiflorum,* native to the Middle East. The poppies are large and held well above the olive-green foliage.

Iceland Poppy

Papaver nudicaule

The glistening, translucent flowers of Iceland poppies are a glowing sight when backlit by the sun. The petals look like tissue paper or crinkled silk. Their spring and early summer splendor in warm parts of the country can be enjoyed throughout the summer in cooler climates. They're short-lived perennials that are best started fresh each year.

Description: A rosette of thin, narrow leaves forms the base. The tall, slender stems are topped by flowers virtually in all colors of the rainbow but blue, with many hues in between. The ring of prominent yellow stamens enhances the colorful blooms. Stem height varies widely from 1 to 2 feet. There are semi-double forms as well.

How to grow: Iceland poppies prefer full sun and a fertile, well-drained soil; otherwise, their requirements are not demanding. Early flowers during cool weather will be the largest. To encourage continued flowering, remove seed heads when they form.

Propagation: By seed. Seeds sown indoors in January will bloom the first season. Plants may also be started the previous summer and overwintered in the garden. In mild winter areas, bloom can start in the winter. Seeds germinate in 10 to 15 days at 55° F. Poppies are tap-rooted plants that do not transplant easily once the tap root is formed. Grow in peat pots and transplant into the garden, pot and all.

Uses: A whole bed of poppies is spectacular. They can also be grown as clumps, groups, or ribbons of plants in mid-border. They're especially beautiful backed by the foliage of hedges or other green plants. They also make good cut flowers. Cut the flowers in early morning just as the buds are showing color, sear the cut ends in an open flame or plunge the stems in hot (not boiling) water for a few moments.

Related species: *Papaver rhoeas,* the Shirley poppy, is the cultivated form of the Flanders poppy, a deep scarlet with black centers. There are many new forms including doubles in pink, white, rose, salmon, as well as red. 'Mother of Pearl' is a selection of pastel shades including gray, blue, lilac, dusty pink, and bicolors.

Related varieties: 'Wonderland' series offers separate colors of white, orange, yellow, pink, and a mix. They're more compact than most, blooming on 1-foot stems. 'Oregon Rainbows' are a mixture of exceptionally large-flowered Iceland poppies, including peach, apricot, cream, picotee bicolors, green, and lavender, as well as more conventional colors.

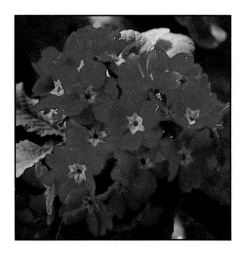

Mexican Tulip Poppy

Hunnemannia fumariaefolia

This Mexican native is a tender perennial grown as an annual in most of the United States. Named for John Hunneman, an English bookseller and plant collector, it's a member of the poppy family, and will bloom all summer through autumn with its sprightly, yellow, poppylike flowers.

Description: Mexican tulip poppy grows from 1 to 2 feet tall. The finely divided leaves are a handsome, blue-gray color. The long-stalked flowers are yellow, 2 to 3 inches in diameter, with bright orange stamens. There is also a double form.

How to grow: Mexican tulip poppies must have full sun to grow and bloom well, and they tolerate drought. Any garden soil is satisfactory as long as it is well-drained. In frost-free or nearly frost-free areas of Zones 9 and 10, it will live as a perennial. In other areas, plant in the spring as soon as danger of frost has passed. Space 10 to 12 inches apart.

Propagation: By seed. Like so many members of the poppy family, it forms a taproot that makes it difficult to transplant. Sow seeds outdoors in place after frost danger has passed. Thin the seedlings to desired spacing. For earlier bloom, start indoors 4 to 6 weeks prior to planting outside. Germinate at 70 to 75° F, which will take 15 to 20 days. When seedlings have three leaves, transplant to individual peat pots that can later be planted into the garden, pot and all.

Uses: Group them in beds and borders, in rock gardens, and beside paths. They grow well in containers on decks, patios, or by doorsteps. Because they tolerate drought, they're good for containers where watering is not regular, although flower size will diminish somewhat. They can be used for cutting.

Related varieties: Glossy, yellow blossoms that set off against the gray-green foliage are the highlight of 'Sunlite.'

Portulaca, Moss Rose

Portulaca grandiflora

Portulaca's profusion of sunny flower colors combined with its toughness make it a natural for difficult garden sites. It will do even better under less difficult conditions. It is a native of Brazil.

Description: Moss roses grow nearly prostrate. They grow as a mat of fleshy leaves with stems topped by flowers. The flowers of newer varieties can reach 2 inches in diameter and are in a myriad of jewel-like colors—lemon-yellow, gold, orange, crimson, pink, lavender, purple, and white. They're enhanced by the bright button of yellow stamens in the center. There are both single and double varieties. The latter is sparked by extra rows of petals.

How to grow: Full sun; light, sandy soil; and good drainage are musts for portulaca, although they respond to adequate moisture with lusher growth and more flowers. Very frost-tender, they should not be planted outdoors until the danger of frost has passed and the ground is warm. Space them 1 to 2 feet apart. The flowers close at night and on cloudy days. Moss rose reseeds vigorously.

Propagation: Sow in place as soon as danger of frost has passed and the soil is warm. For earlier bloom, start indoors 4 to 6 weeks ahead. Seeds germinate in 10 to 15 days at 70 to 80° F.

Uses: Reserve your problem areas for portulaca. They're good container plants that do not languish if you forget to water them one day.

Related species: *Portulaca oleracea* has ornamental varieties with flowers in white, yellow, rose, and red. 'Wildflower' is a mix grown from seed; selections with even larger flowers are grown from cuttings.

Related varieties: 'Sundance' is a mixture of double-flowered varieties. 'Calypso' and 'Sunnyside' are double-flowered varieties.

Primrose

Primula **species and hybrids**

Primroses are favored in mild winter areas. They're also spectacular additions to other gardens for early spring color during cool weather. The two most popular varieties for gardens are *P.* x *polyantha*, bred from a number of species with long stems topped by multiple flowers and *P. acaulis*, featuring many single-stemmed flowers clustered in the center of the plant.

Description: Primrose flowers grow from a rosette of long, narrow leaves. *Acaulis* types will grow up to 8 inches high, while *polyanthus* primroses will grow to 1 foot high. The color range is immense—from a sky color to midnight blue, pinks, reds of all hues, yellow, orange, and lavender. Many of them are centered with a contrasting yellow eye; still others have narrow bands of color in the petals.

How to grow: Where climate is favorable, including the maritime West Coast, they can be grown as perennials. Blooms will start in midwinter through spring with a reprise of color in the fall when weather cools. Elsewhere, they must be grown for spring bloom. Transplant well-hardened plants into the garden as soon as the ground can be worked. Space them 6 to 10 inches apart. Grow them in soil rich in organic matter and keep them moist. In most places, they're happiest with a canopy of high shade.

Propagation: By seed or by division. To break seed dormancy, store in the refrigerator for 3 to 4 weeks before sowing. Sow seeds 8 to 10 weeks before planting in the garden. Seeds germinate in 10 to 20 days at 70° F.

Rose Mallow

Lavatera trimestris

Lavatera is an annual originally from the Mediterranean. It is related to both hibiscus and hollyhock.

Description: Rose mallow grows to 3 to 5 feet by the end of summer. It branches vigorously to form a sturdy bush. Lower leaves are rounded, but upper ones are lobed and toothed. The flowers, borne in leaf axils, are 3 to 4 inches in diameter.

How to grow: Grow rose mallow in full sun in average soil. Make sure soil is well-drained. Soil too rich grows excess foliage to the detriment of flowering. Plant outdoors as soon as the ground can be worked in the spring. Make sure to provide plenty of moisture. Space 1 to 1½ feet apart. Remove spent flowers to prevent seed formation.

Propagation: By seed. Sow in the ground outdoors. Space the seeds thinly to 1- to 1½-foot spacing because thinned seedlings will probably die. For earlier bloom, sow indoors 6 to 8 weeks prior to outdoor planting. Sow in individual peat pots and transplant, pot and all, into the ground outdoors. Seeds germinate in 14 to 21 days at 70° F.

Uses: Lavatera can be used along pathways or walks. Cluster groups of three or more at the end or sides of borders, or grow a row of them mid to rear of the border, depending on border height. Rose mallows make good container plants. Individual specimens make a rounded bush in urns, tubs, and other planters. The pink and white colors also mix well with other flower colors. Lavatera makes good cut flowers.

Related varieties: 'Mont Blanc' has pure white flowers; 'Mont Rose' is rose-pink; and 'Silver Cup' has large, pink flowers.

Salpiglossis, Painted Tongue

Salpiglossis sinuata

A kaleidoscope of color, each flower is dipped in shadings of color and strong veins. Related to petunias, salpiglossis have the same open-faced, trumpetlike flowers. Natives of Chile, they're well worth extra effort to grow.

Description: Unlike petunias, salpiglossis is a relatively upright grower, reaching up to 3 feet in the garden. Flowers are about 2½ inches in diameter. The colors are cream, lemon-yellow, gold, orange, brown, red, scarlet, violet, and near blue. Most of them are overlaid with veins and other patterns of color, making them look like stained glass.

How to grow: Salpiglossis grows best where summers are moderate, in full sun and fertile, well-drained soil. They must have a continuous supply of moisture. Transplant them outdoors in the spring as soon as all danger of frost has passed. Protect them from high winds. As an alternative, push brushwood into the ground around a young plant; the foliage will hide the support as it grows.

Propagation: By seed. Sow seeds indoors 8 weeks prior to planting out. This will allow good-sized plants for setting into the garden after the danger of frost has passed. Seeds should be covered; they need darkness to germinate. Seeds germinate in 15 to 20 days at 70 to 75° F.

Uses: Salpiglossis are ideal for the center of beds or borders as long as other plants cover their somewhat untidy feet. Do the same with containers. Locate them in the center and surround them with lower-growing plants and trailers. They make good cut flowers.

Related varieties: 'Bolero' is a tall strain growing to 2½ feet, with many different flower colors and variants. 'Dwarf Friendship Mixture' blooms on 15-inch plants. 'Kew Blue' has been selected for blue flowers laced with gold veins.

Uses: Primroses can be a highlight of the spring garden in moist, woodland settings and along woodland paths and walkways. Plant them in pockets by streams or ponds. Interplant them with spring bulbs that bloom at the same time. They're also nice with pansies, forget-me-nots, and other spring flowers. In containers, they can be beautifully combined with all of the above and others. An extra bonus is the delightful fragrance many of them have.

Related species: There are between 400 and 500 species and much interest in growing them, including a Primrose Society for aficionados. *Primula malacoïdes,* the fairy primrose, is hardy in California and other mild areas. It is often grown as a pot plant in the spring. *P. auricula* is much grown for variety of flowers, both in the garden and for exhibition at flower shows. *P. japonica* is one of the *candelabra* species with several whorls of flowers growing on tall stems. It is hardy and a perennial.

Related varieties: Some of the favorite *acaulis* types, all in mixtures and separate colors, are: 'Crown,' 'Festive,' and 'Ducat.' The 'Julian' series is a mixture of miniature plants that are hardy and perennial. The favorite *polyanthus* types are the 'Pacific Giant' series.

Salvia, Scarlet Sage

Salvia splendens

Salvias are best known for their spiky color that is dependable in any climate. Adaptable to full sun or partial shade with equal ease, these tender perennials grown as annuals are related to some of the best perennial plants for the garden as well as to sage, which is used for culinary purposes. A native of Brazil, salvia comes in brilliant red, creamy white, rose-colored, and purplish variants.

Description: The native plants are reported to grow up to 8 feet high. In the garden, 3 feet is about as tall as the largest ones grow. There are dwarf variants that grow only 8 to 12 inches. The spikes of flowers are composed of bright bracts with flowers in the center of each. They are either the same color or contrasting.

How to grow: Salvia is a good dual-purpose plant that will perform dutifully in full sun or partial shade. It needs average soil and continuous moisture to perform its best. Transplant plants to the garden after danger of frost has passed and the soil is warm. Depending on variety, space from 8 to 12 inches apart.

Propagation: Although seeds can be sown directly in the garden, earlier sowing indoors will bring earlier flowering. Be sure to use fresh seeds, since they lose their viability quickly. Sow the seeds 6 to 8 weeks before the final frost. The seeds germinate in 12 to 15 days at 70 to 75° F. Do not cover the seeds; they need light to germinate. After germination, reduce the temperature to 55° F.

Uses: Salvia provides some of the purest reds and scarlets in the garden world, and their vertical growth makes them superb accents in the garden. Plant them as spots of color against other colors. They're a classic combination with blue and white for patriotic plantings. Their ability to bloom well in light shade makes them especially useful with pastel colors that tend to fade in the sun. They also make good container plants.

Related species: *Salvia farinacea* is a perennial in milder climates that is now widely used as an annual throughout the country. Its common name is "mealycup sage" for the grayish bloom on its stems and foliage. It grows 18 to 24 inches tall and produces either blue or white flowers. 'Victoria' is the most popular blue; its counterpart is 'Victoria White.' *Salvia patens*, gentian sage, is named for its rich indigo-blue flowers that have a long blooming season.

Related varieties: 'Carabiniere' grows to 12 inches and, in addition to red, has separate colors of coral, shrimp pink, orange, blue-violet, and creamy white. 'Red Pillar' is taller and somewhat later. Tallest reds are 'America' and 'Bonfire,' which will grow to 2 feet in the garden.

Sanvitalia, Creeping Zinnia

Sanvitalia procumbens

Although not a zinnia, sanvitalia has enough resemblance to it to fit its common name of "creeping zinnia." Bright, golden-yellow flowers bloom nonstop all summer until frost. A native of Mexico, it is a member of the daisy family.

Description: The plant is a creeper, growing up to 12 inches in diameter with flowers above topping out at 6 inches. The flowers aren't large, but they're so abundant that they nearly obscure the foliage. The purple or brown centers are a pleasing foil to the yellow petals. Most sanvitalias are singles.

How to grow: Sanvitalia prefers full sun but will adapt to partial shade with less flowering. It is tolerant of most garden conditions. Plant outdoors when all danger of frost has passed and the soil is warm. Space plants 4 to 6 inches apart. Do not overwater or fertilize.

Propagation: By seed. Sow seeds in place when ground has warmed. For earlier bloom, start indoors 4 to 6 weeks before outdoor planting. Seeds germinate in 10 to 15 days at 70° F. Do not cover the seeds; they need light to germinate. Because they do not transplant easily, grow sanvitalias in peat pots that can be planted in the garden, pot and all.

Uses: Since sanvitalia is an annual that likes dry conditions, grow it in rock gardens. Use it as an edging for the front of borders or along sidewalks and paths. It will even bloom near the sunny foundations of houses. It will tolerate dappled shade. Sanvitalia trails well from containers.

Related species: *Wedelia trilobata*, native to Florida and South America, is somewhat similar in appearance with its sunny yellow flowers. It makes a good ground cover in full sun, where it roots as it grows.

Related variety: 'Mandarin Orange' brings a new color to sanvitalia.

Sapphire Flower

Browallia speciosa, viscosa

Sapphire flowers bloom heavily from early spring to fall frost; year-round in sunny windows or greenhouses. They're at their best in cool or coastal gardens, but with partial shade or an eastern exposure they will consistently grow well elsewhere.

Description: *B. speciosa* varieties grow in a loose mound to 18 inches high and as wide, their lax habit allowing them to trail. The most-planted variety of *B. viscosa* ('Sapphire') is a compact, rather stiff plant that doesn't trail.

How to grow: Plant in rich, well-drained soil but keep moist. Plant larger varieties 10 inches apart; dwarf ones 6 inches apart. Browallia is a good shade plant, although with looser habit and sparser flowers. Feed lightly on a biweekly schedule or incorporate a summer-long, slow-release fertilizer in the soil at planting.

Propagation: By seed or by cuttings. Start seeds indoors 6 to 8 weeks prior to planting out after the last frost. Seeds need light to germinate, so do not cover. At temperatures of 70 to 75° F, they'll take 14 to 21 days to germinate. Softwood cuttings taken in the spring or fall root promptly. For large plants in 10-inch hanging baskets, add 4 weeks to the growing time.

Uses: Sapphire flowers are grown in beds, borders, or rock gardens. Compact plants make good edges for a tall border. They are also excellent container plants.

Related varieties: Most planted *speciosa* varieties are the 'Bells': 'Blue Bells Improved,' mid-blue and most popular; 'Marine Bells,' a deep indigo blue; 'Sky Bells,' a clear azure blue; and 'Silver Bells,' pure white. *Viscosa* varieties include 'Sapphire,' deep blue with a white eye; 'Blue Troll,' a dwarf variety in mid-blue; and its counterpart, 'White Troll.'

Scabiosa, Pincushion Flower, Mourning Bride

Scabiosa atropurpurea

This native of southern Europe is like a pincushion with flowers up to 3 inches in size and scores of yellow or white stamens. The original flowers had a sweet scent.

Description: Scabiosa can grow up to 2½ feet tall; modern varieties are shorter. The many branched plants are topped with flowers in white, pink, lavender, and deepest maroon (almost black), from which the name "mourning bride" comes. Both double and single forms are found.

How to grow: Scabiosas grow well in any moderately fertile, well-drained soil. They need full sun. Plant outdoors after all danger of frost has passed, spacing them 8 to 15 inches apart, depending on variety. The taller varieties will need staking, but the shorter ones do not if protected from high winds. Scabiosas are sensitive to water. Apply water in the morning so that it can dry off before night.

Propagation: By seed. Sow outdoors as soon as all danger of frost has passed, thinning seedlings to the proper spacing. For earlier bloom, sow seeds indoors 4 to 6 weeks prior to outdoor planting. Seeds germinate in 10 to 15 days at 70 to 75° F.

Uses: Scabiosa is a delight in cottage gardens and mixed borders. It can also be grown and flowered in greenhouses or in sun rooms through fall and winter. Scabiosa makes good cut flowers.

Related varieties: 'Blue Cockade' has double flowers of rich, lavender-blue. It is a tall, 3-foot variety. 'Dwarf Double' is a mix of colors in white, lavender, lavender-blue, and rose, growing to 18 inches. 'Giant Imperial' features large flowers on long stems, ideal for cutting. They are a mix of lavender-blue, white, rose, and pink. 'Double Mixed' are fragrant, fully double flowers that include the darker colors of purple and deep crimson as well as white and pink.

Scarlet Flax

Linum grandiflorum

This showy annual provides bright red flowers with virtually no care. Each flower lasts a few hours and is followed daily by a procession of new ones. Originally from North Africa, it has become naturalized in parts of the United States.

Description: Scarlet flax grows to 2½ feet tall on slender, branched stems with narrow leaves. The round flowers, up to 1½ inches in diameter, have 5 broad petals. The primary color is shades of red.

How to grow: Grow scarlet flax in full sun in any garden soil, preferably somewhat low in fertility. They perform best in cooler climates. Plants will tolerate mild frosts; in colder climates they can be planted in the fall for late spring bloom. Otherwise, sow in place as soon as the ground can be worked in the spring. Space 4 to 6 inches apart. Water during dry spells. Each plant blooms approximately 4 to 6 weeks. For all season display, reseed at 4- to 6-week intervals.

Propagation: By seed. For earliest bloom in most locations, start seeds indoors 6 weeks prior to outdoor planting. Grow in peat pots to aid in transplanting. Seed germination takes 5 to 12 days at 60 to 70° F.

Uses: Scarlet flax is a good addition to wildflower or meadow gardens. Grow it in clumps in borders or beds and in mixed plantings such as cottage gardens. Plant it also in rock gardens.

Related species: *Linum usitatissimum* has sky-blue flowers that are breathtaking when planted in masses. Height is up to 3 feet. *Linum bienne* is another blue-flowered species that can be grown in the garden.

Related varieties: *Linum grandiflorum rubrum* is a deep red flowered form. 'Bright Eye' is ivory white with chocolate-brown eyes.

Scarlet Pimpernel, Poor-Man's Weather Glass

Anagallis arvensis

The name "Scarlet Pimpernel" was widely popularized by a novel of the French Revolution by Baroness Orczy, whose hero, Sir Percy Blakeney, used the flower as a trademark when he rescued victims from the Reign of Terror. The petals fold up when skies darken before storms or at twilight, not opening again until morning light triggers their rebloom—hence its other common name. A native of Europe and Asia, it is sparingly naturalized in parts of the United States.

Description: A plant whose low-spreading habit causes it to creep over the ground rather than grow upright, scarlet pimpernel's bright flowers provide a twinkling cloud of color. A blue form (*A. a. caerulea*) gives the same light, airy effect. It will rarely grow more than 4 to 5 inches high.

How to grow: Scarlet pimpernel thrives in full sun in ordinary garden soil, but favors sandy, well-drained conditions. Plant 6 inches apart after danger of frost has passed. It will continue blooming all summer.

Propagation: By seed. Seeds germinate in about 18 days indoors at 60° F and may be planted when the danger of frost has passed. They're easily grown by sowing seeds in the garden, then thinning plants to 6 inches apart. They also reseed.

Uses: Scarlet pimpernel is ideal for color in a rock garden. It also makes a good edging for paths or flower borders. Grown in pots on a sunny windowsill, it will continue flowering during fall and winter.

Related species: *A. monellii*, which grows up to 1 foot high, can be grown as an annual. The flowers range from blue with red undersides to pink. *A. tenella*, from the moist soils of southern Europe, bears small, scarlet, bell-shaped flowers on longer stems.

Scarlet Runner Bean

Phaseolus coccineus

In many parts of the world—especially in England and France—the scarlet runner bean is cultivated both as an ornamental and a vegetable. Until recently, the United States has embraced only its ornamental qualities. The lush, thick vines produce clusters of red flowers that are followed by the edible green beans. The Dutch runner bean, *P. c. alba*, has white flowers.

Description: Scarlet runner beans are quick-growing vines with typical, 3-leaflet bean leaves. They grow 6 or 8 feet tall. The bean flowers are borne in clusters like sweet peas. The edible pods that follow are long, slender, green beans.

How to grow: Scarlet runner beans need fertile soil and adequate moisture in full sun. Plant them where they can grow up some kind of support. The beans don't need to be tied—they twine around posts or poles. For covering fences, some kind of twine or netting will be needed for beans to climb. If allowed to grow over the ground, they will form a tangled mass of leaves, and the flowers will be hidden.

Propagation: By seed. Plant the large seeds directly in the ground after danger of frost has passed and the soil is warm. Plant seeds about 3 inches away from fences or posts, spacing them 2 to 3 inches apart. Thin the seedlings to a spacing of 6 to 8 inches. Seeds germinate in 5 to 10 days.

Uses: These quick-growing vines are beautiful when trained up posts, arches, pergolas, or arbors. They make quick-growing screens to break up the garden.

Related varieties: Most seed catalogs list them only as scarlet runner beans and do not select them for special eating qualities. 'Butler' has stringless beans; 'Painted Lady' bears red and white flowers; 'Kelvedon Wonder' is an early variety with long pods; and 'Scarlet Emperor' is named for the color of its flowers.

Schizanthus, Butterfly Flower, Poor Man's Orchid

Schizanthus x *wisetonensis*

Schizanthus revels in cool-weather climates, blooming well in late winter and spring in frost-free climates and other regions with long periods of cool weather in the spring and summer. Where they grow well, the flowers are spectacular. Although flowers are large and open, somewhat resembling butterflies and orchids, they're related to petunias and tomatoes and are native to Chile.

Description: Large clusters of flowers open above the finely cut, fernlike foliage. Compact varieties can grow up to 2½ feet tall and, when loaded with flowers, tend to tumble. The range of flower color is wide: pink, white, lavender, blue, gold, red, and magenta, with many flowers marked with other colors.

How to grow: Schizanthus likes cool, sunny conditions and a rich, moist soil high in organic matter. Under warmer conditions, light shade is good. They must have perfect drainage. Because they bloom best with root restriction, they are most often grown in containers. For garden planting, space them 12 inches apart. Plant outdoors after all danger of frost has passed.

Propagation: By seed. Sow seeds indoors 12 weeks prior to the last frost. Cover seeds; they respond to darkness. Seeds germinate in 20 to 30 days at 60 to 65° F.

Uses: Schizanthus is a natural for containers. It also makes a superb cut flower.

Scotch Thistle

Onopordum acathium

Like ghostly sculptures in the garden, Scotch thistles are so attention-getting that every garden should have at least one for a conversation piece. Not Scotch at all, they're biennials that grow from a small rosette of leaves the first season to tall, silvery branched columns the next year, bloom, and die. Related to both artichokes and true thistles, they have the same distinctive, light purple flowers (perhaps the model for the Scottish national emblem).

Description: The leaves are covered with white, cottony hairs that reflect the light and give it its ghostly appearance. The first year's basal rosette has leaves up to 1 foot in length. The following summer, a large flowering stalk with numerous branches arises from the center of the leaves. The thistlelike flowers are purple when open.

How to grow: Full sun in any garden soil will accommodate Scotch thistle. Plants may be planted into the garden as soon as the ground can be worked. Although their great height would suggest staking, their sturdy stems do not require it. Because they're large, they need plenty of room. Space them 3 feet apart to allow them to develop fully. They will reseed invasively. To control this, cut off flower heads when they lose their purple color.

Propagation: By seed. Sow seeds in late spring to early summer to grow large plants for transplanting into the garden in fall, early enough to become established before freezing. In cold climates, keep plants in a cold frame for spring planting. Seed germination takes 12 to 15 days at 60 to 70° F.

Uses: Grow them against tall fences or as groupings at the rear of large borders. The unopened flower buds may be cut and dried for winter arrangements.

Snapdragon

Antirrhinum majus

Children love snapdragons because they can snap open the flowers. They are also prized because of their columnar stateliness. Snapdragons endure cool weather and are widely planted for winter color in mild-winter areas.

Description: Snapdragons uniformly bear a whorl of flowers atop slender stalks. The best known are ones with snappable flowers, but new kinds have open-faced flowers including double forms. Colors include white, yellow, burgundy, red, pink, orange, and bronze.

How to grow: Plant in rich, well-drained soil with high levels of organic matter. Grow in full sun, fertilize monthly, and water moderately. Space tall varieties 12 inches apart, small varieties 6 inches apart. Pinch tips of young plants to encourage branching. Tall varieties may need staking. After first bloom is finished, pinch off flower spikes to induce new growth and repeat flowering. For cool season bloom in Zones 9 and 10, plant in September.

Propagation: By seed. Germination takes an average of 8 days at 70° F soil temperature. Keep seeds moist, but do not cover, since light is required for germination. For early bloom, sow seeds indoors 6 to 8 weeks before setting outdoors after last frost. Snapdragons may also be sown directly in the garden 6 weeks prior to the last frost when soil is friable.

Uses: Use the tall varieties for the back of the floral border and for cut flowers. Short varieties are good in borders and as edgings for beds. All varieties can be used in containers.

Related varieties: Tall snapdragons include 'Rocket' and open-faced 'Double Madam Butterfly.' Medium varieties, up to 18 inches, are 'Princess' and 'Coronet.' The most popular "mini" is 'Floral Carpet.'

Snow-in-Summer, Ghost Weed

Euphorbia marginata

This annual is a native of the eastern United States. The names "snow-in-summer" and "ghost weed" come from the white, variegated margins on the edges of its leaves. The sap can be irritating.

Description: Snow-in-summer grows rapidly from seedling stage, branching to a small bush 1 to 3 feet tall. The lower leaves are virtually all green, but progressively toward the top, more white appears on leaf edges. When flowering begins, the top leaves are mostly white. The real flowers are tiny, the color coming from the modified leaves called bracts.

How to grow: Snow-in-summer grows well anywhere in full sun—from cool, moist locations to dry, rocky places. It reseeds vigorously. Space plants 12 inches apart.

Propagation: By seed. Sow seeds outdoors after danger of frost has passed. Thin to desired spacing. Or start indoors 7 to 8 weeks prior to planting out. Seeds germinate in 10 to 15 days at 70 to 75° F.

Uses: Plant where large drifts of the green-white combination are wanted to cool the landscape. Snow-in-summer also makes a nice border or temporary hedge for pathways and sidewalks.

Related species: *Euphorbia heterophylla*, "summer poinsettia," has bright red bracts about 4 inches in diameter on plants 2 feet tall. It is also called "Mexican fire plant," "painted leaf," and "fire-on-the-mountain." *Euphorbia lathyrus*, with the common name of "mole plant" or "gopher plant," is often planted because it is supposed to keep moles away, a hotly disputed claim. Other names include "caper spurge." A handsome plant growing up to 5 feet tall, it has long, narrow leaves.

Related varieties: 'White Top' and 'Summer Icicle' are two available selections. 'Summer Icicle' is a dwarf, more compact form growing to 2 feet tall.

Southern Star, Star of the Argentine

Oxypetalum caeruleum

Southern star is worth looking at closely—its buds are pink, opening to a silvery blue star that fades to purple and then to lilac as it ages. The shape of the flower is an exquisite 5-pointed star. A shrubby perennial plant from Argentina, it's used here as an annual except in nearly frost-free parts of Zones 9 and 10 where it will winter over in permanent plantings. It's a member of the milkweed family.

Description: Used as an annual, it has a somewhat different character than its subshrub form in permanent plantings. Young plants have somewhat twining stems topped by clusters of flowers 1 inch in diameter. It can grow to 3 feet in nature, but rarely tops 18 inches in the garden.

How to grow: Southern stars do best in rich, well-drained loam in full sun. Space plants 6 to 8 inches apart. Pinch the plants once or twice to induce bushiness. In midsummer, they can be cut back about halfway to force new growth and extra bloom. Just before frost, plants from the garden can be dug, cut back, repotted, and grown for winter color on sunny windowsills.

Propagation: By seed or cuttings. Plants will bloom about 8 weeks after germination. For early bloom, sow indoors 6 to 8 weeks prior to planting in the garden after all danger of frost has passed. Seeds will germinate in 10 to 15 days at 70°F. Seeds may also be sown directly in the ground outdoors, although this will delay bloom until late summer, except in milder areas.

Uses: Plant them beside pathways and sidewalks or at eye level on banks or above walls for close-up viewing. Use them in containers. Because their growth is upright and somewhat spreading, trailing plants make an attractive addition to containers. Southern stars may also be brought indoors for winter bloom.

Stock

Matthiola incana

Stock is appreciated for its cool, distinctive colors and exceptional fragrance in cool season gardens. In mild winter regions, it's grown as a winter/early-spring annual for bloom before the weather gets torrid. In maritime or cool mountain climates, it makes a good flower for late spring or summer flowering. A biennial treated as an annual, it's a native of the Mediterranean coast and a member of the mustard family.

Description: Most stock varieties have become well-bred doubles, an upgrade from their wild, single nature. Modern varieties vary in height from 12 to 30 inches, but they're all rather stiff columns surrounded by flowers. The flowers are pink, white, red, rose, purple, and lavender in color.

How to grow: Stock is at its best in the cool, humid weather of foggy, coastal areas, even though some varieties are more heat-tolerant for a longer flowering season elsewhere. Stock will tolerate light frost and is useful for winter bloom in mild climates. Elsewhere, plant as early in the spring as ground can be worked. Moist, well-drained soil high in organic matter is preferred. Stock should be planted in full sun. Space them 8 to 15 inches apart, depending on the size of the variety.

Propagation: By seed. For winter use in mild climates, sow stock in the fall. In other places, sow seeds indoors 6 to 8 weeks prior to when ground can be worked outdoors. Seeds germinate in 7 to 10 days at 70° F. Don't cover the seeds; they need light to germinate. A percentage of seedlings are singles. Doubles are usually the most vigorous seedlings and are lighter in color than the singles.

Uses: Stock is relatively precise in appearance, best suited to formal beds where it can be lined up like soldiers. Plant them where the fragrance reaches passersby—near walks, by doorsteps, and close to heavily frequented places. They're also adaptable to containers, especially if you combine them with informal flowers to break up the rigidity. They're also superb cut flowers, with the scent pervading an entire room.

Related species: *Matthiola bicornis* has a particularly strong scent at night; the daytime flowers are unexceptional, so plant them discreetly.

Related varieties: 'Trysomic Seven Week' stock is the earliest bloomer. It is more tolerant of heat, offering a complete range of stock colors. It grows 15 inches high. 'Dwarf Stockpot' has separate colors of 'Red,' 'Purple,' 'Rose,' 'White,' or all together in a mix. It grows 8 to 10 inches tall.

Sundrop

Oenothera x tetragona

Oenotheras are perennials, biennials, and annuals. They can all be grown as annuals. Those whose flowers open at night are called evening primroses; day-bloomers are sundrops.

Description: This plant forms a basal rosette of long, narrow leaves from which rises a flower stalk, bearing blooms that open from the bottom of the stem to the top. It grows up to 3 feet tall. The flowers, up to 1½ inches in diameter, are open cups of a gold color. Sometimes they are scarlet in bud.

How to grow: Oenotheras require average soil with good drainage in a fully sunny location. Good drainage helps improve winter hardiness of the short-lived perennial species. They are relatively tolerant of dry soils, but steady moisture will improve their growth. Sturdy plants, they do not require staking unless grown in locations with high winds. Plant them in the garden in the spring as soon as the ground can be worked easily. Space them 12 to 15 inches apart.

Propagation: By seed or division. For blooming plants the first year, sow them indoors 10 to 12 weeks prior to outdoor planting. Seeds germinate in 15 to 20 days at 68 to 85° F. Biennial and perennial kinds can be sown directly into the garden the preceding autumn, early enough to develop husky plants prior to freezing weather. Sundrops will reseed vigorously.

Uses: Grow sundrops in the middle or at the back of the border. Group them at the center or at the back of beds. They can also be used in front of low hedges.

Related species: *Oenothera erythrosepala* has yellow flowers. Mature blossoms slowly turn red. It grows to 3½ feet tall. *O. texensis* has rose-colored flowers. Compact plants grow up to 12 inches.

Related variety: 'Highlight' is a blooming selection of *O. tetragona*.

Sunflower

Helianthus annuus

Whether giants of the garden at 15 feet tall or barely topping 1 foot, these natives of North America come in a variety of colors and forms. *Helios* is the Greek word for "sun."

Description: Typically growing from 10 to 15 feet tall, sunflowers have coarse leaves and flower heads up to 1 foot or more in diameter. Although they started out as yellow flowers with brown or purple centers, there are now variations with magenta, white, and orange flowers and still others that are fluffy doubles.

How to grow: Sunflowers prefer full sun and will grow in any soil, except one that is light and well-drained. They're very tolerant of heat and drought. The tall varieties may need staking to prevent the wind from toppling them. Plant the tall varieties 12 to 18 inches apart; dwarf ones at 9- to 12-inch spacing.

Propagation: By seed. Sow seeds outdoors after final frost. However, for earlier bloom, start indoors 4 to 8 weeks ahead. Seeds germinate in 10 to 20 days at 70 to 85° F.

Uses: The dwarf kinds can be used in beds and borders, while the taller varieties are best at the back of the border. They can be used as a screen or as a clump at the end of driveways or along fences. The smaller-flowered varieties can also be used as cut flowers.

Related species: *Helianthus debilis* grows 4 to 5 feet tall with yellow or creamy white flowers. *H. giganteus* is the monster sunflower, growing up to 15 feet tall with dinner plate-sized flowers, 12 to 15 inches across.

Related varieties: 'Piccolo' grows to 4 feet and bears rather graceful, 4-inch, semi-double, gold flowers centered in black. 'Sunspot' has 8- to 12-inch blooms on plants only 18 to 24 inches high. 'Large Flowered Mixed' has yellow, red, bronze, and orange flowers on 5-foot plants.

Sweet Pea

Lathyrus odoratus

In cool maritime or mountain climates, sweet peas will bring their beauty all summer. In Zones 9 and 10, they're best in cool seasons, winter, and early spring. Natives of Italy, the original purple or white flowers now come in many hues.

Description: Sweet peas are vining plants that climb vigorously 6 to 8 feet over fences and other supports. The flowers are pink, white, red, lavender, purple, and almost (but not quite) blue.

How to grow: In mild winter areas, sow seeds outdoors in the fall. Elsewhere, plant as soon as ground can be worked. Sweet peas need full sun and a deep, rich soil. Dig a trench and fill with fertilizer and humus-rich soil. When seeds are up, mulch thoroughly to keep soil cool. When seedlings are 4 inches high, pinch the tips to develop strong side branches. Provide support for them to climb. The shortest varieties need no support. Keep blossoms picked to ensure continuous flowering.

Propagation: By seed. Nick seed coats with a knife and soak seeds overnight in water. Before planting, treat with a culture of nitrogen-fixing bacteria available at garden stores. For earliest plants, start in peat pots 4 to 6 weeks before planting outside. Plant pot and all. Seeds germinate in 10 to 14 days at 55 to 65° F.

Uses: Grow them against fences, over trellises, arches, and pergolas. Plant them on a tepee composed of stakes in the center or at the back of the bed. The dwarf varieties can be planted in the border. As cut flowers, sweet peas are superb.

Related varieties: 'Early Mammoth Mixed' has many colors. 'Bijou' is a variety with a bushy habit, growing to 12 inches and a number of colors. 'Super Snoop,' an early flowering dwarf, grows to 2 feet with a full range of sweet pea colors.

Thunbergia, Black-Eyed Susan Vine, Clock Vine

Thunbergia alata

This quick-growing vine boasts many open-faced flowers, usually with dark centers (hence the name "black-eyed Susan"). Where not struck down by frost it is a perennial, but most climates of the United States grow it as a beautiful annual. The name *Thunbergia* honors a Swedish botanist named Karl Pehr Thunberg.

Description: Black-eyed Susan vine can grow 6 to 8 feet tall in a season and has rough, hairy leaves. The blooms have 5 distinct petals and are symmetrical. Flower color can be white, yellow, orange, or cream. Most of them have dark centers.

How to grow: Generally, it grows best in full sun. It needs average, well-drained soil. Plant seedlings 3 inches away from supports. Space plants 5 to 8 inches apart. Pinch the tips to encourage branching. Since thunbergias climb by twining, netting or strings make good trellising materials. They will need a trellis to climb large posts or solid fencing.

Propagation: By seed or by cuttings. Sow seeds outdoors after the last frost or start seedlings indoors 6 to 8 weeks before outdoor planting. Seeds germinate in 10 to 15 days at 70 to 75° F. Cuttings root easily in a commercial soil mix.

Uses: Thunbergias can be used to cover posts, porches, arbors, pergolas, or fences. They also make good container plants. Plants in containers will also bloom over winter in sunny windows.

Related species: *Thunbergia gibsonii* has somewhat larger flowers in a bright orange color. *Thunbergia fragrans* bears 2-inch wide, white, fragrant flowers. The most available variety is called 'Angel Wings' and blooms in about 12 weeks from seed.

Related varieties: 'Susie Mix' is composed of orange, yellow, and white blooms, either with or without dark centers.

Tidy Tips

Layia platyglossa

This annual is native to southern California. A member of the aster family, it has bright, daisylike flowers—a strong, golden-yellow, with every petal tipped with white. This is where the name "tidy tips" arose.

Description: Tidy tips forms a semi-prostrate bush 1 to 2 feet high and as broad. It becomes more or less mounding in form because of frequent branching. The long, narrow, hairy, green leaves are usually entirely covered by the flowers.

How to grow: Tidy tips needs full sun. It is relatively indifferent to soil, growing well in average, well-drained garden soil. It will survive if drought occurs, although it will benefit from watering. Tidy tips is less tolerant of hot, humid weather and in such climates will perform best in the spring and early summer. Otherwise, it will bloom continuously until fall. Space plants 4 to 9 inches apart in the garden. They need no staking, standing up well to wind and rain.

Propagation: By seed. In mild winter climates, seeds may be sown in the fall for earliest bloom in the spring. Elsewhere, sow seeds outdoors as early in the spring as ground can be worked. To start indoors, sow seeds 6 to 8 weeks prior to planting outside. Do not cover; seeds need light to germinate. Seeds germinate in 8 to 12 days at temperatures of 65 to 70° F. Temperatures above 70° F inhibit germination.

Uses: Plant tidy tips in mixed borders and cottage gardens. They're also ideal in wildflower or meadow plantings. They can be used in containers. Tidy tips make good cut flowers.

Related varieties: Named selections are not available. However, a variety, *L. p. campestris,* is more erect, less branched, and has grayer leaves. Flower petals are typically longer, but they have the same yellow color with white tips.

Tithonia, Mexican Sunflower

Tithonia rotundifolia

Tithonia, along with sunflowers, are the largest, most dramatic annuals for the garden. Some varieties can grow up to 8 feet tall. A native of Mexico and southward, its area of origin is the reason for its common name. Members of the daisy family, they are also related to the sunflower.

Description: Tithonias have rough, hairy leaves on tall, vigorous plants. Shorter varieties are now available that will stay approximately 4 feet tall. The flowers are single and up to 3 inches in diameter. The color is a deep orange-red, even though there is now a variety with chrome-yellow flowers.

How to grow: Tithonia must have full sun, but it will grow in average soil with good drainage. It is one of the most heat- and drought-resistant plants, growing reasonably well in soils of low fertility. Plant in the garden after all danger of frost has passed. Space plants 2½ to 3 feet apart. Do not overwater. Protect the plants from high winds and stake them—this is particularly important in late summer and fall when they are tall and top-heavy.

Propagation: By seed. Seeds may be sown outdoors; for earlier flowering, start them indoors 6 to 8 weeks earlier. Seeds germinate in 7 to 21 days at 70° F.

Uses: Its size and coarseness of the foliage dictates planting it at the back of the border. The color is so intense that it only takes a few plants for impact. It is also useful for covering fences and shielding background eyesores in the garden. Tithonias make good cut flowers as long as the hollow stems are seared after cutting and plunged into 100° F water.

Related varieties: 'Torch' is a medal winner that grows 4 to 6 feet tall, bearing the classic, deep orange-red flowers. 'Yellow Torch' has yellow flowers.

Toadflax

Linaria maroccana

Toadflaxes have flowers that pop open when squeezed—just like snapdragons. Native to Morocco, which their species name reflects, these plants should be better known for their cool season color in warmer climates and all summer blooms in cool locations.

Description: Toadflax grows upright and branches, with flowers covering the upper third of the stems. Leaves are long and narrow. The species has blue-violet flowers with white or yellow markings, but new selections include many other colors as well: blue, lilac, pink, yellow, red, and white. They're still marked with a contrasting lip. They grow up to 1 foot tall, but often stay shorter.

How to grow: Toadflax requires full sun and well-drained soil. Low fertility is preferred over a rich soil. Plant as early as the ground can be worked. Seeds can be sown indoors early or directly in the ground outside. They grow and bloom so quickly that an earlier start is not necessary, except in those areas where early heat would diminish their bloom time. Because they are small, plant or thin them to a spacing 3 to 4 inches apart. Linaria self-sows readily.

Propagation: By seed. Sow outdoors as early as ground can be worked. Indoors, seed 4 to 6 weeks earlier. They germinate in 10 to 15 days at 55 to 60° F.

Uses: Toadflax look great in the rock garden. They can also be planted in drifts in the front of borders or beds. They're lovely overplanted with bulbs. Planting them together with snapdragons combines the same flower type with an interesting contrast in size.

Related varieties: 'Fairy Bouquet' and 'Fairy Lights' are both mixtures containing the linaria colors of white, pink, purple, lavender, and yellow.

Torenia, Wishbone Flower

Torenia Fournieri

Torenia is a colorful, modest-sized plant that thrives in shade and hot, humid weather as a result of its original habitat in Vietnam. The common name comes from the two yellow stamens that arch over the center of the petals.

Description: Torenia forms a compact mound about 1 foot high with many branches. Leaves are oval or heart-shaped. The flowers look a bit like open-faced snapdragons with prominent markings on the petals. The most predominant color in the past was blue, but new varieties are pink, rose, light blue, and white. Most carry yellow, but some may have deep blue or purple markings.

How to grow: Torenias grow best in rich, moist, well-drained soil. They're widely used in frost-free areas for winter and spring display. Elsewhere, they thrive during summer in partial shade. They like high humidity and won't tolerate being dry. Plant outdoors after all danger of frost has passed. Space 6 to 8 inches apart.

Propagation: By seed. Sow seeds 10 to 12 weeks prior to outdoor planting. The seeds are tiny; they are more easily sown evenly if mixed with a pinch of sugar before sowing. Germination takes 10 to 15 days at 70° F.

Uses: Torenia is a good addition to plants that bloom well in semi-shade. Plant them in groups of three or more in woodland bowers; grow clumps along paths or walkways. Because it grows evenly, it's a good candidate for formal beds in sun or partial shade. Torenia is well-adapted to containers.

Related species: *Torenia concolor* is a tender trailing perennial. Its flowers are blue to purple without markings.

Related variety: 'Clown Mixture' has flowers of blue, light blue, rose-pink, and white.

Tuberose

Polianthes tuberosa

The cloying tropical fragrance of tuberoses is pervasive on warm summer evenings—reason enough to grow them but with an added benefit of beautiful white flowers. Reputedly, it was cultivated by the Aztecs in pre-Columbian times, then sequestered in a monastery in France until it was released for wider cultivation. Sharing the secret has been a boon to centuries of gardeners ever since.

Description: Tuberoses grow from bulbous rootstocks with a rosette of leaves, centered by a flowering stem that is surrounded by tubular flowers of exquisite fragrance. Flowering stems are from 1 to 2 feet tall. Both single and double varieties are planted. Not hardy, bulbs must be dug up each fall in cold climates and replanted in the spring.

How to grow: Grow tuberoses in rich, well-drained soil that is high in organic matter and in full sun. Plant in the garden after all danger of frost has passed and the soil is warm. Plant the bulbs 2 inches deep and 6 inches apart. Water them thoroughly during dry weather.

Propagation: By offsets. Smaller bulbs will have formed when you dig the bulbs in the fall. They may be replanted the next year and will bloom the second year. For earlier plants, start them indoors 5 to 6 weeks prior to planting in the garden.

Uses: The pure white flowers on long stems combine well with any garden plants. To enjoy their fragrance, plant groups of them where people pass or congregate. Plant them in containers for the lovely flower form and haunting scent. They're good as cut flowers.

Related varieties: 'Mexican Everblooming' is the widely available, single-flowered tuberose. 'Double Pearl' is the widely planted double form, with each blossom packed with many extra flowers.

Venidium, Monarch of the Veldt, Cape Daisy

Venidium fastuosum

The foliage of this plant is nearly as beautiful as the flowers—a shimmery, silvery reflection of light from the hairy leaves and stems. The large, bright orange flowers have darker centers. There are also less strident colors including yellow, cream, ivory, and white. Natives of South Africa, they belong to the daisy family.

Description: Plants grow about 2 feet tall, are branched, and have long flower stems. The large daisies are up to 5 inches in diameter and have a double row of ray flowers. The dark centers are brownish-purple to almost black. Leaves are finely cut and covered with long, shaggy hairs that create the silvery appearance.

How to grow: As perennials, venidiums grow best in mild, maritime climates with cool, dry summers and frost-free winters. They can be used for winter and spring flowering in parts of Zones 9 and 10. Where summers are hot, venidiums are best grown as spring annuals—to be replaced when humidity and temperatures soar. They must have well-drained soil and full sun. Transplant plants to the garden after the last frost date when the soil is warm. Space them 12 inches apart. Stakes may be necessary if they are not shielded from high winds.

Propagation: By seed. Start seeds indoors 6 to 8 weeks prior to planting in the garden. Seeds germinate in 15 to 20 days at 70 to 75° F. Do not cover the seeds; they need light to germinate.

Uses: Plant venidiums in beds and borders. Grow them in groups at a turn or the end of a pathway. They make good cut flowers, although they will close at night.

Related species: A more compact species is *Venidium decurrens*, with bright yellow flowers.

Related varieties: Each seed company makes its own selection.

Verbena

Verbena x hybrida

Verbenas are garden treasures in areas where few other plants would grow. Some varieties trail; others form mounds of color. Parentage is from species found in subtropical and tropical South America.

Description: The trailing varieties may reach 18 inches in diameter, while the mounding types will grow to about 1 foot high and wide. The flowers are in clusters. The leaves are long, narrow, and notched.

How to grow: Verbenas prefer well-drained, sandy soil with good fertility. They will not grow well in shade or with wet feet. They also need air movement around their leaves to prevent mildew. Plant after all danger of frost has passed. Space plants 12 (upright types) to 18 (trailing types) inches apart.

Propagation: By seed or by cuttings. Verbenas are slow in the early stages. Sow seeds 12 to 14 weeks prior to planting in the garden. Chill the seeds in the refrigerator for 7 days before sowing. Cover the seeds; they need darkness to germinate. They are also sensitive to dampness. Wet the seed flat 24 hours before sowing, sow the seeds without watering, and cover with black plastic until germination. Germination takes 3 to 4 weeks at 75 to 80° F.

Uses: The trailing types are ideal for rock gardens, trailing over walls, and as edgings for garden beds and borders. Use mounding types in beds and borders. Verbena also trails nicely from containers.

Related varieties: 'Showtime' and 'Springtime' series are available as separate colors and as mixes. 'Blaze' is a red variety; 'Crystal,' a white; and 'Delight,' a salmon-pink. These are all trailers. Mounding verbenas include the 'Romance' and 'Sandy' series and 'Trinidad'—a fluorescent-rose color. There are also selections grown from cuttings.

Vinca, Madagascar Periwinkle

Catharanthus roseus

These tropical plants, native to Madagascar, stand up well to heat and humidity. Research is now developing new varieties with additional colors beyond the familiar white, pink, and rose of the past.

Description: Flowers are round, 1 to 2 inches in diameter, and borne at the tips of branches or shoots that bear glossy, green leaves. The flowers of many varieties also have a contrasting eye in the center of the bloom. Two forms are grown: somewhat erect types that form moundlike bushes and virtually recumbent trailers.

How to grow: Vinca is at its best in hot conditions—full sun, heat, and high humidity. Grow in warm, rich, well-drained soil. Avoid overwatering to prevent soil-borne diseases. Plant bush types 8 to 12 inches apart; trailing types 12 to 15 inches apart. Avoid planting outdoors before soil is warm.

Propagation: By seed. Sow seeds 12 weeks prior to setting out after last frost. Germination takes 14 to 21 days at a temperature above 70° F. Maintain warm temperatures after germination and be careful not to overwater.

Uses: Trailing types make colorful ground covers and are good edging plants. More upright plants can either back up trailers in the border or combine with other plants. Both types are good container plants. Their heat tolerance makes them ideal for challenging locations.

Related varieties: Creeping kinds include the 'Carpets': 'Dawn,' pink with a rose eye; 'Pink'; 'Snow,' pure white; and 'Magic Carpet Mixture' of all three colors. Uprights include the 'Little' series: 'Blanche,' pure white; 'Bright Eye,' white with a red eye; 'Delicata,' white with a pink eye; and 'Pinkie,' a rosy pink. A new color in vinca is 'Pink Panther,' a fluorescent coral color.

Persian Violet

Exacum affine

Neither a violet nor from Persia, this plant with jewel-like flowers makes a good garden plant. Actually, Persian violets are from Socotra, a small island near the entrance to the Red Sea, and belong to the gentian family.

Description: As a summer flowering plant in the garden, Persian violets can reach 1 foot or more in height, and are very branched, forming a tightly packed clump. The many small leaves are topped by flowers ½ inch in diameter, most often violet-blue in color, although there are also pink and white varieties. Flowers are sweetly scented.

How to grow: Persian violets are easily grown in sunny, warm, humid locations. They prefer moist, well-drained soil and partial protection from the hottest afternoon sun. Since they are very tender, they can only be planted outside after all danger of frost has passed and the ground has warmed. Space 6 to 9 inches apart.

Propagation: By seed or by cuttings. Sow and cover seeds in a seed flat 4 to 5 months prior to planting out in the garden. The very fine seeds take 14 to 21 days to germinate at a temperature of 70° F. After germination, maintain a temperature not below 65° F.

Uses: Plant Persian violets in formal beds or at the front of borders. They also look good along paths and walkways. Plant in containers where their fragrance as well as their color can be enjoyed. Group them in clusters or plant in window boxes.

Related varieties: The 'Midget' series contains blue- and white-flowered varieties. They're dwarf, growing to 10 inches in the garden. 'Tiddly Winks' is a larger variety. The 'Rosendal' series is compact and, in addition to blue and white, has a variety with lilac-rose color.

English Wallflower

Cheiranthus cheiri

These relatives of mustard are perennials in mild winter areas. But they are most often grown for cool season display. Sweetly fragrant, they're grown by the millions in England.

Description: Wallflowers grow from 1 to 2½ feet tall. Many-branched, they're topped by showy terminal spikes in many colors—ranging from creamy white through yellows, oranges, tans and browns, to chestnut red. Some varieties are double.

How to grow: Wallflowers do best in average, moist soil in sun or partial shade in areas where the nighttime summer temperatures are below 65° F. Space 12 to 15 inches apart. Elsewhere they are best for cool season display in spring or fall. They winter over in Zones 8, 9, and 10.

Propagation: By seed. When grown as annuals, sow seeds indoors 6 to 8 weeks before the last frost is expected. Germination takes 5 to 7 days at 55 to 65° F. When transplanting to individual pots, pinch out the tip of the tap root to encourage a bushy root system. Sow seeds in July or August so that plants can winter over for the earliest spring flowering.

Uses: Plant wallflowers in rock gardens, beds, and borders. They are also pleasant by sidewalks and doorsteps. Wallflowers will bloom all winter in a cool room in sunlight. They make good cut flowers, too.

Related species: *Erysimum hieraciifolium* (*Cheiranthus allioni*) is the closely related Siberian wallflower. There are a number of varieties, including 'Early Wonder Mixed Colors.'

Related varieties: Separate, named varieties include: 'Blood Red,' 'Cloth of Gold,' 'Eastern Queen' (salmon-red), 'White Dame,' and 'Fire King' (orange-scarlet). Available mixtures are: 'Bedding Mixed,' growing up to 18 inches and 'Double Dwarf Mixed,' staying below 15 inches.

Zinnia

Zinnia elegans

Zinnias are among the favorite American garden flowers, loved for their variety of colors, which ranges from bold and brassy to muted pastels.

Description: Zinnias are generally grouped into three classes: tall (up to 2½ feet), intermediate (up to 20 inches), and dwarf (up to 12 inches). Leaves and stems are coarse and rough like sandpaper, while the flowers are in almost every color except blue.

How to grow: Zinnias need full sun and rich, fertile soil high in organic matter. They're best in hot, dry climates. Powdery mildew can be a problem in humid locations. Try to avoid watering from above; plant where there is good air movement. Plant them after the final frost when the soil is warm. Space 6 to 12 inches apart, depending on the size of the variety.

Propagation: By seed. Zinnias grow fast, and early bloom can be achieved in most climates by sowing seeds directly into the soil. For earlier bloom, sow seeds indoors 4 weeks prior to planting out. Seeds germinate in 5 to 7 days at 70 to 75° F.

Uses: Dwarf and intermediate varieties can be used in beds and borders or in container plantings. Taller varieties should move to the back of the border or the cutting garden. Zinnias make good cut flowers.

Related species: *Zinnia angustifolia* is a ground-covering species with a prostrate form and single, golden flowers.

Related varieties: Tall varieties: 'Zenith,' hybrids in many separate colors and a mix and 'Giant Flowers, Mixed Colors,' with a variety of colors and flower forms. Medium varieties: 'Border Beauty,' hybrids in separate colors and a mix and 'Cut and Come Again,' with double flowers on long stems. Dwarf varieties: 'Peter Pan,' hybrids with large flowers on short stems and 'Thumbelina,' tiny plants with miniature flowers.

Index

COMMON NAME	BOTANICAL NAME	PAGE(S)
Everlasting; Strawflower		
Helichrysum; Everlasting	*Helichrysum bracteatum*	16, 82, 108
Honesty; Silver Dollar Plant	*Lunaria annua*	16, 82, 108
Statice	*Statice sinuatum*	16, 82, 108
Xeranthemum	*Xeranthemum annuum*	16, 73, 82, 108
Firecracker Plant	*Cuphea ignea*	17, 108
Floss Flower	*Ageratum houstonianum*	16, 19, 30, 50, 59, 108
Foliage Plants		
Dracaena	*Dracaena marginata*	13, 18, 30, 60, 77, 109
Moses-in-a-Boat; Moses-in-a-Cradle	*Rhoeo spathacea*	13, 16, 18, 57, 109
Polka Dot Plant; Freckle Face	*Hypoestes phyllostachya*	13, 18, 30, 60, 109
Purple Heart	*Setcreasea pallida*	13, 16, 109
Forget-Me-Not	*Myosotis sylvatica*	16, 17, 19, 34, 73, 82, 109
Forget-Me-Not, Chinese; Hound's Tongue	*Cynoglossum amabile*	16, 17, 19, 109
Forget-Me-Not, Summer; Cape Forget-Me-Not	*Anchusa capensis*	16, 17, 19, 110
Four O'Clock; Marvel of Peru	*Mirabilis jalapa*	16, 34, 58, 110
Foxglove	*Digitalis purpurea*	13, 14, 16, 39, 59, 110
Fuchsia; Lady's Ear Drops	*Fuchsia hybrida*	16, 17, 60, 111
Gazania; Treasure Flower	*Gazania ringens*	16, 34, 111
Geranium, Ivy-Leaf	*Pelargonium peltatum*	8, 10, 11, 16, 18, 30, 36, 40, 60, 77, 112
Geranium, Regal; Martha Washington or Lady Washington Geranium or Pelargonium	*Pelargonium domesticum*	8, 10, 11, 16, 18, 30, 36, 40, 60, 77, 112
Geranium, Zonal	*Pelargonium* x *hortorum*	8, 10, 11, 16, 18, 30, 36, 40, 60, 77, 112
Gladiolus; Glad	*Gladiolus hybridus*	16, 58, 60, 83, 113
Godetia; Clarkia; Farewell-to-Spring	*Clarkia amoena*	16, 114
Ornamental Gourds		
Dishrag Gourd; Vegetable Sponge	*Luffa aegyptiaca*	18, 56, 57, 86, 114
White-Flowered Gourd	*Lagenaria siceraris*	18, 56, 57, 86, 114
Yellow-Flowered Gourd	*Cucumis pepo olifera*	18, 56, 57, 86, 114
Ornamental Grasses		
Cloud Grass	*Agrostis nebulosa*	18, 34, 57, 80, 82, 114
Golden Top	*Lamarkia aurea*	18, 34, 57, 80, 82, 114–115
Job's Tears	*Coix Lacryma-Jobi*	18, 34, 57, 80, 82, 114
Quaking Grass	*Briza maxima*	18, 34, 57, 80, 82, 114
Wheat Grass	*Triticum aestivum*	18, 34, 57, 80, 82, 115
Wild Oats	*Avena sterilis*	18, 34, 57, 80, 82, 114
Heliotrope; Cherry Pie	*Heliotropium arborescens*	16, 58, 73, 115
Hibiscus, Chinese; Hawaiian Hibiscus; Rose of China	*Hibiscus rosa-sinensis*	17, 18, 19, 24, 115
Hollyhock	*Alcea rosea*	14, 16, 41, 56, 57, 58, 59, 73, 75, 83, 116
Impatiens; Busy Lizzie; Patience	*Impatiens wallerana*	9, 10, 16, 26, 30, 36, 40, 58, 60, 70, 73, 75, 77, 116
Impatiens, New Guinea	*Impatiens* species	16, 18, 30, 36, 40, 60, 70, 77, 116
Joseph's Coat; Love Lies Bleeding; Prince's Feather	*Amaranthus tricolor, A. caudatus*	17, 18, 117
Lantana	*Lantana hybrida*	16, 17, 18, 58, 83, 117
Larkspur; Annual Delphinium	*Consolida ambigua*	16, 17, 19, 34, 40, 54, 72, 73, 80, 82, 83, 117
Lisianthus; Prairie Gentian	*Eustoma grandiflorum*	16, 17, 19, 30, 73, 118
Lobelia	*Lobelia erinus*	4, 16, 17, 30, 72, 75, 77, 118
Lotus Vine; Parrot's Beak	*Lotus berthelotti*	17, 118
Love-in-a-Mist; Devil in a Bush	*Nigella damascena*	16, 17, 18, 19, 82, 119
Lupine	*Lupinus* species	16, 40, 119
Magic Carpet Plant	*Polygonum capitatum*	17, 120
Mallow; Cheese	*Malva sylvestris*	17, 120
Flowering Maple	*Abutilon hybridum, A. megapoticum variegatum, A. striatum thompsonii*	17, 18, 19, 58, 60, 120
Marigold, Cape; African Daisy; Star-of-the-Veldt	*Dimorphotheca* hybrids	16, 121
Marigold, French; Marigold, American	*Tagetes patula, Tagetes erecta*	9, 10, 12, 18, 19, 34, 41, 42, 50, 56, 57, 68, 70, 73, 75, 80, 82, 83, 84, 121
Marigold, Pot; Field Marigold	*Calendula officinalis*	12, 17, 18, 19, 40, 56, 57, 70, 77, 80, 84, 121
Meadow Foam; Fried Eggs	*Limnanthes douglasii*	18, 122